Di Guoyong

on

Xingyiquan

Volume III

Weapons

Available from **tgl books**

Jiang Rongqiao's Baguazhang

Li Tianji's The Skill of Xingyiquan

Yan Dehua's Bagua Applications

Di Guoyong on Xingyiquan: Volume I, Foundations

Di Guoyong on Xingyiquan: Volume II, Forms and Ideas

Di Guoyong on Xingyiquan: Volume III, Weapons

A Shadow on Fallen Blossoms

Falk's Dictionary of Chinese Martial Arts

Beijing Bittersweet

Shadowboxing in Shanghai

 www.thewushucentre.ca

Di Guoyong

on

Xingyiquan

Volume III
Weapons

Second Edition of Weapon and Partner Play
The 2020 Set Edition

邸国勇
形意拳械精解
2020年修订版

translated and edited
by Andrea Mary Falk
霍安娣翻译，主板

Translation copyright © 2008 Andrea Mary Falk

ISBN 978-1-989468-08-1

All Rights Reserved

Second Edition copyright © 2021 The 2020 Set Edition

Library and Archives Canada Cataloguing in Publication of first editions

Di, Guoyong . Di Guoyong on xingyiquan / translated and edited by Andrea Falk. Translation of Xingyiquanxie Jingjie.

Complete contents: v. 1. Five element foundation -- v. 2. Form and theory -- v. 3. Weapon and partner play. ISBN 978-0-9687517-6-3 (v. 1) ISBN 978-0-9687517-7-0 (v. 2) ISBN 978-0-9687517-8-7 (v. 3)

1. Hand-to-hand fighting, Oriental. I. Falk, Andrea, 1954- II. Title.

GV1 1 12.D5 181 3   20 05   79 6 .815 ' 5   C2 00 5 -90 4 17 3 -0

Volume III of a three volume set. Volume I Foundations. Volume II Forms and Ideas. Volume III Weapons.

Translated and edited by Andrea Falk, Quebec City, QC, Canada

With thanks for the assistance of Di Guoyong, Beijing, China.

Second edition, the 2020 Set edition, by Andrea Falk 2021, Quebec, Canada.

The techniques described in this book are performed by experienced martial artists. The author, translator, and publishers are not responsible for any injury that may occur while trying out these techniques. Please do not apply these techniques on anyone without their consent and cooperation.

TABLE OF CONTENTS

Translator's Preface to Volume III vii
Editor's Preface to the 2020 Set Edition viii

CHAPTER ONE: BROADSWORD

Introduction to Broadsword 1
Broadsword on guard stance 2
Broadsword chop 4
Broadsword drill 12
Broadsword thrust 22
Broadsword slash 30
Broadsword crosscut 39
Five Elements Linked Broadsword form 46

CHAPTER TWO: STRAIGHT SWORD

Introduction to Sword 67
Sword on guard stance 68
Sword chop 70
Sword drill 80
Sword thrust 88
Sword slash 98
Sword crosscut 106
Five Elements Linked Sword form 114

CHAPTER THREE: SPEAR

Introduction to Spear 133
Spear on guard stance 134
Spear chop 136
Spear drill 146
Spear thrust 151
Spear slash 162
Spear crosscut 174
Five Elements Linked Spear form 182

CHAPTER FOUR: STAFF

Introduction to Staff 203
Staff on guard stance 204
Staff chop 205

Staff drill 215
Staff thrust 223
Staff slash 229
Staff crosscut 236
Five Elements Linked Staff form 242

CHAPTER FIVE: TEACHING AND TRAINING SUGGESTIONS
    Teaching suggestions 255
    Training suggestions 260

APPENDIX
Glossary of Chinese terms
    Section I: Parts of the Weapon 265
    Section II: Weapon terminology 265

Pronunciation of pinyin 269

About the translator 272

TRANSLATOR'S PREFACE TO VOLUME III

Volume III of Di Guoyong's three volume translated set (from a two volume original) contains the weapons and the advanced partner form *anshenpao*. I am pleased to have completed this series. Relieved is perhaps more the word, but I am having difficulty coming up with words after this long translation process. I am particularly pleased to have finished the final volume on time to present it at master Di's sixtieth birthday celebration in September 2008.

The font size is smaller and the layout more compact in this third volume to keep the size of the book down. Four weapons, each with five elements, a form, and larger photos, would have made this volume too large to be practical if I had kept the same format as Volumes One and Two. Please understand and forgive the well packed layout.

I took supplemental photos again for this volume to get the front views of the basic postures. The best part of that was when Di Guoyong arrived at our training space with a spear, a staff, a sword and a sabre strapped on his bike and his silk uniform stuffed in the basket.

Some may wonder about the use of the word 'play' in the title. The real work of any style is in the basics and the hand techniques. Once you have mastered the empty hand techniques the ability to do the weapons and partner play is almost instinctive. You still need to train hard to get them right, but they are just too much fun to be 'work '.

The glossary in this volume is specific to the weapons. Volumes one, two, and three together contain a pretty comprehensive overall dictionary for Xingyi.

After hours and hours of photoshopping, I know master Di's postures pixel by pixel, and was constantly amazed how perfect was each and every posture in hundreds and hundreds of photos. I worked from the roll of negatives, so know that he did not take backup photos, it was all one pose – one shot. His descriptions, too, are always clear, concise, and helpful in a practical way, much as is his teaching in person.

The photos in this series are proof of the glowing health and fitness that a life of martial arts training can bring you. Photos and descriptions alone, however, do not give the full flavour of the style or the person. I recommend that you go to Beijing and meet Di Guoyong to get the full impact (no pun intended) of his Xingyi.

I hope that this series contributes to the understanding of Xingyi in the English reading population, and that this population grows in number as martial artists discover the clarity of this particular martial art.

I would like to thank:

The author, Di Guoyong, for his knowledge of and enthusiasm for Xingyi, for his patient teaching, for his help with the translation, and easy agreement to my editing. My parents, William Andre and Mary Elliott Falk, for their painstaking proofreading. And, always, Xia Bohua and Men Huifeng, for teaching me Xingyiquan way back when.

Any mistakes in the book are mine alone.

Andrea Falk

霍安娣

Quebec QC, Canada

June 2008

EDITOR'S PREFACE TO THE 2020 SET EDITION

All three books needed to be redone to enable print-to-order sales, but the original files of the books were lost. As I set up the books again, I went through them to standardise the formatting to make them a more cohesive set. The main changes I made were to move things around. This was in order to even out the sizes of the books as much as possible, because the printer had problems making books of widely different thickness come out with the same look. I tried to do the readjustment in accordance with learning and teaching progressions. I moved the twelve animals to Volume I, to include them as basic techniques to Xingyiquan. I put all the theoretical and teaching discussions, the Protect the Body partner form, and the glossaries to Volume II, making it the next level – learning empty hand forms, more applications, and more thinking about things. Volume III is now specific to the weapons.

I corrected some typographical errors, adjusted some translation, and made some editorial changes while I was doing this work. I had to work on the photos yet again, and one yet again impressed with Di Guoyong's perfection and ease in all the movements and postures. If you already have the books, the original translation was solid, you do not need to buy the new set. This is the final edition of the set, and I really hope there are no remaining errors.

Andrea Falk

霍安娣

Morin-Heights, QC, Canada

January 2021

FIVE ELEMENT BROADSWORD

五行刀

INTRODUCTION TO FIVE ELEMENT BROADSWORD, *WUXING DAO*

The five element techniques of the broadsword are the culmination of the work of previous generations of Xingyi masters who refined, practiced, and synthesized broadsword methods from many martial styles. They developed the broadsword techniques based on the movements, footwork, body work, and power generation of Xingyi's five element empty hand techniques and the methodology of the five elements – metal, water, wood, fire, and earth.

The characteristics of the five element broadsword techniques are: the techniques are simple, power expression is emphasized, and the movements are aggressive, quick, well anchored, and highly applicable. Following the principle of simplicity and effectiveness, there are no flowery or extraneous movements. Emphasis is on deep trained skill and on the power of the body. By principle, broadsword methods fully integrate with body methods. The techniques show a intimidating air, advance and retreat quickly, move abruptly and stop firmly, all fully integrated as one, to manifest the characteristics and flavour of the system of Xingyiquan.

The techniques of the five element broadsword take their name from the five element fist techniques of split, drill, drive (crush, thrust), pound (cannon), and crosscut, and are called broadsword chop, broadsword drill, broadsword thrust, broadsword slash, and broadsword crosscut.[1] Each broadsword element is practised in a short combination that is centered around the attacking technique. For example, the broadsword chop combination contains left and right *hook and chop*, high and low *block and chop*, *coil around the head and chop*, and *wrap the head and chop*. The 'soul' of the broadsword chop combination is the chop. That is to say, chop is the main technique – the other techniques in each combination set up for the chop. The combinations of the other elements have a similar structure – a primary technique set up by short combinations.

Xingyi's five element broadsword form is widespread, though there is great variety within the form due to differences in styles and teachers. The five element techniques are much less known. This is because the individual

---

[1] Translator's note: In Chinese the terms are exactly the same. This works in Chinese, but I have changed the words for weapons techniques to make more sense in English.

techniques are very effective for fighting, so were not taught openly in most Xingyi systems. The five element techniques that I introduce here is a new set that I have created by combining what I learned from many elder masters, what I have studied from books, what I learned from other branches of Xingyi, and what I have developed through my years of training. It keeps the essence and methods of the traditional five element techniques, with some deletions and changes that serve to emphasize the broadsword's flavour and characteristics of simplicity and applicability.

You should have a solid foundation in the empty hand five elements and five element form before learning broadsword techniques. All weapons practice should be based on a solid foundation of fist skills. That means that if your empty hand skills are not solid you shouldn't try to learn weapons yet.

The Xingyi classics say, "Ten thousand techniques start from *santishi*." Santishi is the source of all Xingyi techniques, so you must practise the *santishi* post standing. You get a feel for the requirements, power, intent, and spirit of Xingyi within the post standing. Xingyi weapons are no different You should do post standing in the opening posture with each weapon. This is vital, and after much training you will discover the importance for yourself.

The five element broadsword techniques place great importance on whole body power and connection to the broadsword, so how you hold the hilt is emphasized and the requirements are strict. Only if you hold the broadsword properly can you transmit your body power to the broadsword and move with fluidity. The grip on the hilt must adjust according to the technique, and is called by different names such as pincer grip, hooking grip, or full grip. Broadsword chop uses a full grip, broadsword thrust uses a spiral grip, broadsword drill uses a twisted spiral grip, broadsword slash and broadsword crosscut use a firm full grip. When the broadsword is moving the grip must be supple, and when using power the grip must be firm.

In addition, the left hand must coordinate its actions with the right hand. Within the five element broadsword techniques, the left hand quite often assists by supporting the right wrist, to offset any weakness in the right wrist. In actual use the left hand can hold the hilt as well to add even more power. Xingyi weapons are extentions of the power of the body, you need to apply the power of the whole body through the weapons in each technique.

FIVE ELEMENT BROADSWORD TECHNIQUES

On Guard　　　　　　　　yùbèishì　　　　　　　预备势

The *on guard* position of the broadsword serves the same purpose as *santishi*, so you need to stand a great deal and focus on the requirements and rules to set your position into the ideal shape. During post standing you should pay attention to the feeling in both hands, feel the position of the broadsword in front of the body, and focus on making the body smooth with the broadsword, with your power transmitting to the broadsword. You need to do post standing for a long

CHAPTER ONE: BROADSWORD, *DAO*

time to achieve this feeling. The movements are *Stand at attention hold the broadsword; Transfer the hilt over the head; Retreat and chop.*

ACTION 1: Stand to attention facing forty-five degrees to the line in which you will go. Place the right hand at the side. Cradle the guard in the left hand with the tip pointing up, the blade spine snug to the left arm, and the blade edge facing forward. Press the head up and look forward. (image 1.1)

ACTION 2: Lift the hands by the sides to above and in front of the head. Transfer the hilt to the right hand, releasing the left hand and placing it at the right wrist. Look to the left – the line in which you will go. (image 1.2)

ACTION 3: Retreat the right foot and shift back into a *santi* stance with the weight sixty to seventy percent on the back leg. Chop both hands forward and down from above the head to bring the blade edge angled forward with the tip at nose height. The right hand holds the hilt, pulling back to about a forearm distance from the belly. Close the elbows towards each other, release the shoulders and settle the elbows, so that the broadsword lines up on the midline of the body. Close the chest and stretch the upper back taut. Press your head up and look past the broadsword tip. (image 1.3)

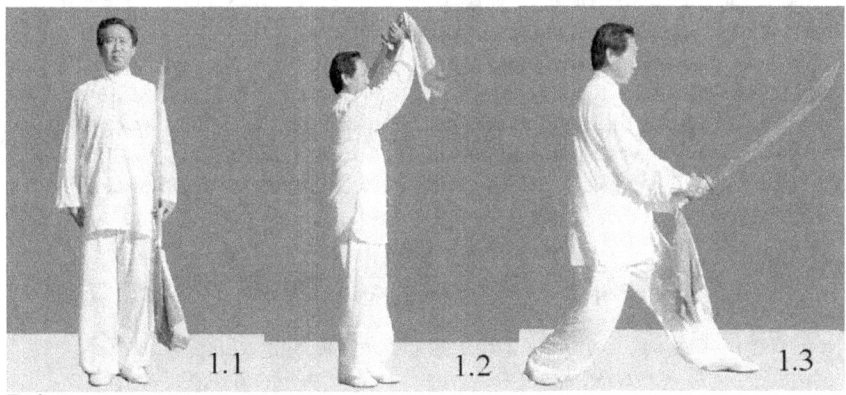

Pointers

- *On guard* is used to start all broadsword combinations and forms, the same as *santishi* is used to commence hand technique practice.
- When setting up for practice, you can start facing the line of practice or at forty-five or ninety degrees to the line. It doesn't matter, choose whichever direction you prefer.
- When lifting the arms be sure to maintain a certain bend in them. When transferring the hilt, use a pincer grip – gripping mainly with the thumb, index, and middle fingers, and only lightly with the ring and little fingers. This hold enables the tip to point down and the blade spine to come around past the left shoulder, across the back to the right shoulder, keeping the blade spine snug to the back and the tip down as it travels. Keep your wrist and grip supple.
- Chop the broadsword forward as you retreat the right foot and sit back.

Do not launch power when chopping, but keep the *qi* full and spirit focused. Once in the final position, pay attention to aligning the three tips: the tip of the feet, the tip of the nose, and the tip of the broadsword. They should be aligned on the same plane on the midline of the body to keep a tight defensive position.

PRACTICAL APPLICATION FOR ON GUARD

This is the same as *santishi* – it is the position taken when facing an opponent. Once you take your position the broadsword is on your midline with its tip, your nose, and your feet lined up, covering the high, mid, and low lines. This position defends your midline while it is prepared to attack. The proper frame of mind for combat is a firm *qi* and a mind at peace, so gather your spirit and still your *qi*.

1. BROADSWORD CHOP

INTRODUCTION TO BROADSWORD CHOP, *PI DAO*

Chop is the technique that most manifests the character of the broadsword. Looking at the shape of a broadsword, its spirit comes out in a chop. The classics say, "the broadsword chops and the straight sword pierces, the spear stabs and the staff strikes." You must practise chop with the ferocity and unyielding spirit of a tiger. Chop is a technique that comes forward and down from above. To use this action you must first set up the conditions for it to work, that is, the broadsword must be raised. The footwork for chop is: left stance, right stance, advance, and retreat. The key techniques for chop are: *Hook left and right and chop; High and low block across and chop; Swinging chop; Coil the head and chop; Wrap the head and chop.*

1a   Right Stance Chop   yòubù pīdāo   右步劈刀

Start from *on guard*. Continue with *Left withdraw, right lifting draw; Left advance, pushing pierce; Right step forward, coil the head and chop.*

ACTION 1: Without moving the right foot, shift back mostly onto the right leg and withdraw the left foot a half-step, touching down. Rotate the right hand, bend the elbow, and lift the hilt at the right of the head. Place the left hand on the right wrist, keeping the left elbow in front of the chest. Turn the blade edge up, with the tip pointing forward and down to sternum height. Close the shoulders, compress the torso, turn slightly rightward. Look past the broadsword tip. (image 1.4)

1.4

CHAPTER ONE: BROADSWORD, *DAO* 5

ACTION 2: Advance the left foot and shift forward. Keep the left hand at the right wrist and push forward with both hands with the blade edge forward and tip angled down. Extend the arms, maintaining a certain flexion, and finish with the broadsword tip at between belly and chest height. Look at the broadsword tip. (image 1.5)

1.5

ACTION 3: Advance the left foot and bring the right foot in to the ankle. Take a loose grip and lift the hilt above the head to bring the broadsword to the left shoulder and around the back to the right shoulder with the tip down and the blade edge out, so that the blade spine is snug to your back. (images 1.6a and b)

1.6a   1.6b

Take a long step forward with the right foot and follow in the left foot a half-step to sit into a *santi* stance. Extend the arms forward to chop forcefully forward and down, and finally pull the right hand back towards the belly. Keep the left hand at the right wrist throughout. Finish with the tip at shoulder height. Press your head up and look past the broadsword tip. (images 1.6 and 1.6 from the front)

1.6   1.6
FRONT

Pointers
- Coordinate the right foot's withdrawal with the rotation and lifting of the broadsword.
- Coordinate the left foot's advance with the pushing pierce.
- The rear foot must step forward quickly and for a good distance, must land firmly, and must land as the broadsword chops.
- Chopping is an integrated power, and must be practised as one movement, with all actions within it connected quickly.

6   BROADSWORD CHOP

1b Left Stance Chop   zuǒbù pīdāo   左步劈刀

Right withdraw, left lifting draw; Right advance, pushing pierce; Left step forward, wrap the head and chop.

ACTION 1: Withdraw the right foot a half-step and shift back without moving the left foot. Rotate the right hand to turn the blade edge out and lift it up to the left side of the head. Keep the left hand on the right wrist. Finish with the tip angled forward and down to sternum height. Keep the right elbow in front of the chest and lift the left elbow. Look past the broadsword tip. (image 1.7)

ACTION 2: Advance the right foot a half-step and shift forward, following in with the left foot to beside the right ankle. Hold the hilt with a spiral grip and push forward with both hands with the blade edge up and the tip forward and down. Keep the left hand on the right wrist. Finish with the tip between belly and chest height. Look past the broadsword tip. (image 1.8)

ACTION 3: Take a long step forward with the left foot and follow in a half-step with the right foot to take a *santi* stance. Hold the hilt with a hanging grip and lift it to the right above the head with the tip down and the blade edge out. Bring the blade spine around the right shoulder, past the upper back to the left shoulder. Adjust the right hand to a spiral grip and bring it over the head, extending the arm to chop forward and down, then pull it back just in front of the belly. Finish with the tip at sternum height, edge down. Keep the left hand at the right wrist throughout. Press your head up, look past the tip. (image 1.9)

Pointers

- All pointers are the same as the *right stance chop*, just reversing right and left. Note that 'wrap ' goes around the

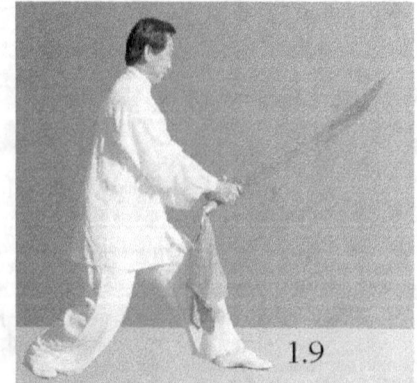

CHAPTER ONE: BROADSWORD, *DAO*

head in the opposite direction as 'coil'.
- Continue on with right and left chop, restricted only by the size of your training space.

1c Chop Turn Around pīdāo zhuànshēn 劈刀转身

Using the <u>left</u> *stance chop* (left foot forward) as example. *Left hook-in step, turn around and present the broadsword; Right advance, pushing pierce; Left step forward, wrap head and chop.*

ACTION 1: Advance the left foot a half-step with the foot hooked in and shift forward onto the left leg. Turn around 180 degrees rightward to face back in the direction from which you came. Bring in the right foot by the left foot, touching the toes down. Keep the left hand on the right wrist. Push forward and up at the right side, circling the tip up and back so that it points back in the direction from which you came. Finish with the blade edge up and the blade spine above the right shoulder. Sit down slightly. Look past the broadsword tip. (image 1.10)

ACTION 2: Advance the right foot a half-step and follow in the left foot. Keeping the left hand on the right wrist, extend the arms not quite fully to push with both hands to the lower front. Finish with the tip between belly and chest height, the blade edge forward. Look past the broadsword tip. (image 1.11)

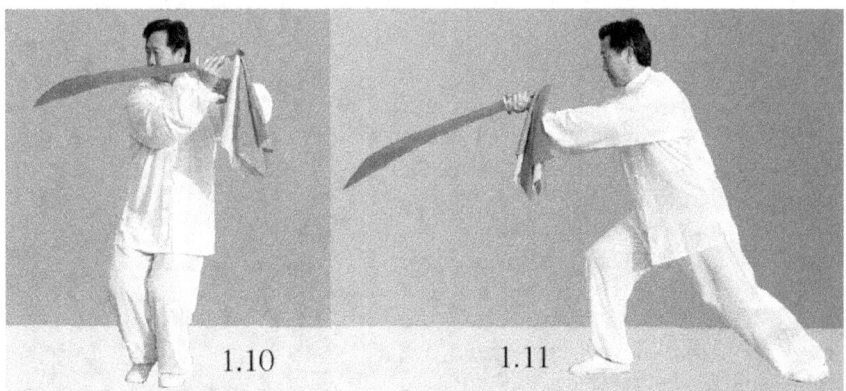

ACTION 3: This movement is the same as that described in action 3 of movement 1b, just in the opposite direction. (see image 1.9)

- The action of *turn around* is the same whether on the right or left side, just transpose the right and left actions. To turn around the other way, step the right foot hooked in and turn around 180 degrees leftward.

Pointers

  o The turn around should be smoothly connected without hesitation. Hook-in and turn around quickly, taking care to first bring the tip up and to circle it back as you turn. The movement should be gentle and the broadsword should wrap around the body snugly. Close the chest

8   BROADSWORD CHOP

and tuck in the abdomen, compressing the torso slightly.
o   After turning, push the broadsword as the foot advances. Chop as the foot steps forward, the same as described above in movement 1b.

1d   Chop Closing Move   pīdāo shōushì   劈刀收势

On arriving back at the starting point, do a *turn around* to face the original direction. *Return and cut across; Wrap the head and change hands; Hold the broadsword in the left hand and flash the palm; Stand at attention holding the broadsword.*

ACTION 1: If the <u>left</u> foot is forward, then withdraw the right foot a bit and shift to the right leg, hooking in the left foot on the spot. Cut flat across with the blade edge facing right at chest height. Extend the left arm to the left to brace out, palm out. Keep both arms slightly bent. Turn rightward and look at the broadsword tip. (image 1.12)

ACTION 2: Shift to the left leg without moving the feet. Rotate the right hand so the palm is up, then back, loosening the grip on the hilt to take the broadsword up over the head and leftward. Circle the broadsword, first placing the blade spine outside the right shoulder, then taking it across the back to the left shoulder in a *wrap the head* movement. Extend the right hand forward to meet the left hand and place the hilt in the left palm. Turn the body leftward. Look at the left hand. (image 1.13)

ACTION 3: Shift back to the right leg and straighten it, bringing the left foot in beside it to stand to attention. Turn the left palm up so that the thumb, ring finger and little finger cradle the guard, and the index and middle fingers wrap around it. Swing the right hand down, right, and then up to above the head, palm up. Hold the broadsword in the left hand with the blade spine snug to the arm and circle it up, rightward, and then down to the left hip. Follow the right hand with the eyes, then snap the head to the left when the right hand flashes, to look to the left. (image 1.14)

CHAPTER ONE: BROADSWORD, *DAO*

ACTION 4: Without moving the feet, let the left hand hang naturally at the side, still holding the broadsword with the blade edge forward and tip up. Bring the right hand down at the right side to stand to attention. Press the head up and look forward. (image 1.15)

1.14 1.15

- If the <u>right</u> foot is forward then in action one retreat the right foot behind the left foot and shift onto the right leg. Cut flat across to the right and back. The rest of the closing is the same as described.

Pointers

- Be sure to move both hands simultaneously during *turn around and cut across,* opening out to brace to right and left. Bring the foot in and flash the palm simultaneously.
- When wrapping the head and changing hands, be sure to adjust your grip on the hilt. Keep the broadsword spine snug to the body, *wrap around the head* must be tight. Be sure to shift the body left and right during the movement.
- The whole movement must be coordinated, fully concentrated, and dignified.

PROBLEMS OFTEN MET IN BROADSWORD CHOP

PROBLEM 1: During *withdraw, lifting draw* the student does not keep the broadsword on the midline of the body, taking it either too far to the right or to the left.

CORRECTIONS: Draw a small circle with the tip, keeping the left hand on the right wrist, so that the tip first circles down from above, and then withdraw and do the lifting draw. In this way it is easier to maintain the tip on the midline.

PROBLEM 2: During *withdraw, lifting draw* the student draws too large a circle with the broadsword tip.

CORRECTIONS: The cause of this error usually is that the student is taking too tight a hold on the hilt. When in movement, the right wrist needs to be able to rotate freely, so the grip should adjust to allow this. Remind the student to first rotate and extend the arm and then raise the elbow to draw the broadsword back.

PROBLEM 3: During *step forward, chop* the broadsword wobbles or sways.

CORRECTIONS: The student should first practise slowly and speed up only when the action is under control. Be sure to first extend both arms forward and then chop down. Pull in the abdomen and press the head up when pulling back, holding the hilt firmly. The hands must use a closing power and the elbows should come in snug to the ribs to keep the blade stable. First find the correct power during slow movement, then gradually speed up.

PROBLEM 4: During *wrap and coil the head* the student does not keep the broadsword spine on the upper back, so that the broadsword technique is not accurate.

CORRECTIONS: The cause of this error usually is that the student is gripping the hilt too tightly and the wrist is too stiff. The student should use a hanging grip so that the tip is able to point down and the broadsword spine is able to come in to the back and shoulders. These actions must be practised over and over, looking for the feeling slowly and gradually.

POWER GENERATION FOR BROADSWORD CHOP

Left withdraw, right lifting draw. Use the power of the waist to draw the arms, which in turn make the broadsword tip draw a circle downward. The torso should compact and settle down, and then rise. The hand lifts the broadsword hilt so that the blade protects the body.

Advance, push. The footwork follows the broadsword. When you push the broadsword forward, use both hand to push forcefully, reaching with the torso and extending the arms. There should be a feeling of pushing and of piercing, with an additional feeling of blocking or knocking aside. This is the hidden meaning within the movement.

Step forward, chop. This must use the fully integrated power of the body. In the final position the broadsword must have a point of focus and must be stable. It must not wobble.

- Broadsword chop is not just a chop forward and down. It must also contain a pulling back, or sawing, action. In this way, it chops, hacks, and slices. Press the head up to lengthen the body. Herein lies the essence of the broadsword. This is one of the most distinctive characteristics of Xingyi broadsword.

Advance, pushing pierce. When pushing, close the chest and stretch the upper back taut, putting a closing-in power into the arms. Advance accurately and firmly with the broadsword. Straighten the back and open the chest when lifting the broadsword above the head. When advancing to chop, withdraw the abdomen and close the chest, and use both hands to chop down. Press your head up forcefully. When pulling the hands back towards the belly, use the power from the lower back, lengthening the torso. Use the power from the whole body and transmit it to the body of the broadsword – the broadsword is an extension of the body

- Grip technique for the chop: adjust the grip on the hilt according to the needs of the techniques.
  - *Withdraw, lifting draw*: the hand turns in and out, and uses a spiral grip.
  - *Coil the head* and *wrap the head*: use a hanging grip.
  - *Chop*: press your head up and use a full grip and settle the wrist.
- When training on your own you may develop strength and power by using a heavy weapon. The weight of a heavy broadsword is up to you, but you must be able to swing it around and to do the techniques correctly. If it is too heavy then you won't be able to do the moves properly. When using a heavy broadsword you should do the moves more slowly, but you must not change any of the technique. This training will improve your body strength and coordination, arm and wrist strength, and help you feel how to use the left hand to assist the right hand.

PRACTICAL APPLICATIONS FOR BROADSWORD CHOP

Looking at the structure of the chop combination, it entails three separate actions: a *withdraw lifting draw,* an *advance pushing pierce,* and a *step forward chop and stab.*

Withdraw, lifting draw is a defensive posture and technique. If, for example, the opponent stabs to your chest with a weapon, you quickly retreat your rear foot a half-step and withdraw your lead foot a half-step. While stepping, rotate your right hand to circle the broadsword tip down to bring the blade edge forward with the tip pointing forward and down to block his weapon with the broadsword body. Then you can follow the line that his weapon stabs to lift and draw back so that it misses its mark.

Advance, pushing pierce can be either an attack or a block. Advance and stab forward with the blade edge forward in a pushing action, following the line of the opponent's weapon to strike his hand and make him lose his hold. You could also stab his belly. You must keep the tip of your broadsword pointing forward on the midline at all times to protect your centre.

Step forward chop and stab attacks by bringing the broadsword around the head. The coiling or wrapping protects your head and chest, in a quick action that both defends and prepares for the following attack. You then step in quickly and as far as you can to get close to the opponent while chopping forward and down. The chop must be aggressive and strong.

- The broadsword is a short weapon so you need to get in close. This means that you must be intimidating, you must have quick footwork, and the actions must be direct. You must dare to attack with no thought of losing, driving straight forward to take down anyone in your way.
- The main power of chop is the forward and downward action, so the main

action is chopping the opponent's head, shoulder, and/or chest. You must use the power of your whole body and apply it through the body of the broadsword, so that your chop is unstoppable. When chopping, you can grip with both hands to get maximum strength. Do not forget to pull backwards as you chop, to add a sawing, slicing action, which increases the damage to your opponent.

- Breathe out when chopping. You may make a sound to augment your strength and give the impression of a tiger leaping from the mountains.

THE POEM ABOUT BROADSWORD CHOP

劈刀歌诀

劈刀气势猛如虎，

遇敌不怵气宜鼓。

缠头裹脑冲进去，

劈刺头顶收腰腹。

The broadsword chop is as fierce as a tiger,

The *qi* is aroused to meet the opponent without fear.

Coil and wrap around the head and charge forward,

Chop and slice, pressing the head up and settling the body core.

2. BROADSWORD DRILL

INTRODUCTION TO BROADSWORD DRILL, *ZUAN DAO*

Broadsword drill is based on the empty hand drill technique of Xingyi. One of the characteristics of Xingyiquan is that almost all Xingyi weapon techniques share the name of a five element or twelve animal model technique. The definition of 'drill' in the martial arts is a forward twisting strike that can go either high or low, and the strike is no different with the broadsword.

Among traditional Xingyi styles there is a broadsword drill that pushes forward with the blade edge forward, tip to the right and blade body flat. Even though the hand holding the hilt turns as if doing an empty hand drill, this is really a broadsword push. When we are holding a broadsword we must bring out the techniques of the broadsword – this sort of technique should not be called a drill, since the broadsword itself is not doing a drilling action. There is also another technique whereby the broadsword is held in both hands, circled in front of the body, and then stabbed forward and up with the blade edge down. This is a straight stab to the head, there is no rotation in the stab – once again, not truly a drill with the broadsword, but similar to the broadsword thrust. I feel that a proper broadsword drill should rotate the blade while stabbing, either upwards or downwards.

The combination for drill is *right stance low drill, left stance high drill, turn around drill*, and *closing move*.

2a Right Stance Low Drill yòubù xiā zuāndāo 右步下钻刀

Start from *on guard*. Continue with *left advance, lifting draw; Right step forward, inverted grip low stab*.

ACTION 1: Advance the left foot a half-step and follow in the right foot beside the left ankle.[2] Keep the knees together and squat slightly on the left leg. Draw a semi-circle in a counter-clockwise direction, finishing with the right hand rotated palm out, the ulnar edge of the right arm up, the right elbow raised to ear height, and arm bent. The blade edge is turned up and angled forward with the tip forward and down between chest and belly height. Keep the left hand at the right wrist throughout the action. Look past the broadsword tip. (image 1.16)

ACTION 2: Take a long step forward with the right foot and follow in a half-step with the left foot, keeping most weight on the left leg. Extend the right arm with the hand in an inverted grip, reaching the right shoulder forward to stab the broadsword tip to belly height, blade edge up. Swing the left palm up to above the head at the left side of the body. The right wrist is at chest height and the broadsword body is angled down. Look past the tip. (image 1.17)

---

[2] Translator's note: Holding the foot at the ankle develops strength, flexibility, and balance. Another way to step is to touch down the foot as shown in the photo. Either way is correct, so I have translated the text as is throughout the book, even when it differs from the photos.

14   BROADSWORD DRILL

Pointers

- As the left foot advances the broadsword knocks down and draws back. These actions must be coordinated with the footwork.
- The inverted grip stab must land as the right foot lands.

2b Left Stance High Drill   yòubù shàng zuāndāo   右步上钻刀

Right advance, wrap and draw; Left step forward, inverted grip stab.

ACTION 1: Advance the right foot a half-step and follow in the left foot to the right ankle. Place the left hand on the right wrist. Circle the blade to the left, up, and then circle right and draw it back, keeping the tip forward throughout. Finish with the right arm bent, the right elbow up, and the torso turned right. Once the right hand has drawn back to the right shoulder, bring it down to the right waist, rotating it palm up to turn the blade edge up. Keep the broadsword tip forward, now at solar plexus height. Keep the left hand at the right wrist throughout the action. Look forward past the tip. (images 1.18 and 1.19)

1.18

1.19

ACTION 2: Take a long step forward with the left foot and follow in a half-step with the right foot, keeping most weight back on the right leg. Circle the left palm across the chest and up to brace / block up above the head with the palm up. Bring the right hand in to the chest, keeping the tip forward and the blade edge up. Extend the right arm while rotating it palm up so that the blade spirals as it stabs forward. Complete the stab with the right hand at chest height and the tip at nose height. Turn the waist, reach the shoulder forward, and press the head up. Look past the tip. (image 1.20 and from the front)

1.20   1.20 FRONT

CHAPTER ONE: BROADSWORD, *DAO*

Pointers

- o Complete the wrapping draw back as the right foot lands. Complete the lower spiraling stab as the left foot lands.
- o Complete all the actions as one movement with no hesitation.

• Connect to *right stance lower drill*, and continue. The number of repetitions is restricted only by the size of your training space.

2c Drill Turn Around   zuāndāo zhuànshēn   钻刀转身

With the <u>right</u> *stance upper drill* as example. *Turn and chop; Withdraw, lifting draw; Right advance, inverted grip low stab.*

ACTION 1: Step the left foot forward, landing hooked in. Do not move the right foot yet. Bring the left hand down to the right wrist. Turn the body around to face in the direction from which you came. Bring the broadsword up and around in a swinging chop. Keep the left hand at the right wrist to put power into the broadsword from both hands. Pivot the right foot onto the straight line and advance it slightly, shifting forward slightly towards the right leg. Chop the broadsword blade to waist height. Look past the tip. (image 1.21)

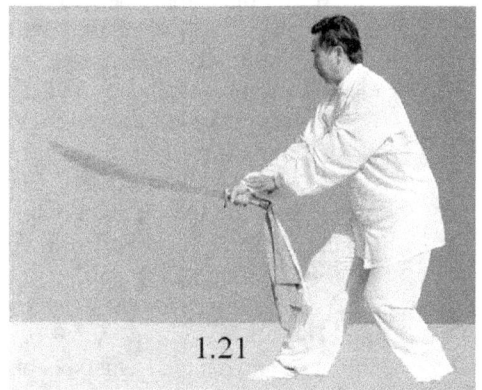

ACTION 2: Shift back to the left leg and withdraw the right foot a half-step to in front of the left foot. Draw the blade back and up without pausing from the chop. Lift the right elbow above the shoulder, bending the arm and rotating the right wrist to bring the ulnar edge up, palm out, hilt at nose height. This brings the blade edge to face forward with the tip angled down at chest/belly height. Turn the body slightly rightward. Keep the left hand at the right wrist throughout, and finish with the left elbow in front of the chest. Look past the tip. (image 1.22)

ACTION 3: Advance the right foot and follow in the left foot a half-step. Extend the right arm with an inverted grip to stab the broadsword forward with the tip at belly height, blade edge up. Reach the right shoulder forward. Brace the left hand up above the head at the left side. The hilt is at chest height, so the blade is angled down. Look past the tip. (image 1.23)

Pointers

- The turn around must be quick. To achieve this, take a considerable hook-in with the right foot. The chop must be forceful, transferring power from the body core to the shoulders, from the shoulders to the elbows, from the elbows to the hands, and from the hands to the broadsword. Do not fully extend the right arm. Use both hands for the chop, turning first, then chopping.
- Continue into *withdraw and draw back* immediately from *chop* with no pause. Shift the weight quickly but with good balance. During the turn around, the weight shifts first to the right leg, and then back to the left leg for the withdrawing step.
- After completing *withdraw and draw back* you must immediately go into *right advance inverted grip low stab*. The two are really one complete movement. Remember always that the end of one move is the beginning of the next move – the power for the following move is gained from the set up in the preceding move. This is a basic principle; always pay attention to getting a smooth and sound power flow.

• If starting from <u>left</u> *stance drill*, step the left foot hooked-in, place the left hand on the right wrist, and rotate inward to turn the blade edge up. From then on the action of *turn around* is the same.

2d Drill Closing Move   zuāndāo shōushì   钻刀收势

If starting from <u>right</u> *low drill*, first do *right retreat, left swinging chop*.

ACTION 1: Slide the left hand to the right wrist. Circle the broadsword so that the tip goes forward, down, and then left, past the left side of the body, lifting the hilt up in front of and above the head. Shift back to the left leg and retreat the right foot, touching down for stability. (image 1.24)

ACTION 2: Retreat the right foot and shift back to the right leg to take a *santi* stance. Swing the broadsword forward and down to chop with the tip at chest height. Pull the hands in towards the belly – keep the left hand on the right wrist. Press your head up and look past the tip. (image 1.25)

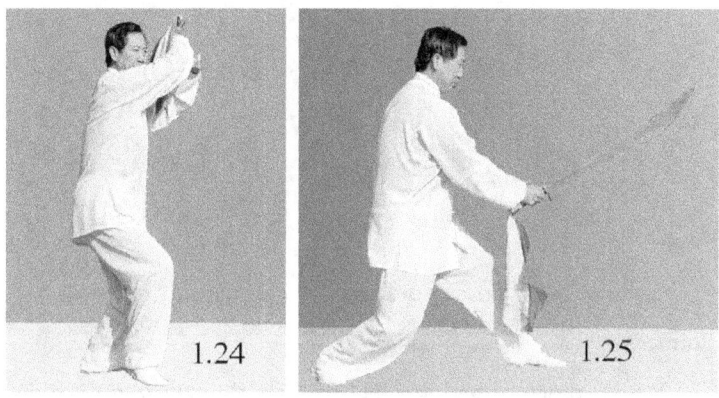

- The rest of *closing move* is the same as described above in *chop closing move*. Turn and right cut; Wrap the head and change hands; Hold the broadsword and flash the palm; Stand at attention holding the broadsword.

If starting from <u>left</u> inverted grip high drill first do *withdraw, right swinging chop*.

ACTION 1: Retreat the right foot a half-step then withdraw the left foot a half-step, so that you are still in a *santi* stance. Lower the left hand to the right wrist. Brandish the broadsword so that the tip goes down and back, swinging past the right side of the body. (image 1.26)

ACTION 2: Swing the broadsword up, then chop forward and down until the tip is at chest height, then pull the hands back towards the belly. Press your head up and look past the broadsword tip. (images 1.27, 1.28)

 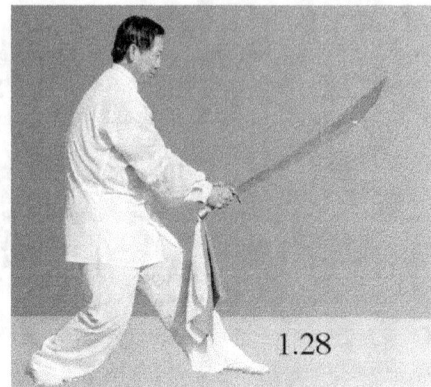

- Continue on to close as described in *chop closing move*.

Pointers

- To properly perform the left or right *swinging chop* the broadsword must pass by the side of the body, so the right hand's grip must adjust. When the tip circles downward the body should turn slightly so that the body leads the shoulders. At this time, lift the right wrist slightly. When the tip moves back, send the right hand forward slightly, extending it forward to assist the momentum of the broadsword so that it smoothly chops forward and down. The tip draws a large circle while the right hand draws a small circle. Try to get a kinesthetic awareness of the hand.
- Complete the chop as the right foot lands behind. Points to consider are the same as those of chop.

PROBLEMS OFTEN MET IN BROADSWORD DRILL

PROBLEM 1: During *right inverted low stab* the student does not control the tip, stabbing too low with not enough forward motion.

CORRECTIONS: The cause of this error is usually that the student has not straightened the wrist, or that his wrist is not strong enough. The student should do wrist strengthening exercises. If he lacks wrist strength, he can bring the thumb under to support the hilt. The student should also focus on the stabbing action to knee height.

PROBLEM 2: The student makes too large a circle with the tip during *right advance lower block and draw*.

CORRECTIONS: The student should extend the arm and turn the wrist, rotating the palm away from the thumb, to lift up. The grip must be supple and the wrist must be lively so that the tip does not draw more than a thirty centimetre circle.

PROBLEM 3: During *right drill* the student stops between the actions for too long a time, losing the power transfer in the body.

CORRECTIONS: Emphasize that right drill is one complete movement. It is taught as two actions for the convenience of learning. Once learned, it must be completed as a single move.

PROBLEM 4: The student uses only the arm to perform *right advance wrap and draw*, so that the movement is not coordinated with the body action.

CORRECTIONS: The broadsword uses the same principle as all Xingyi movements: pre-load back to go forward, pre-load right to go left. The body and both arms are used to give power to the broadsword. During practice the student must focus on the body action, slowly gaining the kinesthetic awareness.

PROBLEM 5: The student does not rotate the wrist enough during the drill. Also, when stabbing, the student uses only the arm and doesn't get power from the body.

CORRECTIONS: Whether stabbing low or high, there must be a twisting action. Drill is a twisting action. If you stab without any rotation, then it is a thrust, not a drill. To launch power into the drill you must turn the waist, reach the shoulder forward, and extend the arm. Pay attention also to assisting the power launch with the left hand. When stabbing the broadsword forward, the left assists by pushing back to balance the power.

POWER GENERATION FOR BROADSWORD DRILL

Right stance low drill: You may step forward or retreat. The right palm must rotate away from the thumb when lowering the blade to block, because the lower block uses the power of the wrist. When lifting and drawing back the blade, use the power of the torso and arm. These actions and transfers of power must coordinate smoothly.

Step forward inverted grip low stab: Step forward and turn the waist, sending the right shoulder forward. Settle and release the shoulder to transfer power to the arm and into the stab. The left hand assists the power launch by bracing back. Settle the torso down slightly to increase the strength of the low stab.

Right advance wrap and draw: Pay attention to the body work. Draw the broadsword back by drawing the arm from the waist. First draw back and then rotate the right hand so that the blade wraps. Use the power of the body core and shoulder, first open and then close. Turn the waist and settle the shoulder to gather power.

- Drill is an inverted grip, twisting stab. In a standard stab the blade edge is down, while in an inverted grip stab the blade edge is up. During the low drill, reach the right shoulder forward and brace the left hand back as you stab. During the high drill, keep the right elbow in front of the chest and send the broadsword forward from the lower back and shoulder. Be sure to keep a certain bend in the arm.

- When circling to block, use the power of the wrist. When lifting and drawing back, use the power of the shoulder and elbow. When stabbing forward, whether high or low, use the power from the lower back and shoulder. The whole body must be connected with no gaps in power.

PRACTICAL APPLICATIONS FOR BROADSWORD DRILL

- The different structure and actions of *left stance drill* and *right stance drill* show two different attacking moves. *Right stance drill* is an inverted grip stab, striking low to the opponent's knee or belly. *Left stance drill* is in reverse stance with the broadsword twisted to stab up, striking high to the opponent's head or chest.

Left advance low block and draw is a defensive move. 'Block ' is a blocking action right or left with the tip down and the blade edge out. 'Draw' is a withdrawing action to the side and back with the tip forward and the blade edge out. Drawing back on the left side is a left draw, and drawing back on the right side is a right draw. The point of contact is the proximal third of the broadsword body, gradually shifting forward as the blade moves back. The full move of draw is a defensive action that includes the block – block and draw work together. The tip draws a counter-clockwise semi-circle in front of the body to catch a weapon stabbing towards the chest, knocking it down to the right so that it misses. Then draw the weapon back, keeping the blade in contact with the opponent's weapon to move in on him. The draw back is also a means of gathering power for the stab. You can advance or retreat, depending on the situation. The footwork needs to be quick and well connected so that you can change from one to the other smoothly.

Right step forward, inverted grip low stab stabs to the opponent's leading knee or thigh, or belly. Keep in line with the opponent's attack and enter into any space that presents itself. A single handed stab is quick, a double handed stab is strong. The key is to advance along the line of the stance, and to have quick footwork. Also, do not be content with one strike – if you miss then immediately flip the wrist to chop the opponent's head or body. Continue to attack with a flurry of moves. 'When learning practise set stances, when using there is no set technique. ' You must move into any opportunity that you see, changing with the situation.

Left high drill first blocks high with the spine of the blade, then slides along the opponent's weapon to draw it back, then turns to stab the opponent's head. When blocking up use the strength of the wrist, when drawing back use the strength of the body, when stabbing forward use the turn of the waist and extension of the shoulder to send power into the blade. The circling action of the blade is the defensive move, controlling the opponent's weapon. The draw back wraps and presses onto his weapon, controlling it so that he cannot make good his escape. Then if he tries to take his weapon away you can follow it to stab.

Quickly stab his head or chest. This twisting stab is called 'snake coiling its body', or 'snake spits its tongue.'

Drill turn around is a means to get turned around to chop someone coming at you from behind. You must extend the arm and chop forcefully. If you can reach his opponent then chop his body, if you can only reach his weapon then chop his weapon. This is both an attacking and a defensive move, and is immediately followed by an advancing inverted grip stab. You must withdraw the foot quickly when turning. You must lift and draw accurately and quickly. You must step forward and stab quickly and forcefully.

- When training broadsword drill you must pay attention to the line that the whole broadsword takes, especially the circles drawn by the tip and the action taken by the hilt. You may make large circles at first. Once the actions are comfortable you should make the circles smaller, as this is more practical. It is often said, "large movements are not as good as small movements, large circles are not as good as small circles." Emphasize quick action – "no technique cannot be dealt with, only speed cannot be dealt with." This is a question of taking the short road or going the long way around. A small circle takes the short road – the hand, blade, and body are quick. If this is based on quick footwork then they will be effective. Entering into the opponent depends on the footwork getting in.

THE POEM ABOUT BROADSWORD DRILL

钻刀歌诀

钻刀如蛇见缝钻,

动作敏捷势势连。

绞带上提下刺膝,

进步上钻找鼻尖。

Broadsword drill is like a snake seeing a crevice and drilling into it.

The actions are quick and nimble and connect one after the other.

Coil around and draw to lift then stab to the knee,

Advance and drill up to find the nose.

3. BROADSWORD THRUST

INTRODUCTION TO BROADSWORD THRUST, *BENG DAO*

Broadsword thrust is based on the five element empty hand technique of driving punch, or crushing fist, and is a forward stab. In broadsword terminology, a thrust is a straight stabbing action with the tip, the arm and blade making a straight line, the power of the body reaching the tip of the broadsword.[3]

The key techniques for thrust are: *left stance thrust, right stance thrust, retreating thrust*. Within the combinations are: *left high hook and thrust, right high hook and thrust, left and right sticking draw and thrust,* and *chop and press and thrust*. There is also a distinction between a single handed thrust and a double handed thrust.

METHOD ONE: DRAW BACK AND THRUST

3a   Right Stance Thrust   yòubù bēngdāo   右步崩刀

Start from *on guard*. Continue with *Left advance, right draw; Right stance thrust*.

ACTION 1: Advance the left foot and follow in the right foot to the left ankle. Lift the right hand to shoulder height, keeping the tip extended forward, the blade horizontal. Rotate the right hand so that the blade edge is up, and turn the body right, pulling the arm back and keeping it bent. Keep the left hand on the right wrist throughout. Look forward. (image 1.29)

ACTION 2: Rotate the right palm towards the thumb and bring it down to between the waist and chest with the palm out. This turns the blade over, the edge once again up.

ACTION 3: Take a long step forward with the right foot and follow in a half-step with the left foot to land behind the right foot with most weight on the left leg. The legs are bent, the left knee behind the right knee, just to the side. Extend the right arm to thrust forcefully forward to chest height, rotating the arm as it moves forward so that the blade edge turns down. The tip points forward at chest height. Keep the right arm slightly bent and transfer power to the tip of the broadsword. Keep the left hand at the right wrist throughout. Press your head up and look past the tip. (image 1.30)

---

[3] Author's note: In normal wushu terminology, *zha* is a thrust and *beng* is a snap. In Xingyi terminology, the broadsword thrust is called *beng dao* because is based on the driving punch – *beng quan*.

CHAPTER ONE: BROADSWORD, *DAO* 23

Pointers

- Complete the rightward draw as the left foot advances.
- The draw and the thrust must connect smoothly in one action. It must be quick and well anchored.
- The stab must be completed as the right foot lands.

1.30

3b Left Stance Thrust   zuǒbù bēngdāo   左步崩刀

Right advance, left draw; Left step forward, thrust.

ACTION 1: Advance the right foot a half-step and follow in the left foot to the right ankle. Pull and draw the right hand back to the left, rotating to turn the blade edge up. Tuck in the right elbow in front of the left shoulder, keeping the blade horizontal with the tip pointing forward. Turn the waist left, tucking in slightly and closing in the chest. Keep the left hand on the right wrist. Look past the tip. (image 1.31)

1.31

ACTION 2: Take a long step forward with the left foot and follow in the right foot to behind the left foot, keeping most weight on the right leg. Rotate the right wrist and bring it in to the left chest to turn the blade edge down, tip still pointing forward at chest height. Take the hilt with the left hand behind the right, then thrust forward forcefully with both hands as the left foot lands (or, for back foot timed, as the right foot comes in). Keep the arms slightly bent, release the shoulders and settle the elbows. The hands complete the thrust at chest height. Look past the broadsword tip. (image 1.32 and from the front)

1.32   1.32 FRONT

24 BROADSWORD THRUST

Pointers

- Draw the broadsword back as the right foot advances. Keep the body well anchored, do not rise or fall. Turn the waist to the left and close the right shoulder towards the left to draw the broadsword leftward. Tuck the right elbow in and rotate the palm towards the thumb. Keep the movement gentle, using the body power.
- Thrust the broadsword forward as the left foot steps forward. Transfer power from the body core to the broadsword. Use both hands to get a stronger thrust, so that the thrust is strong and aggressive, the power reaching to the tip. Breathe out to launch power.

METHOD TWO: HOOK UP AND THRUST

3c Right Stance Thrust   yòubù bēngdāo   右步崩刀

Start from *on guard*. Continue with *Left advance, hook up; Right step forward, thrust*.

ACTION 1: Advance the left foot a half-step and follow in the right foot to the left ankle. Settle the right wrist and take a firm grip to bring the broadsword tip up, the blade vertical with the edge forward, to hook back with the spine. Bring the right arm in to the right side just above the waist to hook back with the broadsword spine to in front of the shoulder. Keep the left hand on the right wrist. Look forward. (image 1.33)

ACTION 2: Take a long step forward with the right foot and follow in the left foot to just behind the right foot, keeping most weight on the left leg. Lift the right hand to the chest and take a spiral grip to bring the tip down to the front to point straight forward. Keep the left hand on the right wrist. Extend both hands out forcefully to thrust forward to just short of straight arms, sending the power to the broadsword tip. The broadsword tip is at chest height. Look past the tip. (image 1.34)

CHAPTER ONE: BROADSWORD, *DAO*   25

3d Left Stance Thrust   zuǒbù bēngdāo   左步崩刀

Right advance, hook up; Right step forward, thrust.

ACTION 1: Advance the right foot a half-step and follow in the left foot to the right ankle. Cock the right wrist and settle the arm down in front of the body so that the broadsword blade hooks back to vertical with the tip up and the edge forward, the spine in front of the right shoulder. Bend both legs to sit slightly, tuck in the abdomen and empty the chest. Keep the left hand at the right wrist. Look forward. (image 1.35)

ACTION 2: Take a long step forward with the left foot and follow in the right foot to just behind the left foot, keeping most weight on the right leg. Lift the right hand to the chest and take a spiral grip to bring the tip down in the front to point straight forward. Keep the left hand on the right wrist. Extend both hands out forcefully to thrust forward to just short of straight arms, sending the power to the broadsword tip. The tip is at chest height. Press your head up and look past the tip.

(image 1.36)

1.35   1.36

Pointers

  o   Complete the hook up and back as the leading foot lands forward.
  o   Complete the broadsword thrust as the rear foot steps forward.
  o   *Left stance thrust* and *right stance thrust* are both complete actions. Do not pause midway through them.

3e Thrust Turn Around   bēngdāo zhuànshēn   崩刀转身

If in <u>*left*</u> *stance thrust*, hook the left foot in and turn around to the right. If in <u>*right*</u> *stance thrust,* step the left foot forward, landing with it hooked in and turn around to the right. *Left hook-in step turn around, crossing cut; Right crossways kick; Left empty stance chop.*

ACTION 1: Step the left foot forward and land with it hooked in, turning the body around to the right to face back in the way from which you came. Pull the right hand back to the left waist, rotating the palm away from the thumb to turn the blade edge out. Then turn the body right and cut across to the right in a flat cut at chest height. Stop when the blade cuts across to the right, bracing out with the left hand at the left, palm facing left. Look forward. (images 1.37, 1.38)

26 BROADSWORD THRUST

ACTION 2: Lift the right knee with the foot turned out, then kick forward and up with a crossways kick to shoulder height. Bend the left leg slightly for stability. Look forward. (image 1.39)

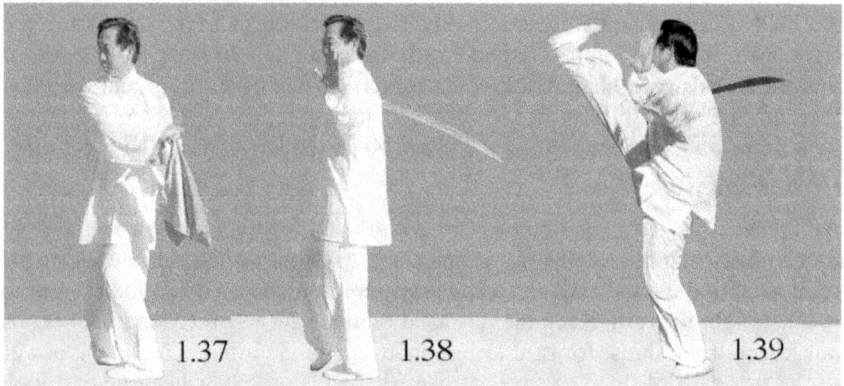

1.37   1.38   1.39

ACTION 3: Land the right foot forward, still turned crossways, and bring the left foot in to squat down, lifting the left heel, with most weight on the left leg. Turn the body right to sit into a resting stance. Rotate the right palm towards the thumb to bring the hilt above the right side of the head with the tip down and the blade edge away from the body, the spine nestled on the right shoulder. Bring it around the upper back to the left shoulder, keeping close all the time. Bring the left hand in to the right wrist or to hold the hilt and chop forward and down forcefully with both hands. The tip is forward, the blade edge down at knee height, the power in the distal third of the blade. Look forward past the tip. (image 1.40)

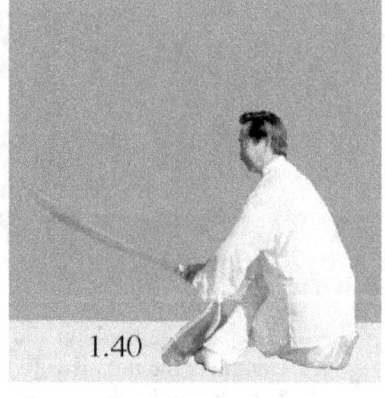

1.40

- Continue on with *left stance thrust*, advancing the leading foot first.

Pointers

- o   The *turn around* for broadsword thrust is similar to the *crushing fist turn around – leopard cat turns over whilst climbing a tree*. It must be done smoothly as one move.
- o   To get turned around with the crossing cut, the left foot must hook-in considerably. It should hook-in to in front of and outside the right foot. First pull the broadsword in to the left side of the body, and then use the turn of the body to put power into the horizontal cut. This is what makes it a strong technique. Be sure to stand steadily on the left leg and gain more power by bracing the left hand out.
- o   The crossways kick is a heel kick. Tuck in the right hip and extend the

knee. Stand firmly on the left leg.

3f Thrust Closing Move   bēngdāo shōushì   崩刀收势

If the <u>left</u> foot is forward then retreat the right foot a half-step and turn while cutting across.

If the <u>right</u> foot is forward then retreat the right foot and turn while cutting across.

The rest of *closing move* is the same as described in *chop closing move*.

PROBLEMS OFTEN MET IN BROADSWORD THRUST

PROBLEM 1: The student lets the blade wobble when thrusting, or thrusts with no point of focus.

CORRECTIONS: This is usually because the wrist is too relaxed and the hold is slack. If the right wrist is not strong enough, press the left hand firmly on it to help out. Settle and release both shoulders and close the elbows in towards each other to send the broadsword tip forwards, letting the forearms follow it. Transfer power from the body core to the shoulders, and from the shoulder to the elbows. Start the move slowly and then speed up, and launch power at the final point of focus. Focus on launching power with accuracy.

PROBLEM 2: During *advance draw the broadsword* left and right, the student takes the right hand too far across to the left or right. The broadsword hilt should not be taken further to the side than half an arm length away from either shoulder.

CORRECTIONS: The student must focus on correct application of the draw. Draw is an action that draws back at the side with the tip pointing forward and the blade edge facing away from the body. A left draw takes the blade to the left side, and a right draw takes the blade to the right side. The student must be sure to take the blade from the front towards the rear, and to pull the hilt back just to beside the right or left shoulder, keeping the tip pointing forward at all times.

PROBLEM 3: When combining the thrust with the hook up, the student does not do a clean thrust, but does an action more resembling a chop.

CORRECTIONS: This is because, after the hook, the student brings the tip down while starting the stab. After the hook he must first bring the tip down to point forward, and then extend the arm to stab. The teacher must watch out for this and correct it immediately. Before the stab, bring the right hand up to the chest, snug to the body – this places the blade horizontal. Then extend the arm to thrust forward, sending the broadsword hilt and tip out in a straight line.

28 BROADSWORD THRUST

PROBLEM 4: The student does not thrust with integrated power, he does not connect the thrust with the step forward. This is a common error.

CORRECTIONS: Explain and correct repeatedly, and have the student practise over and over. At first start with small steps, and fairly slowly, paying much attention to the getting the right feeling. Then gradually increase speed and distance.

POWER GENERATION FOR BROADSWORD THRUST

Draw back in the first method should be gentle, using the waist to draw the shoulder, the shoulder to draw the elbow, and the elbow to draw the hand. When the hand lifts, the chest should be emptied, the upper back stretched taut, the abdomen tucked in, and the weight settled down. This body technique is a slight pre-loading back to gain power for the forward thrust. The body then lengthens when the hand rotates to wrap and press down with the broadsword.

Right draw back: Pay attention to the grip on the hilt. First take a full grip. Then take a spiral grip as you lift the broadsword and draw it back. Then press the hilt down when you rotate the hand to wrap and press down.

Hook: When you knock upwards and hook back, empty the chest, settle the shoulders and sit into the lower back. Take a tight, full grip on the hilt and cock the wrist down. Place the left hand on the right wrist to support it, or you can even hold the hilt with the left hand to get more power.

Thrust: Be sure to keep the blade horizontal, and to keep the tip pointing forward from beginning to end of the action. Empty the chest, stretch the upper back taut, release the shoulders, settle the elbows, turn the waist and reach the shoulder into the stab. Your strength should transfer right through to the tip of the broadsword, so be sure to stab straight and not let the blade wobble. Step quickly and for distance, charging forward with the leading foot and pushing off the rear foot. Release the shoulder and extend the arm, putting a closing power between the arms. Breathe out when launching power, settling the *qi* to the *dantian*. Your power launch must be aggressive, and you must show confidence.

Resting stance chop: Trample the ground when you land the right foot. Do not forget to pull the broadsword back after chopping, to slice in and be ready for a stab. Turn the waist, tuck in the abdomen, and press the head up to gain power in the resting stance. Trample and drop into the stance to chop quickly but with stability. To do this, turn the waist to the right and press the legs together. The stance is low and the power is smooth; the power is integrated and the mind is focused.

- In terms of practical application, there are two types of thrust – a draw back and thrust, and a hook up and thrust. In terms of power application, there are also two types; the connection with the footwork is either front foot timed or back foot timed. That is, stab when the front foot lands or stab when the back foot lands. This variation in power launch also occurs in the driving punch.

CHAPTER ONE: BROADSWORD, *DAO*   29

- Broadsword thrust should show a strong forward stab. The technique must be accurate, the footwork must be quick, the power must be integrated, the spirit must be strong, the body should look like a swimming dragon. Pay attention to the body action and the power, drawing back to pre-load for the forward thrust.

PRACTICAL APPLICATIONS FOR BROADSWORD THRUST

Looking at the structure of the thrust combinations, thrust is a reactive strike. The main technique is a strong stab to the chest, belly, or other sensitive areas. The forward charging drive is similar to the driving punch of the five elements.

Advance draw and *advance hook up* are both defensive moves. If a short weapon is stabbing towards your chest, draw it back as you step in, so that the weapon is taken off line. If a long weapon is coming in with a chop to the head or a stab to the chest, hook up strongly, connecting with the distal third of the broadsword to catch the weapon and take it off line.

Step forward thrust continues directly from the defensive move. Whether from the draw or the hook up, switch immediately to the stab, getting in close without haste. The stab must be stable, accurate, and aggressive. Do not get sloppy. The stab will only work if the draw or hook has taken the opponent's weapon slightly off line. You need to finish the defensive move so that you can slide along the opponent's weapon to stab his chest or belly. You can also slide along a long weapon to slice his arm or hand.

- In using the footwork you can retreat the leading foot and then advance, or you can step aside a little and then advance. Use whatever footwork is needed. The main thing is, because you have a short weapon, when you advance you must get in close to the opponent – your footwork must be quick and agile. Courage is the key word – you must dare to attack and have a strong will to win.

- The main technique of thrusting is the straight line stab to the chest or belly, but you must be attentive to any adjustments made by your opponent. If you miss your target or your opponent blocks your stab you must be able to change your technique immediately.

- You should also be able to use a variety of deceitful tactics such as 'pretending you don't know how to fight ' or 'feinting first then attacking'. In general, you need more than skill, you need to further develop, practise, and deepen your combative knowledge and experience.

The Poem About Broadsword Thrust

崩刀歌诀

崩刀身法似游龙，
左右挂带护我中。
刀进身进全凭步，
粘顺其械扎其胸。

The body action of the broadsword thrust is like a swimming dragon,

Hooking or drawing to right and left to protect the midline.

Getting the broadsword and the body in depends on the footwork,

Stick to and follow the opponent's weapon to stab his chest.

4. BROADSWORD SLASH

INTRODUCTION TO BROADSWORD SLASH, *PAO DAO*

Broadsword slash is based on cannon punch, or pounding fist, of the five element techniques. The main technique is an oblique upward slice to right or left. The slice technique is an upward slicing action with the blade edge facing up, the power in the distal third of the blade. A normal slice is done with the forearm rotated and the broadsword at the right side of the body. An inverted grip slice is done with the palm rotated away from the thumb and the broadsword at the left side of the body. Slash is the opposite of chop. A chop is done with the blade edge down, and comes forward and down from above. A slash is done with the blade edge up, and comes forward and up from below. Traditionally the Xingyi slash is practised as just a slice. I have added a diagonal hack to bring out the attacking nature of the broadsword and give an additional technique. The slash and hack techniques work well together, and the combination practice is more realistic.

The key techniques for slash are: *left stance slash* and *right stance slash*. The *left stance slash* combination is: *Right retreat, right draw; Left advance, slice; Right step forward, diagonal hack.* The *right stance slash* combination is: *Left retreat, left draw; Right advance, inverted grip slice; Left step forward, diagonal hack.*

4a Left Stance Slash   zuǒbù pàodāo   左步炮刀

Start from *on guard*. Continue with *Right retreat, right draw; Left advance, slice; Step forward, hack.*

CHAPTER ONE: BROADSWORD, *DAO*   31

ACTION 1: Retreat the right foot a half-step and then withdraw the left foot a step, shifting back with most weight on the right leg. Bend the right leg and touch down the left foot in front of the right foot. Turn the right palm away from the body to rotate the blade edge diagonally upwards. Bring the right hand up and back at the right side to draw the blade back to the right side of the head. The hand is at eyebrow height and the blade level with the edge up and the tip pointing forward. Keep the left hand on the right wrist throughout. Turn the body right, flex the waist and contain the chest. Look forward past the tip. (image 1.41)

1.41

ACTION 2: Take a long step to the forward left with the left foot and follow in a half- step with the right foot, keeping most weight on the right leg. Circle the blade back and down at the right side, turning right and keeping the left hand on the right wrist. Continue to circle the blade, rotating the right palm towards the thumb to slice upwards to the forward left, blade edge up and tip pointing to the forward left. Finish with the right arm slightly bent, the hand at eyebrow height and broadsword tip at shoulder height. Swing the left arm up to block with the arm bent, palm up above the head at the left. Turn the waist, and reach the right shoulder forward slightly. Follow the broadsword tip with the eyes, looking just past the tip throughout the action. (image 1.42)

1.42

ACTION 3: Advance the left foot a half-step and bring the right foot past the left ankle then step it out to the forward right. Follow in the left foot a half-step, keeping most weight on the left leg. Relax the hold on the hilt to lower the tip and draw a circle with the blade at the right side, using the right hand as the pivot point of the circle. Once the circle is completed to the front, rotate the right palm away from the thumb and take a full grip, then extend the arm forward and up. Finally, hack forward and down at an angle. Bring the left hand in to the wrist when circling, and keep it there. Pull the hilt down and back at the right side, at the waist. The blade edge is down, the tip at chest height,

1.43

pointing in the direction that the action is moving. Put power to the blade body, press your head up, and look past the tip. (image 1.43)

Pointers

- Slash is one continuous movement. Combine the three actions together smoothly.
- Complete the upward slice and backward draw with the right retreat and left withdraw of the feet, so that feet and hands work together.
- Advance the left foot and slice the blade in the same diagonal direction, landing both at the same time with integrated power.
- During *step forward hack,* the right foot should first come in to the left foot and then step out. Circle the blade as the right foot comes in, lifting the blade. Hack down as the right foot steps forward.

4b Right Stance Slash   yòubù pàodāo   右步炮刀

Left retreat, draw; Right advance, inverted grip slice; Step forward, hack.

ACTION 1: Retreat the left foot a half-step then withdraw the right foot a half-step, shifting back to the left leg. Bring both hands together up and back to the left side at eyebrow height. Rotate the right palm to face towards the body. Hold the blade edge up with the tip pointing to the forward right. Tuck in the right elbow in front of the chest as the left foot retreats. Turn leftward and draw the blade back to the left. Look past the tip. (image 1.44)

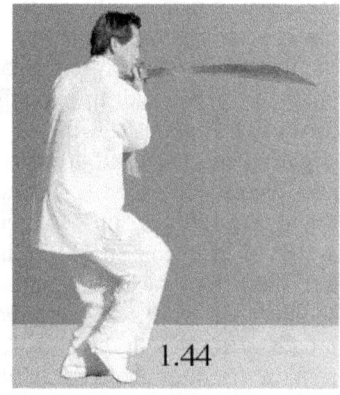

ACTION 2: Take a spiral grip, turn the body leftward and rotate the right hand to circle left and down to circle the blade at the left side of the body. Advance the right foot to the forward right and follow in the left foot a half-step, keeping most weight on the left leg. Continue to circle the broadsword, turning the body rightward and rotating the right palm away from the thumb, to slice up to the forward right. Finish with the blade edge up and tip pointing diagonally forward at shoulder height, the right arm slightly bent and the hand at eyebrow height at the forward right side. Send the right shoulder forward into the slice. Watch the movement of the blade tip throughout. (images 1.45, 1.46 and 1.46 from the front)

CHAPTER ONE: BROADSWORD, *DAO*

1.46

1.46 FRONT

ACTION 3. Advance the right foot a half-step, bring the left foot past the right ankle, then take a long step with the left foot out to the forward left. Follow in the right foot a half-step, keeping most weight on the right leg. Relax the hold of the right hand and circle the broadsword tip down, using the hand as the pivot point of the circle, so that the blade hooks down in a circular action outside the left arm. Use the spine of the blade to hook. Once the blade circles to above the head, take a firm grip and extend the arms to swing the blade forward and down to hack diagonally. Keep the left hand on the right wrist throughout. Finish by pulling the hilt in to the left waist, blade edge down and tip at chest height, tip slightly angled to the straight line. Send power to the body of the blade. Turn the waist slightly left, press the head up, and look past the tip. (image 1.47)

1.47

Pointers

- The movement of broadsword during the left and right slashes are basically the same, but since you hold the broadsword in the right hand your actions are quite different. The methods and power applications differ.
- In *left stance draw* the right hand must first send the blade tip forward at the right side. Then retreat, turn the waist, close the shoulders, flex the arms, and tuck in the elbows. And finally draw the blade back to the left, using the power from the body core to integrate the blade with the body.
- Complete the inverted grip slice as the right foot advances.
- *Step forward, hack*: to cut strongly down to the front is a chop, to cut strongly down to an angle is a hack.

4c Slash Turn Around   pàodāo zhuànshēn   炮刀转身

From the <u>right</u> stance angled hack. *Right hook-in step turn around; withdraw, right draw; left advance slice.*

ACTION 1: Step the right foot to hook-in in front of the left toes and shift onto the right leg, turning around to the left to face back in the way from which you came. Keep the hands at the right waist, the left hand still on the right wrist. Press your head up and look past the tip. (image 1.48)

ACTION 2: Withdraw the left foot to touch down beside the right foot, staying on the right leg. Extend the arms to slice up with both hands to the left front, broadsword tip forward and blade edge up. After withdrawing the foot, draw the blade back to the right side of the head, turning the body slightly right. Look forward past the tip. (image 1.49)

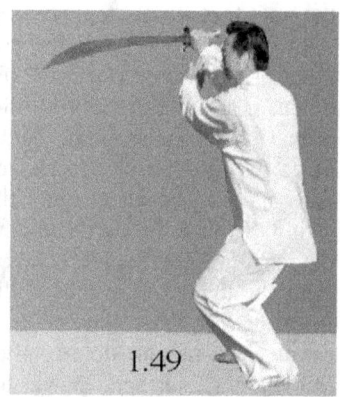

ACTION 3: Step the left foot to the forward left and follow in a half-step with the right foot, keeping most weight on the right leg. Keep the left hand on the right wrist and circle the broadsword back and down on the right side, turning the body right. Keep the broadsword moving and slice it up to the forward left, rotating the right hand to bring the blade edge up. The tip points to the forward left at shoulder height and the hilt is at eyebrow height. Keep the right arm slightly bent, turn the waist, and reach the right shoulder forward slightly. Follow the broadsword with the eyes, looking always past the tip. (image 1.50)

- Continue on with *right advance, angled hack*.

- If you start *turn around* from *left advance, angled hack*, then hook-in the left foot and turn around. Then continue with *right withdraw, left draw*, and so on, just transpose the right and left actions.

Pointers

- You must hook-in and turn around quickly, so need to hook the foot considerably to get around. Do not take a big step, but hook-in well, so that the turn around is stable.
- When turning, the broadsword stays at the side and comes around with the body, it does not move by itself. Wait until you are facing around in the other direction, before extending the arms forward and lifting the blade. Then when you withdraw the foot draw the blade back. Be sure to keep this order so that the movement is agile and quick, coordinated and gentle.

4d Slash Closing Move   pàodāo shōushì   炮刀收势

On arriving back at the starting point, do another *turn around*. If in a *left* angled hack, then do *left withdraw, right hook down; Left advance, swinging chop*.

ACTION 1: Without moving the right foot, shift onto the right leg and bend it to stand firmly, withdrawing the left foot to in front of the right foot. Extend the arms forward, rotate the right hand, and loosen the grip to circle around the wrist, hooking the broadsword tip down and bringing the broadsword spine on the right side of the body. Keep the left hand on the right wrist throughout. Look forward. (image 1.51)

ACTION 2: Advance the left foot a half-step forward without moving the right foot, to settle into a *santi* stance. Use the momentum of the broadsword to swing up and then chop forward and down. The position and use of power is the same as the normal chop. (image 1.52)

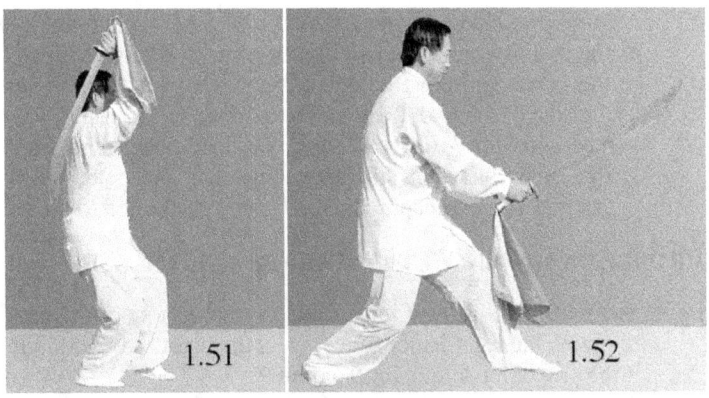

- The rest of the closing move is the same as that of the broadsword chop

36 BROADSWORD SLASH

closing move: Wrap the head and change hands; Hold the broadsword and flash the palm; Stand at attention holding the broadsword.

If the right foot is forward then do *Right withdraw, left hook*; *Right retreat, swinging chop*.

ACTION 3: Withdraw the right foot to the left foot without touching down, shifting onto the left leg. Extend the arms forward and rotate the right hand to turn the blade edge up. Then circle the blade with the right wrist at the pivot point of the circle so that the tip is down, then hooks back to the left side of the body. Keep the left hand on the right wrist throughout and look forward. (image 1.53)

ACTION 4: Shift back and retreat the right foot without moving the left foot, shifting most weight onto the right leg in a *santi* stance. Swing the blade up then forward and down to chop. The final position is the same as a normal *chop*. (image 1.54)

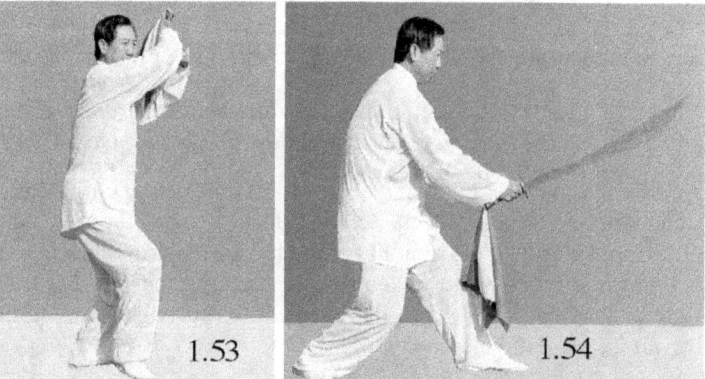

- The rest of the movement is the same as the *chop closing move*.

Pointers

- Hook the blade down as the foot withdraws. The hook technique uses the broadsword spine as point of contact. The wrist must be supple and the movement must be quick. Be sure to keep the broadsword snug to the side of the body, whether hooking to left or right.
- The chop in *closing move* may be done gently and slowly, as long as the hands and feet still arrive together. Keep the spirit full and use internal power, keeping the body fully connected to the weapon.

PROBLEMS OFTEN MET IN BROADSWORD SLASH

PROBLEM 1: During *retreat and draw*, the student doesn't draw an adequate circle with the right hand, so just pulls the broadsword straight back. This is not the proper technique for the draw.

CORRECTIONS: The definition of draw is to pull back from the front at the side, keeping the weapon horizontal. The right hand must first rotate to that the blade edge is angled up. Prior to drawing back, the blade must first reach forward. Then retreat the foot, turn the waist, and draw the blade back. The movement should be gentle and coordinated, not hard and strong.

PROBLEM 2: The student has no point of focus in *advance and slice,* often sending the blade too high.

CORRECTIONS: The slice should strike and be focused straight forward. Once the blade moves past the body then it should be slicing forward. Once the blade has reached shoulder height then the hand and arms should stop rising, and the power should come from the shoulder and waist. Take a firm grip on the hilt and pay particular attention to controlling the position of the shoulder and elbow.

PROBLEM 3: The student is inaccurate in the placement of the *step forward angled hack*, or steps the rear foot through without passing by the other foot, or steps forward to the wrong place.

CORRECTIONS: The rear foot must come in to the other foot first, this is the characteristic stepping pattern of Xingyi – shin rubbing stepping. Then step out to forty-five degrees. If the feet are placed correctly, take a perpendicular line from the midpoint of the line between them. The hack is then done diagonally at a forty-five degree angle.

POWER GENERATION FOR BROADSWORD SLASH

Withdraw and draw: First rotate the right palm away from the thumb, then lift the broadsword and draw it back. Use the waist to bring the shoulder back, which brings the elbow back, which brings the hand holding the broadsword back, so that power transfers from the body to the broadsword.

Slice: The right hand draws a small circle to make the broadsword draw a large circle. Rotate the right palm towards the thumb as it slices up, taking a spiral grip. Put power to the midsection of the blade. Turn the waist and reach the shoulder forward.

- In Xingyi, the techniques of chop and hack both have a characteristic action – a pull back at the end. In the first action of swinging up, extend the arms, lengthen the torso and expand the abdomen. When chopping or hacking down, settle the shoulders and elbows and pull the arms, contain the chest, tuck in the abdomen, and press the head up.

BREATHING CYCLE FOR BROADSWORD SLASH

Once you are comfortable with the actions, you should improve your deep skill by co-ordinating breathing with the actions. The actions guide the breathing and the breathing synchronizes with the actions. In this way you can find the power in the movements and find the whole body power.

- Inhale as you withdraw the foot and draw the broadsword back to gather

power.
- Exhale as you advance and slice, launching power.
- Use a short quick inhalation as you step forward and hook down or swing up before the hack. Then exhale quickly as you step forward and hack. Settle the *qi* to the *dantian*.
- Use a long and gentle inhalation during the closing, as it is a gentle move. Settle the *qi* to the *dantian* and connect the whole body together.

PRACTICAL APPLICATIONS FOR BROADSWORD SLASH

- Looking at the structure of the slash combination, it contains a draw, a slice, a hook, and a hack. This gives a short, practical combination similar to a sparring combination. The combination is very practical while showing the flavour of Xingyi and the characteristics of the five element techniques.

Withdraw and draw defends against a stab to the head, chest, or abdomen. Retreat or withdraw a step to dodge out of the way, and reach the body of the blade forward to meet the opponent's weapon. Then follow its direction and draw it back so that it misses its target. Whether or not you succeed depends on mastering the crucial moment; 'you can't be late, and you can't be early'. You have to wait until the opponent's weapon is within your space. This is easy to say but hard to do. You need to practise this and gradually get used to it and master the timing. Practice with a partner feeding techniques, to get a feel for the timing. Then you can gradually develop the ability to defend yourself with the technique.

Step forward slice goes in along the line of the opponent's stance to slice to the belly or chest, or to go on the line of his weapon, slicing up to his wrist or forearm, or to his leg. The key to getting in is to take a long, quick step. When going smoothly along the line of his stance you can move his weapon out of the way as you get in. The classics say, "Short can be made long with quick entering footwork." Your footwork must be quick and you must dare to use it to get the body in close.

Step forward hook and hack starts with a defensive action against a stab to your chest or belly made as the opponent, for example, dodges to the side and comes into the opening made when you completed a slice up. You quickly hook the tip down to catch his weapon with your blade spine, then quickly enter, using both hands to lift your broadsword, then hack down, using the full force of your back and shoulders. A double grip makes the hack much stronger. The classics say, "a single handed hold is supple and used in normal situations. A double handed hold is strong and should be used for fighting." If the opponent blocks the hack then you put the strength of your whole body into the blade and hack whatever you can catch – his body or his weapon.

- Slash is a powerful technique so you should show a strong and confident attitude like a leopard cat. You should charge straight in with the belief that you can't be blocked or stopped. You should always train with this attitude.

THE POEM ABOUT BROADSWORD SLASH

炮刀歌诀

炮刀气势如猫豹，

撤步后带进步撩。

上步挂劈势要勇，

手脚齐到方为妙。

The broadsword slash has the spirit of a leopard cat,

Withdraw and draw back, then advance and slice.

Step forward to hook and hack ferociously,

The secret lies in the hands and feet arriving as one.

5. BROADSWORD CROSSCUT

INTRODUCTION TO BROADSWORD CROSSCUT, *HENG DAO*

Broadsword crosscut is a horizontal cutting action from left to right, and right to left. The footwork is the same as the empty hand crosscut, following a zigzag line. Of course, the technique differs with a weapon, so you need to start again at the beginning. The weapon must become one with the body. You must learn how to fully utilise the character of each weapon with each technique – each weapon has its own characteristics due to its structure and use, and each original technique of the five elements or twelve animals has its characteristic power.

Broadsword crosscut contains two techniques: a brandishing check and a crossing cut. The brandishing check is a mix between two techniques. It has the large movement of a brandish,[4] but the blade is not absolutely horizontal, so it is not a pure brandish. There is a checking technique in this movement, but it is larger than a pure check. The crossing cut is a crossing hack with the blade horizontal.

The key techniques for crosscut are: *left stance crosscut, right stance crosscut, step forward crosscut, retreat crosscut,* and *turning crosscut.*

---

[4] Translator's note: a brandish is a large, flat circling block, usually overhead. A check is short, hard knock to the side.

5a Right Stance Crosscut   yòubù héngdāo   右步横刀

Start from *on guard*. Continue with *Left advance, right brandishing check; Right step forward, crossing cut.*

ACTION 1: Advance the left foot a half-step and follow in the right foot to the left ankle. Keep the knees together and bend the left leg slightly to stand firmly. Bring the hands from the belly forwards and up to the chest, about a forearm length away from the body, until the broadsword tip is at head height. Brandish the broadsword to circle the tip forward and right, then back, and then around to the left. Once the tip is in front of the left shoulder, turn the right palm down so that the blade edge is forward. During the brandish the right hand rotates outwardly then inwardly. Turn the body left. Keep the left hand on the right wrist throughout. Follow the broadsword tip with the eyes. Finish looking forward. (image 1.55)

ACTION 2: Take a long step to the forward right with the right foot and follow in a half-step with the left foot, keeping most weight on the left leg to sit into a *santi* stance. Using a spiral grip, palm down, cut diagonally across to the forward right with the blade flat. Keep a 120 degrees bend in the right arm and keep it at shoulder height. Turn the body rightward slightly. The tip finishes the cut angled to the forward right at shoulder height. Keep the left hand on the right wrist throughout. Press your head up and look at the broadsword tip. (image 1.56)

Pointers

- Brandish the broadsword as you advance the left foot. Draw a conical shape with the hilt and tip – the hilt as the point and the tip as the large circle.
- Take a considerable step forward with the right foot and follow in the left foot quickly, timing the footwork with the horizontal cut.
- The crosscut is one movement, do not pause midway through the action.

5b Left Stance Crosscut   zuǒbù héngdāo   左步横刀

Right advance, left brandishing check; Left step forward, left crossing cut.

CHAPTER ONE: BROADSWORD, *DAO* 41

ACTION 1: Advance the right foot a half-step and follow in the left foot to the right ankle. Keep the knees and thighs together and bend the right leg to stand firmly. Lower the broadsword to chest height and circle the tip left and back. When the right hand is in front of the face, brandish the broadsword around to the right to in front of the right shoulder. At this time the right palm is up. When brandishing the broadsword, the tip circles higher than the head and the right hand draws a small horizontal circle in front of the chest. When the tip arrives in front of the right shoulder, bring it down to shoulder height and place the blade flat with the edge facing forward. During the action, first turn the body left and then right. Keep the left hand on the right wrist throughout. Press the head up. Watch the broadsword tip throughout the action. (image 1.57)

ACTION 2: Take a long step to the forward left with the left foot and follow in a half- step with the right foot, keeping most weight on the right leg. Take a spiral grip on the hilt with the palm up and cut across horizontally, taking the blade forward and diagonally left. The blade edge faces left, the right arm stays slightly bent, the hand is at shoulder height and the tip is slightly higher than the shoulders. Turn the body slightly to the left and reach the right shoulder forward slightly. The tip finishes pointing at the same angle as the left foot. Keep the left hand on the right wrist throughout. Press your head up and look past the tip. (image 1.58 and from the front)

Pointers

- Complete the brandishing check as the right foot advances.
- The broadsword must arrive at the same time as the foot in the crossing cut, using the power of the whole body.

5c Crosscut Turn Around   héngdāo zhuànshēn   横刀转身

From *right* stance crosscut. Right hook-in step, turn around, left brandishing check; Left advance, crosscut.

42   BROADSWORD CROSSCUT

ACTION 1: Hook-in the right foot to the outside of the left foot and shift onto the right leg, turning around to the left to face in the way from which you came. Lift the left foot by the right ankle. Lift the hilt to nose height, rotating the palm away from the thumb and lowering the tip to waist height with the blade angled forward and down, the blade edge out. Once you are turned around, lower the hilt to chest height and brandish the tip up, left, back, and then right. Keep the right wrist lively, rotating as the blade circles to finish with the palm up in a spiral grip. Keep the left hand on the right wrist throughout. When the broadsword circles to the right shoulder the blade edge is forward. Watch the blade as it moves and then look forward. (image 1.59)

ACTION 2: Take a long step to the forward left with the left foot and follow in a half-step with the right foot, keeping most weight on the right leg. Cut across forward and left forcefully with both hands. (image 1.60)

- If from *left* stance crosscut the action of *turn around* is the same, just transpose right and left.

Pointers

o   The action and requirements of the crossing cut are the same as described above.
o   The turn around should be smooth, stable and quick, done as one movement.
o   The leading foot must hook-in well, landing outside the rear foot. This gets the body turned around easily and sets up for the next step. The more the foot is hooked-in the easier it is to push off for the next step.
o   When hooking-in to turn around, as the hilt is raised and the blade lowered, contain the chest and abdomen. Crouch the body down slightly to protect it.

5d   Crosscut Closing Move   héngdāo shōushì   横刀收势

The closing is the same as *broadsword slash closing move*.

If in *right* stance crosscut, then step the right foot back with *right retreat left hook down* before the *left advance chop*.

If in *left* stance crosscut, then move the left foot with *left withdraw, right hook down* before the *left advance, chop*.

The rest of the closing is the same as usual.

PROBLEMS OFTEN MET IN BROADSWORD CROSSCUT

PROBLEM 1: The student hangs on too hard when trying to brandish the broadsword so that it can't move smoothly.

CORRECTIONS: The grip must adjust and the wrist must be relaxed. Hold firmly to check, then loosen the grip to brandish.

PROBLEM 2: The student brandishes the broadsword completely over the head.

CORRECTIONS: The student should keep the right hand about a foot in front of the chest. When the hand makes a small circle in front of the chest, the tip makes a large circle above. So the broadsword tip draws a circle in front of the body, like a vertical cone. This is an effective defensive move, while swinging wildly over the head is not.

PROBLEM 3: The student does the crossing cut with a straight arm.

CORRECTIONS: If the arm is straight then the body's power cannot transfer through it and the strength will be weak. The student must pay attention to maintaining a certain flexion in the arm throughout the move. To connect the broadsword to the body, the optimum elbow angle is 135-150 degrees.

PROBLEM 4: When the student cuts forcefully he creates considerable momentum, so he cannot control the force or direction of the blade. This is a common error.

CORRECTIONS: First use both arms to brandish the blade, then, to cut across, wait until the blade is almost to the final point and bring the arms in slightly. This connects the blade more to the body, gives it power and keeps it under control. This is the sawing, slicing power of Xingyi broadsword.

POWER GENERATION FOR BROADSWORD CROSSCUT

The *brandishing check* works together with the advancing footwork. First use the broadsword spine to check to the side and then circle with the brandishing action. The right wrist must move easily, rotating throughout the action. The wrist draws a small circle so that the broadsword tip draws a large circle in front of the body. The broadsword forms a cone, that is, as the hilt lowers the tip rises. When launching power, launch from the body core to transfer to the shoulder, elbow, hand, and broadsword. This movement should be gentle and coordinated, using the body.

The crossing cut should be prepared for with a pre-loading action. Gather power to the right before launching to the left, and vice versa. This gives more power transfer from the body to the broadsword. Just before launching power, take a firm grip on the hilt. Keep the right arm bent and use the left hand to assist. Co-ordinate this with the breath, breathing out to get more power. Put the power of the whole body into the body of the broadsword and focus forward.

- The power launch of crosscut is not simply a cut across to the side. It should contain a sawing, slicing power as well. Turn the body and sit into the buttocks to make a slicing action so that the strike is more damaging. This is one of the main characteristics of Xingyi broadsword.

- The power of the turn around must fully utilize the spinning of the body, so swing the broadsword around without stopping. The power should go through all segments of the body out to the broadsword tip. Be careful to control the direction and angle of the crosscut after this.

BREATHING CYCLE FOR BROADSWORD CROSSCUT

- Inhale as you advance the leading foot with the brandishing check, to gather power.
- Exhale as you step forward with the crossing cut, launching power.
- Hold the breath briefly as you turn quickly around.

Use a long inhalation and exhalation during the closing, as it is a gentle move.

PRACTICAL APPLICATIONS FOR BROADSWORD CROSSCUT

- The core technique for broadsword crosscut is the crossing cut to either side. This can also be called a horizontal hack. Crosscut can attack high, middle or low – high is to the head, middle is to the chest, and low is to the waist. It is said, 'broadsword crosscut has the spirit of a raging elephant'. You want to bring out the direct charging spirit of an angry elephant. Its strength has no equal, there is nothing that can stop it. If you train like this, then when you want to use the technique you should be able to do the same.

Advance brandishing check is a combination of brandish and check. Check is a short knock to the side, using the fore-section of the broadsword spine to knock the opponent's weapon offline. Brandish is a horizontal turning, usually used to connect movements smoothly and gather power for the following movement. Brandishing check first checks, and then brandishes, to prepare for the following cut. If the opponent stabs towards your head or chest, once the weapon enters your space, that is, once he is within reach of your blade tip, knock his weapon aside with the end of your blade so that he misses you. Then stick to his weapon and draw it back borrowing his power to advance a half-step.

Step forward crossing cut is an attack meant to kill, and is the heart of the broadsword crosscut combination. The check has taken the opponent's weapon aside, and the brandish has gathered your power. You can now charge in with a horizontal cut, combining your hands with your leading foot, your *qi* with your will, and your strength with your *qi*. Spot your opponent and launch power forcefully into the cut. As usual, this move depends on quick and long footwork. As the classics say, "stepping slowly means losing, stepping quickly means winning." The power of the crosscut comes from the turn and pause in rhythm of the waist – first cutting and then slicing. If you use the crosscut effectively, really using the power of your whole body, then I think that there is no way the opponent can deal with you.

Crosscut turn around takes care of an opponent behind you, so you must get around quickly. Lift the hilt to bring the broadsword body around your head, protecting your head and upper body, then immediately step forward and cut across. The saying "left is coil the head, right is wrap the head ' means that they are the same technique, just done differently in the different directions because the broadsword is held in the right hand.

- You must use the crosscut according to the situation, do not try to use it as if the technique is set in stone. Think about the situation between yourself and your opponent. If you feel he is stronger, then use strategy. If you feel he is weaker, then attack strongly.

THE POEM ABOUT BROADSWORD CROSSCUT

横刀歌诀

横刀气势如怒象，
左右上步横冲撞。
腰肩带手刀拨云，
横折锉刺找敌项。

Broadsword crosscut has the spirit of a raging elephant.

Step in with a charging, ramming power, cutting left and right.

Check and brandish, sending the power from the back and shoulders to the hand and blade.

Cut across with a short sawing slice to seek out the opponent's neck.

6. FIVE ELEMENTS LINKED BROADSWORD

INTRODUCTION TO THE FIVE ELEMENTS LINKED BROADSWORD, WUXING LIANHUAN DAO

The Five Elements Linked Broadsword form is a short form that combines the foundation of the five element techniques with additional broadsword techniques. It is quite widespread and popular among traditional Xingyi practitioners.

Looking at the structure of the form, it contains all the five elements plus a few new moves such as *wheel around lift knee and chop, cross step hook down swinging chop, lift knee high stab,* and *leopard cat climbs a tree*. So, although short, it is rich in content. It is tightly and logically structured with smooth power transfer, good practicality, aggressive power moves, and strong attitude. The form has a clear rhythm, and each short combination links together quickly and smoothly. The hands and feet work smoothly together, the power combines gentle and hard, and the whole form is complete and full. The attitude is confident and solid as a mountain.

Performed well, the form can fully show the flavour and characteristics of Xingyi weapon play. If you want to perform it well, though, you must have a good foundation in the broadsword five element techniques. Once you are comfortable with the actions, power, and use of the techniques then it is easy to learn the form. Where Xingyi broadsword differs from most other broadsword methods is in the body power – the use of the fully integrated power that connects the body integrally with the broadsword. If you have not mastered the five element techniques then it is most difficult to master the form.

NAMES OF THE MOVEMENTS

1. Opening Move
2. Chop: Right Step Forward, Chop
3. Thrust: Step Forward, Hook Up, Stab Forward
4. Drill: Withdraw, Inverted Grip Low Stab
5. Chop: Step Forward, Hook Down, Swinging Chop
6. Drill: Lift Knee, Inverted Grip High Stab
7. Turn Around and Hide the Broadsword
8. Thrust: Step Forward, Hook Up, Stab Forward
9. Chop: Wheel Around, Lift Knee and Chop
10. Slash: Step Forward, Right Slice, Swinging Hack
11. Crosscut: Right Step Forward, Brandishing Check, Crossing Cut
12. Crosscut: Left Step Forward, Brandishing Check, Crossing Cut
13. Drill: Right Step Forward, Outer Block and Draw Back, Inverted Grip Low Stab
14. Drill: Left Step Forward, Wind Around and Draw Back, High Stab

CHAPTER ONE: BROADSWORD, *DAO*

15. Leopard Cat Climbs a Tree: Step Forward, Heel Kick, Resting Stance Chop
16. Thrust: Step Forward Wrap and Draw Back, Stab
17. Leopard Cat Turns Over Whilst Climbing a Tree: Turn Around, Crossing Cut, Heel Kick, Resting Stance Chop

(The following moves are repetition back in the returning direction)

18. Thrust
19. Thrust
20. Drill
21. Chop
22. Drill
23. Turn Around and Hide the Broadsword
24. Thrust
25. Chop
26. Slash
27. Crosscut
28. Crosscut
29. Drill
30. Drill
31. Leopard Cat Climbs a Tree
32. Thrust
33. Leopard Cat Turns Over Whilst Climbing a Tree

(Closing combination)

34. Thrust
35. Closing Move

Description of the Movements

1. Opening Move qǐ shì 起势

The whole action is the same as setting into *ready stance*. The movements are *Stand at attention holding the broadsword; Transfer the hilt over the head; Retreat and chop.*

ACTION 1: Stand at attention facing straight ahead or forty-five degrees to the line of the form. Let the right arm hang at the side, and nestle the broadsword guard in the left hand. The broadsword tip points up, the spine nestles into the left arm, the edge is forward. Press your head up and look forward. (image 1.61)

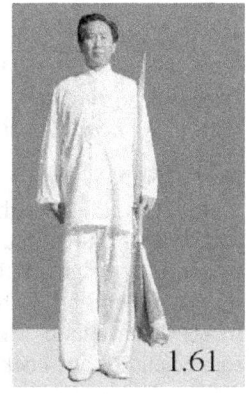

1.61

ACTION 2: Raise the hands at the sides until they arrive in front of and above the head. Bring the hilt to the right hand and release the left hand, placing it on the right wrist. Look at the right hand as it comes up, then look to the left. (images 1.62, 1.63)

1.62

1.63

ACTION 3: Retreat the right foot and shift back, bending the right leg and keeping the left leg a bit more straight, to sit into a *santi* stance. Chop forward and down, the blade edge facing forward and down, the tip pointing forward at nose height. Pull the right hand in towards the belly, about a forearm length away. Keep both arms slightly bent, close the elbows towards each other, release the shoulders and settle the elbows, contain the chest and stretch the upper back taut. Keep the blade on the body's midline. Keep the left hand at the right wrist throughout. Press your head up and look past the tip. (image 1.64)

1.64

Pointers

- Keep the arms naturally bent when lifting them. Turn a bit to the left when transferring the hilt to the right hand, and take the hilt with a pincer grip.
- Complete the chop as the left foot retreats and you shift back. Do not launch power for the chop, do a full, focused, slow move.

2. **Chop** pīdāo 劈刀

Withdraw, lifting draw back; Advance, push away; Right step forward, coil around the head and chop.

ACTION 1: Withdraw the left foot a half-step without moving the right foot. Shift back onto the right leg and lift the left heel, touching the toes to the ground. Rotate the right palm away from the thumb and lift it at the right side to in front of and to the right of the head, also lifting the elbow. Keep the left hand at the right wrist and bring the elbow in front of the chest. The broadsword tip points forward throughout, and first circles left and down in front of the belly, then rotates and draws back as it is lifted. In the final position blade edge is up and the tip angles down to the front at chest height. Contain the chest, tuck in the abdomen, turn a bit to the right, and look past the tip. (image 1.65)

ACTION 2: Advance the left foot and shift forward without moving the right foot. Extend both arms, the left hand still at the right wrist, to push the blade edge forward, the tip staying angled down at chest/belly height. Keep the arms slightly bent. Look past the broadsword tip. (image 1.66)

ACTION 3: Take a long step forward with the right foot and follow in the left foot a half-step to take a *santi* stance. Loosen the hold of the right hand and bring it up over head at the left so that the broadsword tip points down, the blade edge is out, and the spine is on the left shoulder. Bring the blade around to the right shoulder, passing snugly along the upper back, then extend both arms to chop forcefully forward and down. Pull the right hand back towards the belly. keeping the tip at chest height. Keep the left hand on the right wrist. Press your head up and look past the blade tip. (images 1.67, 1.68)

Pointers

- Rotate and draw back the broadsword as you withdraw the left foot. When you advance and push the blade, follow the blade with the footwork. When you step the right foot forward the footwork must be

fast and for distance, and land as the blade chops.
- The movement must be completed without stopping, especially actions 2 and 3. The actions must be quick and connected. Broadsword chop must also contain a sawing, or inward slicing, power.

3. Thrust   bēngdāo   崩刀

Left step forward, hook up; Right step forward, stab forward.

ACTION 1: Step the left foot forward and follow in the right foot to the left ankle. Take a full grip with the right hand and cock the wrist down, pulling the hilt down to the right belly. The broadsword tip hooks up in front of the right shoulder with the blade edge forward. Keep the left hand at the right wrist. Both hands are at waist height. Look forward. (image 1.69)

ACTION 2: Take a long step forward with the right foot and follow in the left foot to just behind the right foot, most weight on the left leg. Lift the right hand to chest height and change to a spiral grip to bring the tip down to point straight forward. Extend both arms forcefully forward, keeping them slightly bent, to stab forward to chest height. Send the power out to the broadsword tip. Reach the right shoulder forward slightly. Keep the left hand on the right wrist throughout. Look past the tip. (image 1.70)

Pointers
- Complete the hook up as the left foot lands. Be sure to bring the broadsword spine towards the right shoulder.
- Complete the stab as the right foot lands. Do not let the blade wobble. Keep the whole movement continuous and coordinated.

4. Drill   zuāndāo   钻刀

Left retreat, lifting draw back; Right advance, inverted grip low stab.

ACTION 1: Retreat the left foot and shift back towards the left leg, withdrawing the right foot a half-step and touching the toes down. Rotate the right palm away from the thumb, to circle the tip left and down. Then lift and draw the blade back, lifting the right elbow to draw the blade edge up with the tip angled down to chest height. Turn slightly to the right. Keep the left hand on the right wrist throughout. Look past the tip. (image 1.71)

ACTION 2: Advance the right foot and follow in the left foot a half-step, keeping most weight on the left leg. Using a spiral grip with the hand inverted, stab forward and down to finish with the tip at knee height and the blade edge up. Swing the left hand up to the left to brace out, arm bent, above the head. Look past the broadsword tip. (image 1.72)

Pointers

- o Complete the rotation, lifting, and drawing back the blade as the left foot retreats. Lift the blade by using the weight shift, withdrawing the right foot, and lifting the elbow. Use the turn of the body to draw the blade back.
- o Complete the low stab as the right foot steps forward – foot and broadsword tip landing simultaneously. Turn the waist, reach the right shoulder forward and brace the left hand up and back to assist the power launch.

5. **Chop**   pīdāo   劈刀

Left step forward, left hook down; Step forward, swinging chop.

ACTION 1: Step the left foot forward in front of the right leg, landing hooked out. Don't move the right foot, but lift the heel and bend both legs in a crossover stance. Take a full grip on the hilt with the right hand and lift the bent wrist slightly to circle the broadsword tip down, left and back. This hooks with the broadsword spine. Turn the body left, circle the blade at the left side then lift it. Stab the left hand down under the right armpit. Look at

the tip. (image 1.73)

ACTION 2: Take a long step to the forward right with the right foot and follow in a half-step with the left foot to sit into a *santi* stance. Rotate the right palm away from the thumb to turn the blade edge up, then swing the right hand up, forward, and down to waist height to chop with the broadsword tip at chest height. Circle the left hand down, left, and up to brace out at the left side of the head. Look past the tip. (image 1.74)

Pointers

- Hook the broadsword down as the left foot does the cross-step. Turn the body to the left and close the shoulders. As the broadsword hooks to the lower left, stab the left hand under the right armpit, so that the two arms perform complimentary opposite actions.
- The right foot must step forward quickly and for distance, and the left foot must follow in immediately. The swinging chop must have balance in all directions – up and down, forward and back.

6. Drill   zuāndāo   钻刀

Lift knee, inverted grip high push.

ACTION: Advance the right foot a half-step and shift to the right leg. Bend the right leg slightly for stability and lift the left knee. Bend the right arm and do an elbow cover, rotating the right palm towards the thumb to turn the palm up. This draws a semi-circle with the broadsword to the left, up, and then right. The blade is flat, the edge forward and tip pointing to the right. Press down slightly with the blade. Lower the left hand to the right wrist. As the left knee lifts, push forward and up with the horizontal blade to nose height. Keep the right arm slightly bent. Look past the blade. (image 1.75)

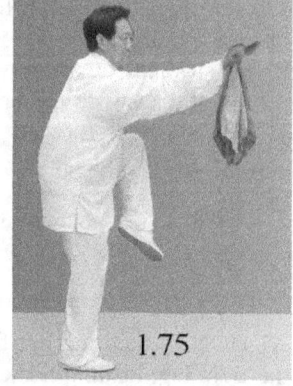

Pointers

- The lift knee and the broadsword push must be coordinated, integrating the upper and lower actions. Be sure to rotate the right hand and bend the arm, so that the blade body draws a horizontal circle to block. Tuck in the abdomen and contain the chest. Then push forward.

CHAPTER ONE: BROADSWORD, *DAO*

- o   This is a traditional alternate method of doing broadsword drill.

7. Turn Around and Hide the Broadsword   huíshēn cángdāo   回身藏刀

ACTION: Rotate the right foot on the spot to turn around 180 degrees to the left. Bend the right knee and land the left foot to sit into a *santi* stance. Lift the hilt past the head with a pincer grip with the blade edge down and the blade body on the right shoulder. Wrap the blade past the upper back to the left shoulder. Keep the left hand at the right wrist. Take a full grip and bring the blade forward, down and then pull back at the right side, keeping the blade on the thigh with the tip forward. Push the left hand forward to shoulder height. Look past the left hand. (image 1.76)

Pointers

- o   Turn around, land the foot, chop and pull back all as one coordinated movement. Turn around quickly, paying attention to the angle.
- o   The turn around may also be completed as a <u>chop</u>, keeping the blade in front. Pull the blade back just in front of the belly, place the left hand on the right wrist, and press the head up more.

8. Thrust   bēngdāo   崩刀

Left advance, hook up; Right step forward, stab.

ACTION 1: Advance the left foot a step and follow in the right foot to the left ankle. Bend the left leg and press the knees together. Send the blade forward then take a full grip and cock the wrist to pull the hilt back to the right side, which brings the tip up, hooking the blade back to the right shoulder with the blade edge forward. Keep the left hand on the right wrist. Look forward. (image 1.77)

ACTION 2: Take a long step forward with the right foot and follow in the left foot to behind the right, in the same short stance as a driving punch. Keep the left hand on the right wrist, lower the broad-

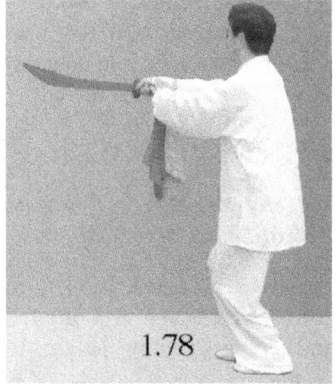

54   FIVE ELEMENTS LINKED BROADSWORD FORM

sword tip to point forward, then stab forcefully forward at chest height. Look past the tip. (image 1.78)

9. Chop   pīdāo   劈刀

Hook-in and wheel around. Lift knee, chop.

ACTION 1: Advance the right foot a half-step, landing hooked-in and shifting to the right leg, to turn the body around to the left 180 degrees to face in the way in which you came. Take a hanging grip with the right hand, rotate the palm towards the thumb and lift the hilt so that the blade edge is to the left. Turn the left palm out and swing it up past the face to the upper left of the head. Look towards the left hand. (image 1.79)

ACTION 2: Stand firmly on the right leg, keeping the knee bent, and lift the left knee. Circle the left hand forward and down, then back and up to the upper left of the head with the palm out and the arm bracing outward. Use a spiral grip with the right hand and circle it up, forward, then down to waist height, arm bent, so that the blade does a swinging chop and the tip finishes at chest height. Reach the torso forward slightly. Send the power to the distal third of the broadsword blade and look past the tip. (image 1.80)

Pointers

o Hook-in the right foot before turning around. The more you hook-in the easier it is to turn.
o The three actions – wheel around, lift the knee, and chop – are one movement. Co-ordinate the hands to assist each other. When launching power, turn the waist and send the shoulder forward, tuck in the abdomen and contain the chest. Reach the torso forward slightly. Use a firm grip on the hilt.

10. Slash   pàodāo   炮刀

Left step forward, carry and draw; Right step forward, inverted slice; Left step forward, hack across the wrist.

ACTION 1: Land the left foot forward, hooked-out. Rotate the right palm towards the thumb to bring the blade edge up, and lift it to draw across towards the left at eyebrow height, tip pointing to the forward right. Turn the body slightly to the left. Keep the left hand on the right wrist. Look past the tip. (image 1.81)

ACTION 2: Step the right foot forward diagonally to the right without moving the left foot and shift forward. Using a spiral grip, circle the right hand left, down, and then forward again to complete an inverted grip slice. The right palm is rotated away from the thumb at head height with the arm bent, the blade edge up, and the tip pointing forward. Send the power to the distal third of the blade. Keep the left hand at the right wrist. Look past the tip. (image 1.82)

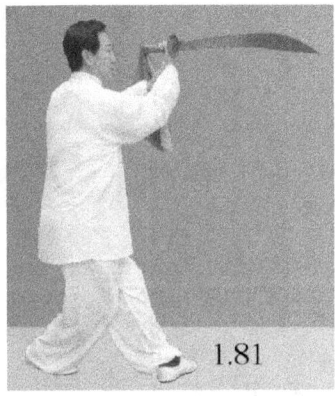

ACTION 3: Shift forward without moving the right foot. Bring the left foot in to the right ankle then step it out to the forward left. Follow in the right foot and shift the weight equally between the legs. Circle the blade vertically with the wrist as the pivot point, so that the tip goes down, left, back, and then up and forward to chop in a wrist cutting action. Keep the left hand at the right wrist. Keep the broadsword moving, and extend the right arm with a full grip to hack down, pulling the blade back to the left side. Finish with the tip at chest height. Press your head up and look past the tip. (images 1.83, 1.84)

Pointers

- The right hand must complete the lift and draw as the left foot lands hooked- out. Turn the waist, close the shoulders, and cover with the elbow to draw the hand and thus the broadsword to the left. The movement is gentle. Keep the legs slightly bent and sit the torso slightly down.
- The inverted grip slice must be completed as the right foot lands. The

blade must stay close to the body as it circles in the slicing action. Transfer power from the waist to the shoulder, from the shoulder to the arm, and from the arm to the blade.
o In the wrist cutting action the right wrist draws a small circle, so the wrist must be supple. When hacking down, first extend the arm and lengthen the back. Then contain the chest, tuck in the abdomen, settle the shoulders and elbows, and pull in. Be sure to press the head up.

11. Crosscut héngdāo 横刀

Left advance, right brandishing check; Right step forward, crossing cut.

ACTION 1: Advance the left foot a half-step and follow in the right foot to the left ankle. With the left hand supporting the right wrist, extend the arms forward and up to bring the broadsword tip forward and check to the right. Then brandish in a circle back, and finally come around to the left in front of the body, tip forward. To do this, the right wrist first rotates palm towards the thumb and then palm away from the thumb to bring the palm down in front of the left shoulder. Turn the body to the left. Follow the tip with the eyes during the movement. (image 1.85)

ACTION 2: Take a long step to the forward right with the right foot and follow in a half- step with the left foot, keeping most weight on the left leg. Take a spiral grip and turn the waist to the right to cut the blade horizontally across to the right, keeping the right elbow bent at about 120 degrees. Bring the hand and broadsword tip across at shoulder height in line with and pointing in the same direction as the right foot. Look past the tip. (image 1.86)

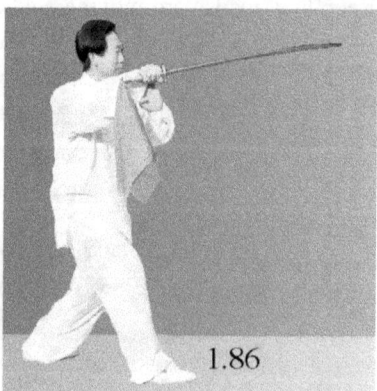

Pointers

o Coordinate the brandishing check with the step of the left foot. First check to the side and then brandish around. Adjust the grip so that as the right hand draws a small circle the broadsword draws a large circle in front of the body. Be sure to move the blade by the movement of the body and arms, not just the wrist. The action is gentle and coordinated.
o When cutting across, you need to add a short sawing in power to the crossing cut by turning the waist and sitting the buttocks at the end of

the movement. Exhale to put more power into the strike, transferring the power of the whole body into the blade.

12. Crosscut héngdāo 横刀

Right advance, left brandishing check; Left step forward, crossing cut.

ACTION 1: Advance the right foot a half-step and follow in the left foot to the right ankle. With the left hand supporting the right wrist, lower them slightly to chest height, then draw a small circle to the left, back, then forward, so that the broadsword tip draws a large circle right, forward, left, back, and then again to the right. Rotate the right palm up in front of the right shoulder, the blade angled up at head height. When the tip arrives at the right shoulder then lower it to shoulder height, blade edge forward. Follow the tip with the eyes during the movement. (image 1.87)

ACTION 2: Take a long step to the forward left with the left foot and follow in a half-step with the right foot, keeping most weight on the left leg. Take a spiral grip and turn the waist to the left to cut the blade horizontally across to the left, pointing in the same direction as the left foot. Finish the cut with the right palm up, the blade edge to the left, and the tip at nose height. Keep the left hand on the right wrist. Look past the tip. (image 1.88)

 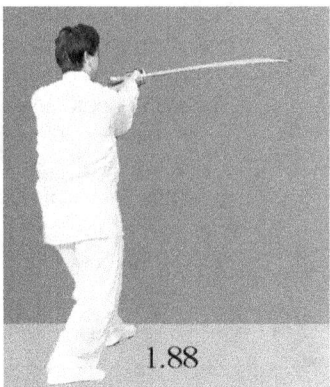

1.87   1.88

Pointers

o Points to consider are the same as those for movement 11, *right crosscut.*

13. Drill zuāndāo 钻刀

Left advance, right outer block and draw back; Right step forward, inverted grip stab down.

ACTION 1: Advance the left foot a half-step and follow in the right foot to the left ankle. Lower the right elbow slightly to first block to the right with the blade spine. Then rotate the right palm away from the thumb and flex the right wrist to bring the broadsword tip left and down. Then lift the right elbow and bend the elbow, pulling the hand back to draw the blade back, edge up and tip forward at chest height. Keep the left hand at the right wrist throughout. Look past the tip. (image 1.89)

58   FIVE ELEMENTS LINKED BROADSWORD FORM

ACTION 2: Take a long step forward with the right foot and follow in a half-step with the left foot. Extend the right arm to stab forward in an inverted grip, blade edge still up and tip pointing forward. Finish with the elbow slightly bent, the blade tip at chest height. You may keep the left hand on the right wrist or swing it up by the head at the left side.

Look past the tip

(image 1.90)

Pointers

- As the left foot advances the blade needs to complete three actions: block with the spine to the right, block across and down to the right, and then lift and draw back. The broadsword's action must be continuous, smooth, and quick.
- The stab is completed as the right foot steps forward. Extend the right wrist and keep a firm grip. You may press the thumb under the hilt to help keep the tip up. The stab is downward with the blade angled down, the exact height of the tip is determined by the placement of the hand.
- The two actions must be closely connected to use the power transfer within the torso.

14. Drill   zuāndāo   钻刀

Right advance, entangle and draw back; Left step forward, inverted grip stab up.

ACTION 1: Advance the right foot a half-step and follow in the left foot to the right ankle. Draw a clockwise trapping circle with the blade tip, first lowering it, then taking it left, up, and finally right, drawing it back at the right side and lowering it to the waist. Rotate the blade edge up with the tip forward at chest height. Keep the left hand at the right wrist. Look past the tip. (image 1.91)

CHAPTER ONE: BROADSWORD, *DAO*

ACTION 2: Take a long step forward with the left foot and follow in a half-step with the right foot, keeping most weight on the right leg. Slice the left hand across in front of the body to block up at the upper left, palm up above the head. Extend the right arm forward to stab up with the blade edge up. Finish with the right hand at chest height and the broadsword tip at nose height. Turn the waist and reach the right shoulder forward. Press the head up and look past the broadsword tip. (image 1.92)

Pointers

- Entangle and draw back as the right foot advances, completing all movement at once. Be sure to use the waist so that the power of the body transfers to the arm and thus to the blade. Complete the trapping action before drawing back.
- Land the stab as the left foot lands. Lengthen the lower back, release the shoulder forward, and extend the arm. Swing up the left hand to assist the power launch of the stab.

15. Leopard Cat Climbs a Tree   límāo shàngshù   狸猫上树

Advance, wrist cut, separate broadsword, heel kick; Resting stance chop.

ACTION 1: Lower the left hand to the right wrist. Use a pincer grip to lower and pull the broadsword tip back outside the right arm. Then circle it in a vertical circle up and forward, rotating to that the blade edge is down. Advance the left foot a half-step. Swing the blade down and back. Swing the left hand down and to the left. Lift the right knee and kick to chest height with the foot turned out across. Bend the left leg to stand firmly. Look past the kicking leg. (image 1.93)

ACTION 2: Land the right foot forward, hooked out, and follow in the left foot slightly to sit into a resting stance. Lift the right hand over the head and bring the left hand in to meet the right wrist. As the right foot lands, chop forward and down with the blade, then pull the hands back toward the belly, the blade at waist height. Press your head up and look past the tip. (images 1.94, 1.95)

FIVE ELEMENTS LINKED BROADSWORD FORM

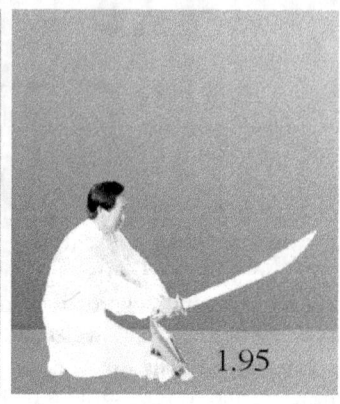

Pointers

- Complete the whole movement as one smooth continuation – but make sure that the actions are correct and the techniques clear.
- Keep the right wrist supple to be able to swing, hook, and circle the broadsword down and out to the right.
- Chop down as the right foot lands, turning the waist and closing the hips.

16. Thrust   bēngdāo   崩刀

Right advance, wrap and draw back; Left step forward, stab.

ACTION 1: Advance the right foot a half-step and follow in the left foot to the right ankle. Extend the broadsword forward then rotate the blade edge up and pull it back to the right shoulder, keeping the tip forward. Turn to the right and pull back until the right hand is in front of the right chest. Keep the left hand on the right wrist. Look past the tip. (image 1.96)

ACTION 2: Take a long step forward with the left foot and follow in the right foot to behind the left foot, most weight on the right leg, in the normal stance for a driving punch. Rotate the right hand and extend it forcefully to stab the blade forward, turning the edge down. The blade is level with the tip forward at chest height. Send the power forward to the tip. Keep the left hand on the right wrist. Look past the tip. (image 1.97)

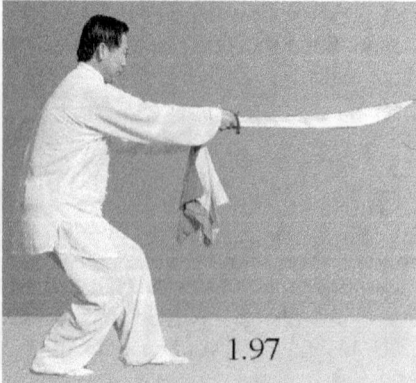

Pointers

- Wrap and draw the blade as the right foot advances. This is a gentle action. Use the waist, shoulder, and arm to draw the blade around and back, and be sure to rotate the right hand.
- Stab forward as the left foot lands, using integrated power. Take a long step and land firmly. Stab strongly into the blade.

17. Leopard Cat Turns Over Whilst Climbing a Tree

límāo dào shàng shù   狸猫倒上树

Hook-in turn around, crossing cut; Right heel kick; Resting stance chop.

ACTION 1: Step the left foot forward, land hooked-in, and turn fully around to the right. Rotate the right palm down and pull the blade back to the left side with the edge out. Open out both hands to either side, cutting flat across to the right with the blade at chest height and bracing the left hand out to the left. Look forward. (images 1.98, 1.99)

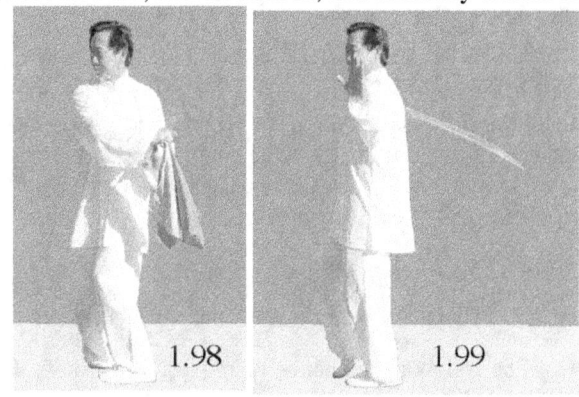

ACTION 2: Lift the right knee and then do a crossways heel hick forward and up to shoulder height. Stand firmly on the left leg. Look forward. (image 1.100)

ACTION 3: Land the right foot forward, pushing it down crossways, and bring in the left foot to sit into a resting stance. Change the right hand to a spiral grip, rotate it. and lift the hilt above the head so that the broadsword tip drops at the right shoulder. Bring the left hand in to the right wrist. Chop forward and down, bringing the hands down to hip height with the broadsword tip at waist height. Press the head up slightly. Look past the tip. (image 1.101)

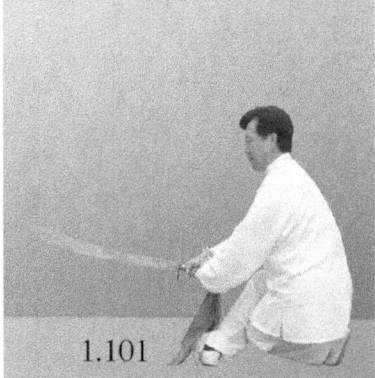

62   FIVE ELEMENTS LINKED BROADSWORD FORM

Pointers

- o   Hook-in considerably to be able to turn around smoothly. Cut the blade around to the back while turning. Turn quickly and cut with power.
- o   The other points to consider are the same as for movement 15.

18. Thrust   bēngdāo   崩刀

Right advance, wrap and draw back; Left step forward, stab.

ACTION 1: Advance the right foot a half-step and follow in the left foot to the right ankle. Extend the broadsword forward then rotate the blade edge up and pull it back to the right shoulder, keeping the tip forward. Turn to the right and pull back until the right hand is in front of the right chest. Keep the left hand on the right wrist. Look past the tip. (see image 1.96, and reverse the direction)

ACTION 2: Take a long step forward with the left foot and follow in the right foot to behind the left foot, most weight on the right leg, in the standard stance for a driving punch. Rotate the right hand and extend it forcefully to stab the blade forward, turning the edge down. The blade is level, with the tip forward at chest height. Send power forward to the broadsword tip. Keep the left hand on the right wrist. Look past the tip. (see image 1.97, and reverse the direction)

Pointers

- o   This is the same as movement 16, but going in the other direction.
- •   The following sequence of moves, 19 through 33, is the same as the first section, moves 3 through 17, repeated in the other direction. Perform the *turn around* again when you get back to the starting place, another *step forward thrust* in the original direction, and then close the form.

19. Thrust   see move 3.
20. Drill   see move 4. (images 1.102 and 1.103)

CHAPTER ONE: BROADSWORD, *DAO* 63

21. **Chop**   see move 5.
    (image 1.104)

22. **Drill**   see move 6.
23. **Turn Around and Hide the Broadsword**   see move 7.
24. **Thrust**   see move 8.
25. **Chop**   see move 9.
26. **Slash**   see move 10. (images 1.105, 1.106)

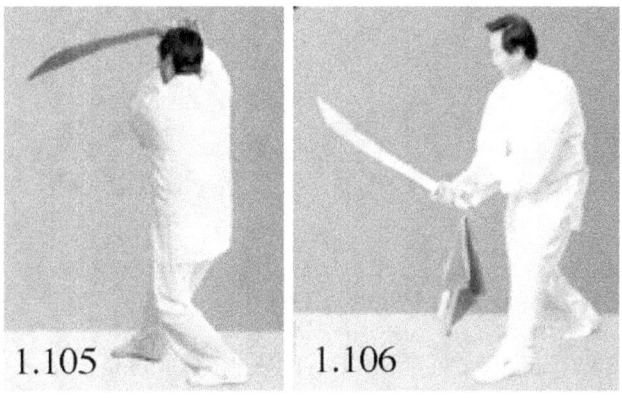

27. **Crosscut**   see move 11. (image 1.107)

28. Crosscut see move 12. (image 1.108)

29. Drill see move 13.

30. Drill see move 14. (image 1.109)

31. Leopard Cat Climbs a Tree   see move 15.
32. Thrust   see move 16.
33. Leopard Cat Turns Over Whilst Climbing a Tree   see move 17.

You are now moving in the original direction.
34. Thrust   see move 16.

35. Closing Move   shōu shì   收势

Return and cut across. Wrap the head and change hands; Hold the broadsword in the left hand and flash the palm; Stand at attention holding the broadsword.

ACTION 1: Retreat the right foot a bit and shift to the right leg, hooking in the left foot slightly on the spot. Cut flat across with the blade edge facing right at chest height. Extend the left arm to the left to brace out, palm out. Keep both arms slightly bent. Turn rightward, brace out with both arms, and look at the broadsword tip. (image 1.110)

ACTION 2: Shift to the left leg without moving the feet. Rotate the right hand so the palm is up, then lift it over the head at the right, loosening the hold to place the broadsword spine outside the right shoulder on the back. Circle the right hand to the left, taking the blade across the back to the left shoulder in a *wrap the head* movement. Extend the right hand forward to meet the left hand and place the hilt in the left palm. Turn the body leftward. Look at the left hand. (image 1.111)

ACTION 3: Shift back to the right leg and straighten it, bringing the left foot in beside it to stand to attention. Turn the left palm up so that the thumb, ring, and little fingers cradle the guard, and the index and middle fingers wrap around the hilt. Swing the right hand down, right, and then up to above the head, palm up. Hold the broadsword in the left hand with the blade spine snug to the arm and circle it up, rightward, and then down to the left hip. Follow the right hand with the eyes, then snap the head to the left when the right hand flashes, to look to the left. (image 1.112)

ACTION 4: Without moving the feet, straighten the left hand naturally at the side, still holding the broadsword with the blade edge forward and tip up. Bring the right hand down to the right side and stand to attention. Press the head up and look forward. (image 1.113)

Pointers

- Brace out with both hands simultaneously during the turn around and cut across.
- Bring the foot in and flash the palm simultaneously.
- When wrapping the head be sure to adjust your grip on the hilt. Keep the broadsword spine snug to the body – the wrap must be tight. Be sure to shift the body left and right during the movement.
- The whole movement must be well coordinated, fully focused, and dignified.

FIVE ELEMENT SWORD

五行劍

INTRODUCTION TO FIVE ELEMENT SWORD, *WUXING JIAN*

Previous generations of Xingyi masters developed the five element sword techniques. They examined a multitude of sword techniques in many styles, deleted what they felt was superfluous, selected the best, the most practical and those which would best represent the flavour and character of Xingyiquan. They created five sword techniques, which they named after the five elemental fist techniques of Xingyiquan. The names of the techniques are sword chop, sword drill, sword thrust, sword slash, and sword crosscut – the same as the five element fists.[5]

The traditional five element sword techniques are simple and practical with no extraneous movements, and emphasize deep skill. The footwork, body actions, power applications, and five element theory of Xingyi empty hand are combined with techniques that are characteristic of the sword. Each of the five short combinations is practised on its own, and contain both a left and a right-sided technique.

The five element sword techniques are not commonly practised in traditional circles. There are three possible reasons for this. One: teachers felt they were too valuable to teach openly, so they lost transmission. Two: few teachers knew them. Three: students did not like to learn and practise them because they seemed too simple and plain. The sword's five element form is, however, very popular and widespread. The form is built on the five techniques, but people do

---

[5] Author's note: In this book I have kept the traditional names but have included modern terminology for clarity. For example, *beng* is the word used in Xingyi weapons terminology for a straight thrust, as it is like *beng* [crushing or driving punch]. In standard weapons terminology *beng* is a snap up, while *ci* [pierce] is the standard terminology for a straight thrust with a sword. Similarly, what we call *pao jian* [sword slash] is normally called a *liao* [slice up]; and what we call *heng jian* [sword crosscut] is normally called a *pingzhe* [flat cut].
Translator's note: The names are slightly different in English for clarity. I have kept the names different from the modern terms, though, and in keeping with the Xingyi feeling.

not realize that real deep skill comes from training the individual techniques.

Each weapon has its own character, techniques and uses. The sword is considered the master of the short weapons, or the king of all weapons. The shape of the sword determines how it is used. The sword is a short weapon with a relatively light, straight, double-edged blade that tapers to a sharp tip. This blade makes it an agile weapon that allows you to adapt techniques quickly. In addition to the character of the sword itself, you must respect the nature of the Xingyi sword. The manner in which we use the sword in Xingyi – the footwork, bodywork, power, and application – is quite different from most other styles. The Xingyi sword techniques are highly practical and at all times show the flavour and characteristics of empty hand Xingyi. It is said in martial arts that the weapon is an extension of the arm, and in Xingyi this is certainly true – the weapons are fully integrated with the body. The movements are weighty and well anchored, the techniques are practical, and the power is integrated. Xingyi sword can be classified as a 'static sword'. That is, each completed position is held, each and every position can be seen clearly, and a clear distinction is made between action and stillness. The positions are well anchored and firm, it is suffused with power, defense and attack can be seen clearly, there is interplay between gentle and hard, and the bearing is resolute. The five sword techniques must be built on the foundation of the five element hand techniques. Without this foundation, you cannot master the sword techniques.

FIVE ELEMENT SWORD TECHNIQUES

On Guard   yùbèishì   预备势

The *on guard* position is the opening of any Xingyi weapon form or practice session, equivalent to the empty hand left *santishi*. For the sword, this means to stand in *santi* stance with the sword ready in the right hand. *On guard* is the beginning of any practice session or fight, so it is important to collect the mind. It must be done as post standing to develop the correct habits for holding the sword and prepare the way for the other techniques.

The actions are: *Left hand holds the sword behind; Transfer the sword over the head; Left santi stance, chop.*

ACTION 1: Stand to attention, press the head up, and look forward. Place the right hand at the side with the hand in sword fingers shape (thumb tucked onto bent little finger and ring finger, other fingers straight). Hold the hilt upside down with the left hand, with the thumb, ring and little fingers on the guard and the index and middle fingers extended along the hilt. The arms are naturally extended at the sides and the sword is vertical, the tip up and the flat of the blade snug to the left arm. Face forward or in the direction in which you will practise. (image 2.1)

ACTION 2: Lift the hands by the sides to above and in front of the head. Transfer the hilt to the right hand. Release the left hand and form the sword fingers shape. Unless otherwise stated, the left hand will remain in sword fingers shape throughout all the movements from now on. Look forward. (images 2.2, 2.3)

ACTION 3: Retreat the right foot and shift back towards the right leg to sit into a left *santi* stance. Chop forward and down from above the head to bring the tip angled forward at nose height. The right hand holds the hilt, pulling back to about a foot distance from the belly. Keep the right arm slightly bent, release the shoulders and settle the elbows. Line up the blade on the midline of the body with the blade standing.[6] Keep the left hand at the right wrist throughout. Press the head up and look past the sword tip. (image 2.4)

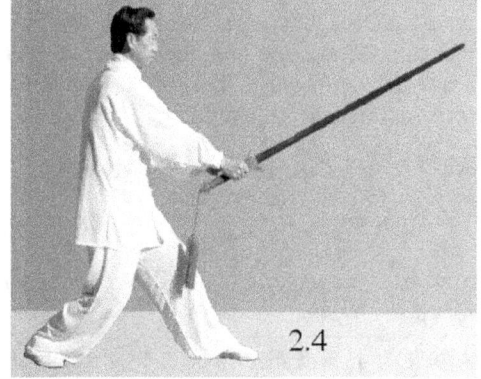

Pointers

- When you lift the sword to the side in the left hand it must not wobble. The flat of the blade must be pressed to the forearm so that it is lifted behind the arm.
- Be careful to make a clean and firm hand transfer above the head.
- Chop forward and down as the weight shifts back, pressing the head up at the same time.
- Perform the actions smoothly connected. Show an attitude of combat preparedness even though there is no power launch, Keep focused and show vitality and well-anchored power. Settle the *qi* to the *dantian*. Do

---

[6] Translator's note: A 'standing' blade is the edges 'standing' vertically. If the sword were horizontal, the edges would align up and down. A 'flat' blade is the edges lying flat. If the sword were horizontal, the edges would align side to side. A sword strike may be 'flat', 'standing', or angled, independent of the angle to which the tip points. For example, a horizontal pierce may use either a standing or a flat blade.

70 SWORD INTRODUCTION

- not perform the movement quickly or with overt force.
- You should practise the final position as a post standing exercise. Pay particular attention to lining up the blade along the midline of the body, with the three tips aligned – tip of the feet, tip of the nose, and tip of the sword.

1. SWORD CHOP

INTRODUCTION TO SWORD CHOP, *PI JIAN*

Sword chop is similar to the empty hand split and uses the same type of integrated body power. Sword chop uses a standing blade to chop forward and down. The power must reach the blade of the sword.

The traditional techniques of sword chop include: *hook and chop, swinging chop, straight chop,* and *angled chop*. Footwork includes: *right stance chop, left stance chop, advance chop, retreat chop*. There are also a *left and right swinging chop* and a *left and right hook up and down to chop*. The main traditional technique is the *left and right hook up and chop*, and the *left and right hook down swinging chop*. The other techniques are mainly slight differences in footwork or order of combining the moves.

METHOD ONE: HOOK DOWN AND CHOP

1a Right Stance Chop   yòubù pījiàn   右步劈剑

Start from *on guard*. Continue with *Left advance, right hook down; Right step forward, chop.*

ACTION 1: Advance the left foot a half-step and follow in the right foot to the left ankle. Keep the knees together and stand firmly on the bent left leg. Lift the right hand to the shoulder, rotating the palm towards the thumb so the sword tip draws a vertical circle at the right of the body, first pointing down, then back. Lift the right hand slightly to nose height as you finish the circle, lifting the sword tip. Turn the body slightly to the right. Keep the left hand at the right wrist throughout. Follow the sword tip with the eyes then look forward. (image 2.5)

2.5

ACTION 2: Take a long step forward with the right foot and follow in a half-step with the left foot, keeping most weight on the left leg to sit into a sixty/forty *santi* stance. Take a full grip with the right hand to chop forward and down with a standing blade. Pull the right hand in to about a foot away from the belly, so that the sword tip finishes at shoulder height. Keep the left hand at the right wrist throughout. You may also take the hilt with the left hand during the chop

CHAPTER TWO: SWORD, *JIAN* 71

to do a stronger, double handed chop. Lengthen the lower back, press the head up, and settle the shoulders and elbows. Look forward. (image 2.6, and from the front)

Pointers

- o   Complete the hook down at the right side as the left foot advances. Keep the blade close to the body. Keep the wrist loose and rotate the palm towards the thumb to accomplish this.
- o   Complete the swinging chop as the right foo t steps forward. The whole body must be connected through to the sword blade, so the sword and foot must arrive simultaneously.
- o   The hook and chop is one combined movement, and must be done without hesitation so that the hook sets up the chop.
- o   The chop must arrive accurately with a point of focus. Every chop must be clean and sharp. Using a double-handed grasp can give more control. Do not get carried away and use so much force that the sword blade wobbles.

1b Left Stance Chop   zuǒbù pījiàn   左步劈剑

Right advance, left hook down; Left step forward, chop.

ACTION 1: Advance the right foot a half-step and follow in the left foot to the right ankle. Lift the right hand to in front of the face, then rotate the palm away from the thumb so that the palm faces right and the thumb is down. This brings the sword tip down and back to circle and hook at the left of the body. Bend the right elbow and lift it to shoulder height, dropping the right hand to chest height. Keep the left hand at the right wrist throughout.
Turn slightly to the left. Look at the sword tip.
(image 2.7)

SWORD CHOP

ACTION 2: Take a long step forward with the left foot and follow in the right foot a half-step, keeping most weight on the right leg in a sixty/forty stance. Take a firm grip with the right hand and bring the sword up and forward, extending the arm to chop forward and down. Then pull the hilt back to about thirty centimetres from the belly, bringing the sword tip to shoulder height. Keep both arms slightly bent. Keep the left hand at the right wrist throughout or take the hilt with the left hand to do a stronger double-handed chop. Release the shoulders and settle the elbows. Sink the *qi* to the *dantian*. Press the head up. Lengthen the torso slightly. Look past the sword tip. (image 2.8)

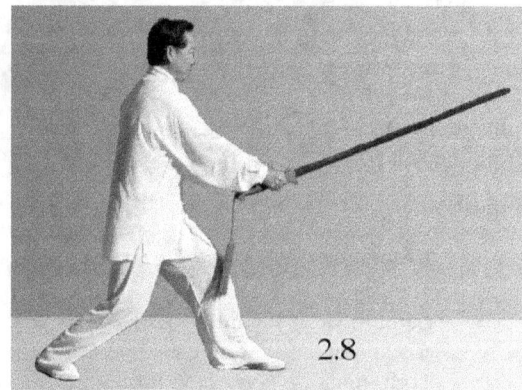

Pointers

- o   The points to consider are the same as *right stance chop*, the only difference being which foot is forward.

- Continue on with *right chop* and *left chop*, restricted only by the size of your training space.

METHOD TWO: HOOK UP AND CHOP

1c   Right Stance Chop   yòubù pījiàn   右步劈剑

Start from *on guard. Left advance, scooping hook up; Right step forward, chop.*

ACTION 1: Advance the left foot a half-step and follow in the right foot to the left ankle. Extend the right arm forward slightly to lower the sword tip to chest height. Then take a full grip and sit the right wrist down, bending the arm and bringing the hand to the right side of the chest, tucking the elbows in snugly to the ribs, to scoop up and hook back with the sword tip. Keep the left hand at the right wrist or grasp the hilt on the other side, palms facing each other, right hand above the left. The right hand and sword hilt are vertical in front of the chest. Draw the right shoulder back slightly, angle the torso slightly, and bend the left leg. Look forward. (image 2.9)

ACTION 2: Take a long step forward with the right foot and follow in a half-step with the left foot, keeping most weight on the left leg. Grip the hilt with both hands and extend the arms to chop forward and down, then pull in to about thirty centimetres from the belly. The sword tip completes

the chop at shoulder height. Sit into the buttocks, tuck in the abdomen, lengthen the back, press the head up, and look past the sword tip. Your power should reach the sword blade. (images 2.10, 2.11)

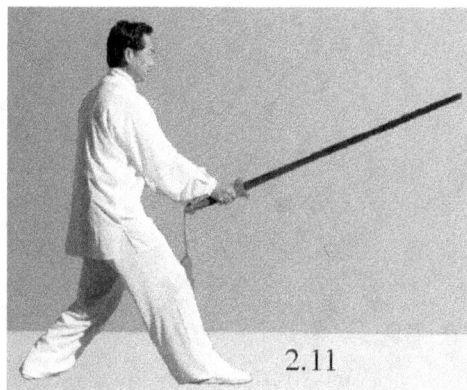

Pointers

- Complete the scooping hook as the lead foot advances a half-step. Complete the chop as the rear foot steps through and lands. The sword arrives as the feet arrive, so that hands, feet, and sword work as one.
- Although these actions are described separately they are one movement and must be done continuously. The hook up must be quick and the chop must be strong.

1d Left Stance Chop   zuǒbù pījiàn   左步劈劍

Right advance, scooping hook up; Left step forward, chop.

ACTION 1: Advance the right foot a half-step and follow in the left foot to the right ankle. Take the hilt in both hands and extend both arms slightly to lower the sword tip to solar plexus height. Then take a full grip, cock the wrists down, and bend the arms, pulling back to in front of the left chest with the elbows snug to the ribs to scoop the tip up and hook back. The sword finishes with the blade vertical in front of the left chest. Pull the left shoulder back a bit and angle the torso slightly, bending the right leg. Look forward. (image 2.12)

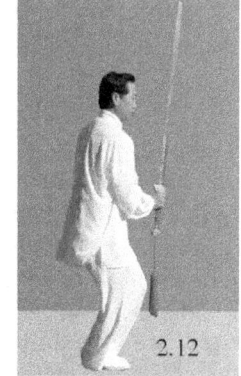

ACTION 2: Take a long step forward with the left foot and follow in the right foot a half- step, keeping most weight on the right leg. Extend both arms with both hands holding the hilt to chop forward, then pull both hands down and back to about thirty centimetres in front of the belly. Finish the chop with the tip at shoulder height, sending the power to the sword blade. Sit into the buttocks, tuck in the belly, lengthen the back, press the head up, and look past the sword tip. (images 2.13, 2.14)

SWORD CHOP

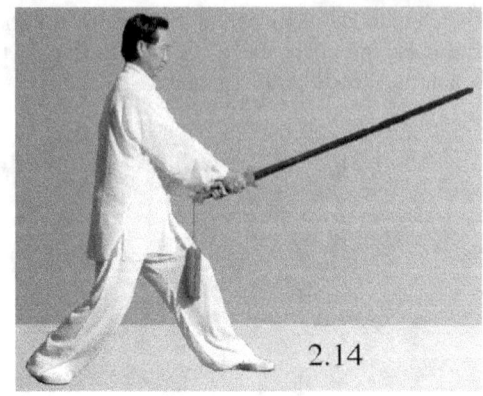

Pointers

- o Points to consider are the same as *right stance chop*.

• Continue on to repeat, limited only by the space available.

1e Chop Turn Around   pījiàn zhuànshēn   劈剑转身

Using the <u>*left*</u> *stance chop* as example.
Left hook-in step, lift; Right step forward, chop.

ACTION 1: Hook-in the left foot to in front of and just outside the right foot. Shift onto the left leg and lift the right foot at the left ankle. Rotate the right hand and lift it above the head, lifting the hilt with the sword tip angled down. Support the right wrist with the left hand. Look past the sword tip. (image 2.15)

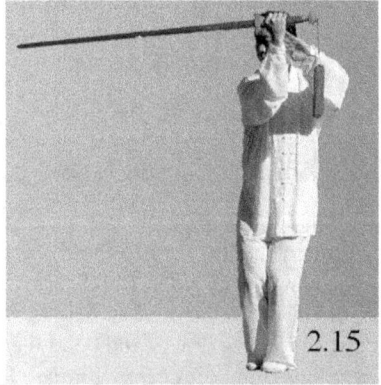

ACTION 2: Turn the body around 180 degrees to the right to face back in the way from which you came. Step the right foot forward and follow in a half-step with the left foot, with most weight still on the left leg, forming a sixty/forty *santi* stance. Lower the right hand to do a swinging chop forward, then pull it back in front of the belly. The sword tip finishes at shoulder height. Keep the left hand at the right wrist. Press the head up. Look past the sword. (images 2.16, 2.17)

2.17

- The basic action of *turn around* is the same whether on the right or left side, just transpose the right and left stepping. To turn around the other way, step the right foot hooked in and turn around 180 degrees leftward. With the right foot hook-in step, to turn around to the left, rotate the right palm towards the thumb. Use a hanging grip to keep the sword blade close to the body.
- Note that with the left foot hook-in step, to turn around to the right, the right palm rotates away from the thumb as it lifts the sword. Use a pincer grip to keep the sword blade close to the body.

Pointers

- Lift the sword as the foot hooks in.
- Be sure not to knock yourself with the sword blade.
- Chop with the sword as you turn around and step forward. This movement should be fast and strong.

1f Chop Closing Move   *pījiàn shōushì*   劈剑收势

On arriving back at the starting point, do a *turn around* to face the starting direction. Once you are in *left stance chop* then do *closing move: Right retreat, draw the sword; Stand at attention and transfer the sword; Left hand holds the sword behind.*

ACTION 1: Retreat the right foot a half-step and shift to the right leg, extending the left leg and turning the foot in. Lift the right hand and pull it back to in front of the right shoulder, palm in, so that the sword blade is horizontal at shoulder height with a standing blade. Bend the left arm and turn the palm out, placing the hand on

2.18

the guard with the thumb down. Turn the body ninety degrees to the right. Look past the sword tip. (image 2.18)

ACTION 2: Grasp the guard with the left hand upside down with the thumb, ring, and little fingers cradling the guard. Align the index and middle fingers along the hilt so that the blade is flat on the left forearm. Lift the left hand and extend it, circling to the left to lower at the left side so that the sword is vertical at the left side. Circle the right hand down, left, and then up to above the head at the right, palm up and arm bent to brace. Withdraw the left foot and stand up with the feet together. At first follow the right hand with the eyes, then turn the head to look left when the right hand flashes above the head. (image 2.19)

ACTION 3: Do not move the feet. Swing the right hand down to the side and open to a normal palm shape. Turn the head to look forward. Do not move the left hand. At this point you are at attention, and the practice is completed. (image 2.20)

2.19   2.20

Pointers

- The footwork and sword work must be well coordinated: pull the right hand back to draw the sword back with the blade horizontal, retreat the right foot, and shift back.
- The left hand must take the sword hilt accurately and immediately snug the flat of the blade to the forearm. Extend the index and middle fingers along the hilt to press and control it. Circle the hands coordinated together and with the withdrawal of the left foot. Pay attention to the actions and spirit of the eyes.
- After you have completed *closing move* you should still show full spirit. Settle the *qi* and calm the mind.

PROBLEMS OFTEN MET IN SWORD CHOP

PROBLEM 1: The student holds the hilt too tightly during the hook down so that the wrist is stiff and the sword cannot move smoothly, making the whole movement uncoordinated.

CORRECTIONS: First of all, you must explain the different ways of gripping the hilt. Then you must explain how each gripping technique combines with each sword technique. For the hook down, the right palm must rotate towards the thumb and then hook down, using force on the hook down. When turning, the grip must be relaxed so that the sword can circle quickly and stay close to the body.

PROBLEM 2: During the chop the student loses control due to the momentum of the sword. The blade is unstable, not coordinated with the body, or even wobbles.

CORRECTIONS: The student should start out not putting too much force into the chop, and gradually increase the force as he gains control. He should also start out slowly and gradually increase the speed as he gets used to it.

PROBLEM 3: During the hook up and chop, the student lifts the hilt up too high to do the scooping hook upwards, lifting above the shoulder. This makes the blade touch the body, which should never be done with a sword.

CORRECTIONS: Explain to the student that this action is made up of two techniques – a scoop and a hook up. He must first sit the wrist down to scoop and then pull the arm back to hook up. In this way the sword is first brought vertical and then pulled back. He also must be careful to place both hands in front of the chest so that the blade is not pulled back into his body.

POWER GENERATION FOR SWORD CHOP

Right hook down and chop: the right hand needs to take a relaxed grip and rotate the palm towards the thumb with a supple wrist to complete an effective hook down. The hand and hilt complete a small circle while the sword blade completes a large circle. When bringing the blade up you should lengthen the body core, lift the shoulder and draw the elbow. When chopping forward you should first extend both arms forward, and then move down and pull back in. Tuck in the abdomen, contain the chest, sit into the lower back, press the head up, release the shoulders, and settle the elbows to give full body power to the chop.

- Chop is not a simple chop down. It does a sawing, inward slicing, action to complete the movement, pulling and gathering towards the body. This is a characteristic of Xingyi's sword chop. This method lengthens the line of action of the blade and increases the power of the chop.

- When chopping, respect the theories of Xingyi's power application: "use a firm grip to strike " and "launch power after the halfway point." That is to say, when launching power to chop, take a full, firm grip on the hilt. The sword circles into the chop, so wait until it has completed half of the circle, then augment its momentum with your power launch. In the first half of the circle, keep your grip and wrist relaxed. As the sword blade arrives over the head then firm up and launch power forward to chop down.

- The technique scoop is applied with the sword tip, while hook is applied with the sword blade. The *scooping hook* in the chop combination unites these two techniques. First scoop then hook, but all in one continuum. When scooping, extend the arm and cock the wrist down. When hooking, bend the arm and pull in. When scooping/hooking to the left be sure to pull the hilt in to the left chest. When scooping/hooking to the right be sure to pull the hilt in to the right chest. Contain the chest, bend the lower back,

78 SWORD CHOP

contract the belly, and compress the torso to gather power.

- To chop you must draw a circle with the hands, first up, then forward, then down, and then back in towards the body. Lengthen the torso as you raise the hands. Extend the arms as you reach the hands forward. Settle the elbows as you lower the hands. Tuck in the belly and press the head up as you pull the hands in. In this way you use the whole body throughout the strike. The sword blade does not simply chop down, but saws or slices in towards the body at the end of the action.

Turn around: Gather power as you hook-in and lift the sword. Launch power as you turn around and chop. Transfer power from the lower back to the shoulders, from the shoulders to the arms, and from the arms to the blade. The right hand draws a circle above the head, so the hand moves the hilt, transferring the action and power to the blade. As the hand arrives at the upper front, it rotates to turn the blade to standing in preparation for the forward chop.

BREATHING CYCLE FOR SWORD CHOP

- Inhale as you advance and hook, whether hooking up or down.
- Exhale as you step forward and chop. Settle the *qi* to the *dantian*.

Use long and deep breathing when practising slowly. Use a long inhalation and a short, sharp exhalation when practising quickly.

PRACTICAL APPLICATIONS FOR SWORD CHOP

- The sword is a relatively short and light weapon, so this needs to be taken into account when applying its techniques. The blade is narrow and thin with a sharp tip and two sharp edges, so its movements are light and agile. Because of its structure you should avoid clashing directly with an opponent's weapon. Techniques should be done firmly and gently – never with overt force, but not weak, either. You need deft power with a confident attitude to play the sword.

Chop: This is a chop down from above, and so is an attack. The target is the opponent's head, hand or arm, or body. You can turn a defense into an attack by directly chopping down on an opponent's straight oncoming weapon. To chop an opponent's weapon you must first step aside so that the sword chops down a bit at an angle, crossing with the weapon. As soon as you make contact with the weapon, advance to pierce, scoop or slice up. Do not be content with one strike, but always continue with successive attacks without giving the opponent any breathing space. If you can seriously hurt him then he will lose the capacity to fight.

Hook down and chop: Looking at this movement, the hook down to left or right is a defensive move, defending yourself from a straight stab towards or below your centre. You cannot use the thin, light and short blade to directly block, so the hook is a technique that follows along the line of action to deflect from your

CHAPTER TWO: SWORD, *JIAN* 79

midline. You must retreat or dodge to the side while hooking down. Then you advance to chop, moving in with the body and sword simultaneously. Chop to the head, body, or arm. You can chop either with a one handed grip or a two handed grip. Ordinarily the one handed grip is used as it is agile, but the two handed grip is much stronger and is used for real combat.

Hook up and chop: This primarily defends against a high stab. First scoop, then hook. When you scoop up, don't go past your head. When you hook back don't go past your shoulder. This technique will defend against a straight stab from almost any weapon. You need to step a bit to the left when hooking on the right side, to dodge the attack. Touch the opponent's weapon with the scooping action, then slide along it with the hooking action to deflect it and draw it into the empty space. The immediately follow up, sliding along his weapon to chop his hand or body. This attack depends on getting in quickly with the feet, body, and hands. Getting in close with ferocity lengthens the range of the sword.

- The chop can also be combined with other techniques. For example, you can first chop onto the opponent's weapon and immediately follow up with a step in pierce to his chest. Or you can first chop down then and then snap the wrist up to cut his hand or arm. Or you can follow the chop with a step in crossing cut, or with a slice up, to slice the opponent's chest, head, hands or arm. You must be able to follow up the chop smoothly with many techniques to take advantage of whatever opportunity presents. 'When the technique changes in the heart, the method comes out in the hands'.

- When you do the hook up or hook down you should be ready to advance or retreat as needed, but you will usually retreat. You need to react to whether or not the opponent gets into your zone of defense. To have the appropriate reaction time you need to recognize 'old and young '. 'Old ' is when the opponent gets too deeply into your zone, and 'young ' is when he doesn't get in enough. In an 'old ' situation, you haven't defended on time. In a 'young ' situation the opponent can change easily. So this is the window of opportunity that you need to master. You must react when the opponent's weapon gets thirty centimetres into your zone of defense. As soon as the opponent's weapon has entered your zone you must stick your sword to his weapon. As his weapon advances you follow his force to draw him off target. If he retreats then you can go along with this and advance, stabbing his arm or body. When using the hook you must pay attention to the opponent's balance; if he hasn't entered deeply into the attack then you must not attempt an attack, but prepare to defend against a second or third attacking technique. Use agile stepping and tight defensive measures to protect yourself. Of course, 'saying is not doing'. As Sunzi said: "There are no fixed moves in the opponent's weapon, just as there is no fixed shape in water. You must change with the opponent to gain victory.'

THE POEM ABOUT SWORD CHOP

劈剑歌诀

劈剑技法最平长,

左右上下挂劈忙。

上步抡劈随身走,

劈中带刺内中藏。

The most common technique of the sword is the chop.

Hook left or right, up or down, and follow up with a chop.

Step in with a swinging chop to follow the opponent.

There is a hidden draw and sawing slice in the chop.

2. SWORD DRILL

INTRODUCTION TO SWORD DRILL, *ZUAN JIAN*

Sword drill gets its name from the empty hand drill of the five elements. When drill is done as a hand technique the fist rotates as it moves forward and up. When done as a sword technique, drill uses a twisted grip. The right hand rotates to turn the under edge of the blade as the blade pierces forward, to complete a drilling action. The rotation turns the under edge of the blade up for the high drill or forward for the low drill. For the <u>low</u> pierce the right palm is rotated away from the thumb so that the under edge of the blade is angled forward and the sword tip points forward and down, usually in a right, or aligned, stance. For the <u>high</u> pierce the palm is rotated towards the thumb to turn the under edge of the blade up and the tip forward and up, usually in a left, or reverse, stance.

The combination for drill is *right stance drill, left stance drill, turn around drill*, and *closing move*. The right low drill combination contains an entangle with a lift. The left high drill combination contains a wrap with a draw. The low pierce is to the knee, while the high pierce is to the head.

2a Right Stance Drill yòubù zuānjiàn 右步钻剑

Start from *on guard*. Continue with *left advance, entangle and lift; Right step forward, low pierce*.

ACTION 1: Advance the left foot a half-step and follow in the right foot by the left ankle. Rotate the right palm away from the thumb to bring the under edge of the blade forward. Lift the right elbow to lift the blade with the arm bent, and draw the hand up and back to in front of the right shoulder. Keep the left hand at the right wrist, following along with the action of the right hand. This action will make the sword tip circle counterclockwise left, down, right, and up, finishing angled forward and down at belly height. At this point, turn the body a bit to the right. The left elbow is in front of the chest. Look at the sword tip. (image 2.21)

ACTION 2: Take a long step forward with the right foot and follow in a half-step with the left foot to take a *santi* stance. Thrust the right hand in an inverted grip forward and down to chest height as the right foot lands, to pierce with the sword tip to front at knee height. Reach the right shoulder forward and almost fully extend the arm. The thumb / forefinger web of the right hand is forward and down. Swing the left hand up to the left of the head to brace out with the arm, keeping it rounded. Look past the sword tip. (image 2.22)

Pointers

- Complete the circling entanglement with the blade as the left foot advances.
- Complete the low pierce as the right foot steps forward. The power must reach to the sword tip. Be sure to rotate the right hand into an inverted grip so that the under edge of the blade is turned forward. The right hand must control the sword blade so that the tip pierces forward and down. You may brace the thumb against the guard to prevent the sword tip from dropping.

2b Left Stance Drill   zuǒbù zuānjiàn   左步钻剑

Right advance, entangle and draw; Left step forward, twisted pierce to the throat.

ACTION 1: Advance the right foot a half-step and follow in the left foot to the right ankle. Bend the right leg and keep the knees together. Bring the left hand to the right wrist. Circle the right hand to make the sword tip circle left and then up to the right. When the tip arrives up, bend the right arm and draw the hand back to beside the right shoulder and turn the body a bit to the right. (image 2.23)

82   SWORD DRILL

Then rotate the right palm towards the thumb and bring it down to the waist, palm up, turning the under edge of the blade up. Keep the sword level and pointing forward at all times during these actions. Bend the waist and settle the chest, turning slightly right. Look past the sword tip.

ACTION 2: Take a long step forward with the left foot and follow in a half-step with the right foot. Use a spiral grip and extend the right hand in front of the chest to pierce forward with the palm heart up. The under edge of the blade will be on top, the tip at head height, the arm slightly bent, and the right hand at chest height. Swing the left hand up to the left side, above the head, arm rounded to brace out. Reach the right shoulder forward slightly. Press the head up. Look past the sword tip. (image 2.24)

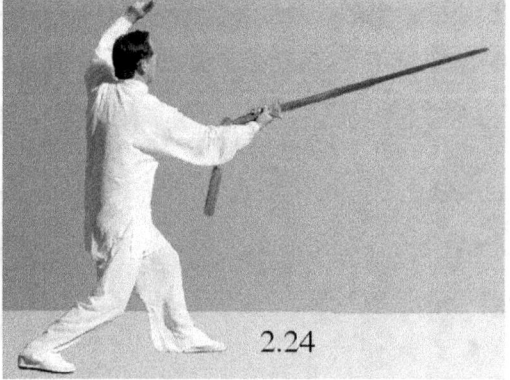

Pointers

- o Complete the entangling circle and draw back with the blade as the right foot advances.
- o Complete the pierce as the left foot steps forward. Both feet and hands must work together to balance the power.
- • Connect to *right stance drill*, and repeat right and left until you run out of space.

2c   Drill Turn Around   zuānjiàn zhuànshēn   钻剑转身

Using the *left stance drill* as example. *Turn and crossing cut; Right withdraw, entangle and lift; Right advance, low pierce.*

ACTION 1: Hook-in the left foot on the spot to turn around 180 degrees to the right to face back in the way from which you came. Hook-out the right foot so that it points straight, and shift onto the right leg to take a bow stance. Lower the left hand to the right wrist and rotate the right palm away from the thumb so that the palm faces down and the blade is horizontal and flat. Brandish the sword as the body turns, to cut horizontally back at chest height. Bring the right hand to the right front. Swing the left hand horizontally to shoulder height at the left.

Look forward after you have turned around. (image 2.25)

ACTION 2: Shift back to the left leg, bending it, and withdraw the right foot a half-step, touching the toes down. Draw the blade in a flat circle up, left and down. Keep the left hand on the right wrist. First rotate the right palm towards the thumb to turn the palm up, then circle the hand while rotating the palm away from the thumb so that the blade tip points down. Bend the right arm and lift the elbow, bringing the hand in front of and above the right shoulder so that the blade is angled down and forward, and the tip at waist height. Look past the tip. (image 2.26)

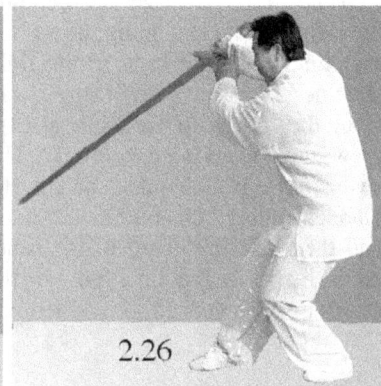

ACTION 3: Step the right foot straight forward and advance the left foot a half-step. Extend the right arm forcefully forward and down, palm facing right at chest height, to pierce the blade tip to knee height. Swing the left hand up above the head at the left, bracing out with the arm rounded. Look past the tip. (image 2.27)

Pointers

- Complete the turn as one move.
- Complete the hook-in step and horizontal cut with force. Transfer power from your waist to your arm to the body of the blade, cutting flat around to the rear. Be sure to shift onto the right leg when you hook-in and turn around, and reach with the torso and the arm to cut. Pretend you are cutting an opponent behind you.
- The pointers for *withdraw and lift*, and *advance and pierce down* are the same as above. The only difference is that the right palm first needs to rotate towards the thumb and circle. Once the sword tip is pointing down to the left, then rotate the right palm away from the thumb. The right hand draws a small circle to make the sword tip draw a large

circle. The movement must be coordinated, tightly knit, and be connected throughout the whole body.

2d Drill Closing Move   zuānjiàn shòushì   钻剑收势

If starting from *left* drill.

ACTION: Retreat the left foot a half-step and shift to the right leg, bending the right leg and extending the left leg. Pull the right hand back to the right shoulder, rotating the palm away from the thumb to face forward, to draw the sword straight back. The sword blade is at shoulder height, the blade standing. Open the left hand and then take the guard in the hand, palm facing forward. Look at the sword tip. (image 2.28)

If starting from *right* drill.

ACTION: Retreat the right foot behind the left and shift to the right leg, bending the right leg and extending the left leg. (image 2.29)

- The rest of *closing move* is the same as sword *chop closing move*.

Pointers

  o Whether the left or right foot is forward, the <u>right</u> foot moves back and the <u>right</u> hand pulls the sword back. When the left foot is forward the hand must rotate as it pulls back, so be sure to keep the blade flat. Be firm and stable when taking the hilt in the left hand. Lift the left elbow so that the flat of the blade is pressed along the outside of the forearm.
  o The entire movement must be connected and well anchored, and must be focused to the end. The upper and lower actions must be coordinated. Be sure to show clarity in the eyes.

PROBLEMS OFTEN MET IN SWORD DRILL

PROBLEM 1: During the *left advance entangle and lift* action of *right drill*, the student draws too large a circle with the sword tip as he does the counterclockwise circle with the blade. This results in the blade moving stiffly with poor coordination, as well as being an ineffective technique.

CORRECTIONS: The main reason for moving stiffly or with poor coordination is that the student is holding the hilt too tightly, which makes the wrist very stiff. The student must learn to loosen up the wrist, and adjust to use the grip appropriate to each movement and technique. For example, piercing needs a spiral grip, chopping needs a full grip, lifting needs a pincer grip, cutting needs a full grip, and slicing needs a spiral grip.

PROBLEM 2: The student drops the tip during the *step forward inverted grip low pierce* of *right drill*. The tip hangs, with not enough forward piercing action.

CORRECTIONS: The student must understand that this is a pierce to the knee, not the foot, so the tip must pierce forward and down, not just down. The student may not have enough wrist strength to pierce when the wrist is rotated in this way. He should reach the wrist forward and grip the butt end of the hilt firmly with the ring and little fingers. This will help him to control the direction of the sword tip. If this grip does not solve the problem, he may slide the thumb onto the guard to lift the front end of the hilt and grip firmly with the other fingers.

PROBLEM 3: The student has no power in the *low pierce*.

CORRECTIONS: Poor feeling for the *low pierce* causes this to be an awkward action. The student must practise quick and long stepping. When launching power, he should turn the waist, reach the shoulder forward and extend the arm. He must focus on applying power in a sequential and integrated way. First advance one foot, then prepare power in the waist and turn, reach the shoulder forward, extend the arm, so that when the other foot lands the sword tip arrives. If he pierces in this way then the sword will have power.

PROBLEM 4: During the *right advance entangle and draw back* action of *left drill* the student makes too big a circle with the right hand, and separates the actions of entangling and drawing.

CORRECTIONS: The student must first understand the action. The technique of entangle uses the fore section and tip of the blade, while that of draw uses the midsection of the blade. He must first entangle and then draw, but the entangling action contains a draw, and draw is the continuation of the entangle. So these two techniques must be done as one action. The method of correction is to repeat this technique over and over to get a feel for it.

PROBLEM 5: During the *left step forward twisted pierce to the throat* of *left drill*, the student lets the blade wobble, and the tip has no point of focus. Another error is to not twist the blade over sufficiently, so that the under edge is not on top.

CORRECTIONS: The tip will never pierce effectively if the blade wobbles. Firstly, the student must step firmly. When he extends the right arm he should keep a slight bend in the elbow, reach the shoulder forward, and roll the elbow in, so that the hand can rotate more easily. He must rotate the hand fully so that the under edge of the blade is on top. When practising this technique, the student must concentrate on leading the tip forward, following it with the arm, and using the power of the whole body to urge it forward. He must seek out the meaning of the words lead, follow, and urge.

POWER GENERATION FOR SWORD DRILL

Advance, entangle and lift: The left foot advances and the sword lifts and draws back, so you must first rotate the palm away from the thumb to circle the sword left and down to entangle. Then lift the elbow and pull the right shoulder back to lift and draw the sword. The body of the blade should feel like it is sticking to an opponent's weapon and drawing it back. The movement must be weighty and well anchored, and the mind must be focused. The body sits down slightly at this time.

Step forward, low pierce: Turn the waist, reach the shoulder forward, and extend the arm to pierce down. The left hand must swing to the upper rear left to give an equal and opposite force to balance the action of the right hand and give more power to the blade that is piercing to the lower front right. This balances the diagonal power line so that the body and weapon are as one. The posture is rounded, the power is full, the movement is smooth, and the strength is integrated.

Advance, wrap and draw: Keep the bodywork gentle and rounded. Transfer power from the waist to the shoulder, from the shoulder to the elbow, from the elbow to the hand, and from the hand to the blade. When drawing the sword back be sure to turn the under edge of the blade up. When lowering the hand to the waist, rotate the palm towards the thumb gradually as it lowers. Contain the chest and store power in the lower back, so that the move has a hidden technique of wrapping and pressing down. Keep the sword tip pointing forward at all times throughout the action.

Step forward, twisted pierce to the throat: Rotate the blade as it pierces forward, so that it finishes with the blade standing and the under edge up. Keep the waist relaxed and turn, reaching the shoulder and elbow forward in a settled way. Just as the sword pierces, urge forward from the lower back to the shoulder, shoulder to elbow, elbow to hand, and hand to sword, sequentially and consecutively to transer the power of the whole body into the tip of the blade.

BREATHING CYCLE FOR SWORD DRILL

- Inhale as you entangle and lift, or entangle and draw.

- Exhale as you step forward or advance and pierce.

Breathe slowly, deeply, and evenly when practising slowly, still breathing out for the piercing actions.

PRACTICAL APPLICATIONS FOR SWORD DRILL

- The main targets of drill are the throat and the knee. The high drill can target the head, face, neck, throat or chest. The low drill can target the belly, knee, thigh, or shank. The right drill withdraws, entangles and lifts, then advances to pierce the knee. The left drill advances, entangles and draws, then steps forward to pierce the throat.

Right drill entangles, lifts, then pierces down. The entangling action is defensive, used when the opponent stabs a bit below your centre. You may retreat, advance, or dodge, whatever is appropriate, so your footwork must be quick and agile. If the opponent comes in strongly you should retreat your rear foot then withdraw your lead foot. Connect the front half of your blade to the opponent's weapon and deflect it to the right and down, encircling it as you move. Connect your blade to use the lift and draw to stick and draw the opponent's weapon back to take him off target. Then you can advance and pierce to the knee or thigh. As it says in the classics, "Move like a running rabbit with your body like the wind; eyes are bright, hands are fast, body and feet are light."

> Pay attention whether you advance, retreat, or withdraw that you are using the footwork to keep out of the way of the opponent's attack, and using the sword to gently lead his weapon. Never use a sword to strike or block directly against another weapon. The blade of a sword is easily damaged by hard contact with another weapon. This is what the classics mean when they say: "skill is in dodging, control to the angle."

Left drill advances, entangles, draws back, and then steps forward to pierce up. The entangle, draw, twist and press down takes care of the defensive needs, and the pierce to the throat is the attack. The sword tip circles leftward and upward to knock aside a stab to the upper body. At the same time stick the sword blade to his weapon and use his force to draw him in, then twist your arm and rotate your wrist to wrap up and press his weapon down. As he tries to get away, step forward quickly to pierce to his head or chest. When you are dodging out of the way be sure to press his weapon down, pressing it forward.

Turn around is a method of dealing with an attack from behind. When you cut horizontally as you turn, you can slice the opponent's chest or head if he has come within your space. You must turn and slice quickly. If the opponent has not come in close then you at least hinder his attack with your cut. Once you have turned then you can use whatever technique is appropriate to attack. For either of these situations to work you must be sure to cut around directly behind you as you turn, and control the momentum of the sword, keeping control of the focus and direction. If you swing too wide then you will leave a gap for the opponent to enter.

THE POEM ABOUT SWORD DRILL

钻剑歌诀

钻剑技法快中求，

巧闪旁扼步法游。

绞剑上提下刺膝，

缠带裹压反刺喉。

The techniques of sword drill are quick and seek out the midline,

Stepping as if swimming, dodge and control off to the side.

Entangle with the sword to lift up and pierce down to the knee,

Coil and draw, wrap and press, and pierce with an inverted blade to the throat.

3. SWORD THRUST

INTRODUCTION TO SWORD THRUST, *BENG JIAN*

Sword thrust is based on the empty hand technique of driving punch, or crushing fist, which is a relatively level straight punch with the right or left fist. So as long as the blade edge is standing and the tip pierces straight forward, the technique is considered a thrust. In sword terminology this is normally called a pierce, but in Xingyi, all weapons techniques are named after the empty hand technique that they resemble.[7]

Sword thrust uses the same integrated power as the crushing punch, sending the power of the whole body out to the tip of the sword. The main technique during the thrust practice is the straight pierce itself. Within the combinations are hook, check, entangle, and draw. There is also a distinction between single handed thrust and double handed thrust – the single handed being quick and agile, and the double handed being strong and aggressive.

There are variations in the way the sword thrust is done in different regions and between different teachers, but all use a straight piercing action. I will describe two variations. One is *hook, check, thrust*, the other is *entangle, draw, thrust*.

---

[7] Translator's note: I have translated *beng* as thrust, rather than using something like 'crushing sword'. In this way the term is different from the usual word, pierce [*ci*], but still makes sense in English and gives the feeling of the technique. In the book, for clarity, the full technique is called sword thrust, while the stabbing action alone is called pierce.

Method One: Hook, Check, Thrust

3a Right Hook, Check, Thrust   yòu guà bō bēngjiàn   右挂拨崩剑

Start from *on guard*. *Left advance, right hook, check; Right step forward, pierce.*

ACTION 1: Advance the left foot a half-step and follow in the right foot to by the left ankle. Bend the legs, keeping the knees together. Open the left hand and grasp the hilt behind the right hand. Cock both wrists and bend the arms, pulling the hilt back beside the right waist so that the sword tip draws a circle up and back to finish pointing up with the blade vertical at the right side. Do not allow the blade to touch the body – keep it about twenty centimetres away. Settle the chest and tuck in the belly, tuck the elbows in to the ribs, turn the torso slightly to the right. Look forward. (image 2.30)

ACTION 2: Bring the hands, still both on the hilt, up to the solar plexus, which brings the sword tip down to chest height. The tip now points forward with the blade horizontal and standing. Take a long step forward with the right foot and follow in the left foot to behind the right foot, into the same short stance used for the crushing punch. The weight is on the right leg, the legs are slightly bent. Forcefully thrust forward with both hands, almost fully extending the arms, to pierce forward at chest height, sending the power to the sword tip. Press the head up and look forward. (image 2.31)

3b Left Hook, Check, Thrust   zuǒ guà bō bēngjiàn   左挂拨崩剑

Right advance, right hook, check; Left step forward, pierce.

SWORD THRUST

ACTION 1: Advance the right foot a half-step and follow in the left foot without touching down. Bend the arms and cock the wrists to bring the hands in to the left side of the waist, tucking the elbows to the ribs. This circles the sword tip forward, up, and then back to hook up and check with the tip up and the blade vertical in front of the body. Settle the shoulders down, contain the chest, tuck in the belly, press the head up, and look forward. Place the sword blade about twenty centimetres in front of the left shoulder. (image 2.32)

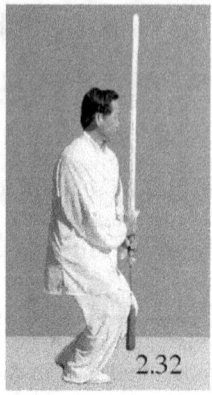

ACTION 2: Take a long step forward with the left foot and follow in the right foot to just behind the left foot, in the same stance as used in the crushing punch. Lift both hands to the chest to bring the sword tip forward and down to chest height. As the left foot lands, thrust forward forcefully with both hands to pierce forward at chest height. Keep the arms slightly bent, release tension in the shoulders, settle the elbows, and send your power to the sword tip. Press the head up and look past the sword tip. (images 2.33 and 2.33 from the front)

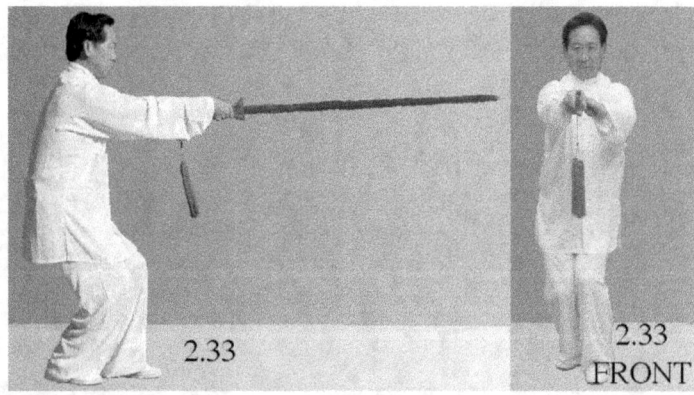

Pointers

- Cock the wrists to hook up and check as the foot advances, whether left or right.
- Thrust forward as you take the long step forward. Make the step long and quick, and land as the sword completes the pierce. Send power out to the sword tip.
- There are two actions but they must be done as one movement without a break. The forward step must be quick and go for distance. The landing must be stable, and the follow-in step must be quick.
- Use a full grip for the hook up and a spiral grip for the pierce.

Method Two: Entangle, Draw, Thrust

3c Right Entangle, Draw, Thrust yòu jiǎo dài bēngjiàn 右绞带崩剑

Start from *on guard. Left advance, entangle and draw to the right; Right step forward, pierce.*

ACTION 1: Advance the left foot a half-step and follow in the right foot to the right ankle. Bend both legs and keep the knees together, standing firmly on the left leg. Place the left hand at the right wrist. Rotate the right palm away from the thumb and lift it, then draw it back on the right side to in front of the right shoulder, drawing a counter-clockwise circle with the sword tip. Draw the sword back on the right side, tucking the left elbow in at the solar plexus. Turn the torso slightly to the right. The sword tip has drawn a small circle in front, keeping the blade horizontal. Look past the sword tip. (image 2.34)

ACTION 2: Take a long step forward with the right foot and follow in a long half- step with the left foot to about a foot length behind the right foot, putting most weight on the left leg. Extend the arms forward to pierce with a standing blade. You may grasp the hilt in both hands or keep the left hand at the right wrist. Keep the arms slightly bent and the blade horizontal at chest height. Reach the right shoulder forward slightly and send power to the sword tip. Press the head up and look past the sword tip. (image 2.35)

3d Left Entangle, Draw, Thrust zuǒ jiǎo dài bēngjiàn 左绞带崩剑

Right advance, entangle and draw to the left; Left step forward, pierce.

ACTION 1: Advance the right foot a half-step and follow in the left foot to beside the right without touching down. Place the left hand on the right wrist. Draw a clockwise circle at the front with the sword tip, then draw it back to the left. Rotate the right palm towards the thumb and draw it back to in front of the left shoulder, palm up and elbow tucked in to protect the heart. Turn the torso slightly to the left. Keep the blade horizontal. Look past the sword tip. (image 2.36)

SWORD THRUST

ACTION 2: Take a long step forward with the left foot and follow in with the right foot. Extend the right hand forward to pierce the sword straight to chest height. Keep the right arm slightly bent. Either support the butt with the left palm or place it on the right wrist. Press the head up and look past the sword tip. (image 2.37)

Pointers

- The footwork of the second method is the same as that of the first – bring the rear foot through to step forward into the pierce. The only difference is that method one uses a hook up and method two uses an entangling action with the sword. The hook moves directly back while the entangle circles back, so they are different uses and power applications.
- Complete the entangling draw to the side as the foot advances. Draw back to the right when the left foot advances, and draw back to the left when the right foot advances.
- As the foot steps through to pierce, complete the action of the foot with the sword, both arriving at the same time.
- Complete the actions as one movement, do not hesitate between them.

3e Thrust Turn Around   bēngjiàn zhuànshēn   崩剑转身

Continue the thrust combination until you run out of space. If the <u>right</u> foot is in front then step the <u>left</u> foot forward with a hook-in step. If the <u>left</u> foot is forward then hook it in on the spot. *Left hook-in, turn around, horizontal cut;*

CHAPTER TWO: SWORD, *JIAN* 93

Right crossing heel kick; Resting stance, chop.

ACTION 1: Hook-in the left foot outside the right toes and shift onto the left leg. Bend the left leg slightly and grip the ground with the toes to stand firmly, and lift the right foot by the left ankle. Bring the sword back to in front of the left chest, rotating the right palm down to place the blade flat with the edges to left and right. Turn the body around 180 degrees to face back in the way from which you came. Bring the right hand around with the body turn, so that the sword cuts horizontally across from left to right in front of the body, finishing at the right side at shoulder height. Open the left hand out horizontally to brace out to the left at shoulder height. Keep the arms slightly bent. Look forward. (image 2.38)

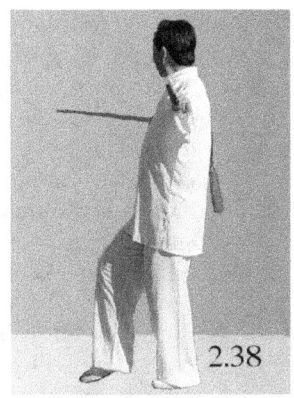

ACTION 2: Lift the right knee and dorsi-flex the right ankle, turning the foot out. Kick forcefully forward and up to waist height. Stand firmly on the left leg. Look forward. (image 2.39)

ACTION 3: Land the right foot forward, keeping it hooked out, and follow in the left foot a half-step. Squat on the left leg with the heel up and slightly extend the right leg, to sit into a resting stance with the weight mostly on the left leg. Lift the right hand above the head while rotating it palm towards the thumb to hang the hilt. This causes the sword to brandish down and then up above the head. Bring the left hand in above the head to settle onto the right wrist. Once the right foot has landed, chop forward and down with the sword until the blade is horizontal at waist height. The right hand finishes in front of and above the right knee. The left shoulder is forward of the right shoulder, so that the torso is turned about forty-five degrees. Press the head up. Look past the sword tip. (image 2.40)

- Continue on with *advance, hook and thrust*.

SWORD THRUST

Pointers

- Turn around in one movement without pausing. Stop for an instant in the resting stance, showing stability in the stance.
- *Sword thrust turn around* is the same general move as the empty hand turn around *leopard cat turns over whilst climbing a tree*. It consists of a hook-in step with a wrist turn, a turn around with a horizontal cut, a crossing kick, and a resting stance with a chop. There is only a turn around to the right, not to the left. Be sure to turn around quickly. Be sure, also, to keep the head up and back straight. The left hook-in step must be well hooked and placed outside the right foot, so that the body can get turned around and the kick can be done comfortably.
- Swing the left hand out horizontally as the sword cuts across, to assist power transfer to the right hand.
- Tuck in the belly when lifting the right foot, and tuck in the hip when kicking. Do not throw the hip forward into the kick. Kick at least to waist height, but it is best to kick to shoulder height. Kick as soon as the sword tip has passed the midline in its cut. You must not kick too early or too late – kick just as the sword passes.
- The *resting stance chop* is also called *dragon model chop*. You may half-sit in a scissor stance if need be. When you land from the right kick, be sure to advance the foot as much as possible to stomp forward and down. Complete the chop down as you land into the resting stance. Press the head up as the sword chops down. Gain stability by pressing the legs tightly together and tucking the arms into the ribs. Release tension in the shoulders, press the head up, and chop down the midline.

3f   Thrust Closing Move   bēngjiàn shòushì   崩剑收势

Continue back to your starting place and turn around, then close. It doesn't matter which foot is forward. *Right retreat, hold the sword; Stand at attention and transfer the sword; Hold the sword behind in the left hand.*

ACTION: Retreat the right foot behind the left and shift back to the right leg without moving the left foot, to sit into a *santi* stance. Bend the right arm and bring the right hand in front of the right shoulder to pull the sword directly back. Open the left hand with the thumb down and palm out, bending the arm to place the hand on the guard. Hold the blade horizontal in front of the body at shoulder height with the blade standing. Turn the body a bit to the right and look past the sword tip. (image 2.41)

2.41

- The rest of the closing is the same as that of *sword chop closing move*.

PROBLEMS OFTEN MET IN SWORD THRUST

PROBLEM 1: The student hits himself with the blade when hooking up.

CORRECTIONS: Remind the student that touching yourself with the blade of the sword is a grave error in swordplay, as the double edged blade can cut. The student should use a firm grip when cocking the wrist and bringing in the arm forcefully. He must focus on bringing the blade vertical; once the blade is vertical then he should bend the elbow and bring the arm in, keeping the hand in a tight full grip on the hilt to control any movement of the blade. The elbows must be brought tightly in to the ribs, as this also helps to keep the blade away from the body. The hilt should be about twenty centimetres away from the body, and the blade about thirty centimetres away from the shoulder.

PROBLEM 2: Three common errors in *entangle and draw back* are: the student draws too big a circle with the sword tip; he is too stiff when drawing back; he does not smoothly connect the entangling and the drawing back actions.

CORRECTIONS: The entangle must be done with a supple wrist, using mostly the wrist for the action, so that the sword tip draws a circle about thirty centimetres in diameter. The draw back must be done with the waist drawing the arm back, then bending the arm to draw the sword back. Done in this way it cannot be stiff. Although entrap and draw are two different actions, they must be linked smoothly together. First entangle and then draw, but the entangling action contains a draw, and the drawing action contains an entangle. It really is one action with two parts.

PROBLEM 3: Three common errors in pierce are: the student overextends the arms to pierce; the sword tip wobbles with no point of focus; the sword does not arrive at the same time as the stepping forward foot lands.

CORRECTIONS: The student should keep about a 160 degrees bend in the elbow on the final pierce. In this way the power of the whole body can transfer through the arm, and it is also easier to change the technique for defense. The cause of the tip wobbling is usually that the sword and arm are not aligned, the arm and body are not united, the footwork is unstable and the body disunited. The student must grip the hilt firmly and extend the wrist, release tension in the shoulders and sink the elbows, tuck the elbows in to the ribs, contain the chest, stretch the upper back open, press the head up and lengthen the spine, and settle the *qi* to the *dantian*. He should first practise slowly to find all the requirements and then practise more quickly to find the power.

POWER GENERATION FOR SWORD THRUST

Hook and check: The lead foot lands as the hands grip the hilt to bring the sword up and back – hook up is the main technique and check is the secondary technique. That is, when hooking up, there is a hidden power that knocks aside to left or right. When the left foot advances the sword has a slight checking power to the right, and when the right foot advances the sword has a slight checking power to the left. This should not be too large or too obvious a movement. Sit the wrists to bring the blade upright, and bend the arms to bring the blade back to hook. Turn the waist slightly to right or left to take the blade slightly to the side for the hidden check. You may grasp with the hands together or with them spread on the hilt, the right on top and the left underneath. Be careful to stop the blade about twenty centimetres from the body – a sword blade must never hit the body.

Entangle and draw: When the sword 'entangles' in front of the face, whether clockwise or counter-clockwise, both the tip and the hilt should form vertical circles. The central portion is the balance point as the hilt and tip circle. The central balance point stays at all times on the midline of the body as the tip forms a larger circle and the hilt a smaller one. When drawing to the left or right, draw the sword from the waist and arms. Use the strength of the wrists to make stirring circles, and use the strength of the body for the draw back. Sit the body down slightly when drawing back, to gather power.

Pierce: The pierce must be completed exactly as the forward stepping foot lands. The hands must first lift to bring the tip of the sword forward. At this time bend the waist, contain the chest and bring in the arms to gather power. Extend the wrists to pierce. To pierce, send the sword tip forward, drive from the feet into the body, lengthen the back and settle the shoulders. Urge the hands forward from the elbows, and the elbows from the shoulders, breathing out and settling the *qi* to the *dantian* so that the power reaches to the sword tip, causing the blade to quiver. Lower the hands slightly and lengthen the back when piercing the sword tip forward. Lower the sword with a gathering power. Press the head up with the final pierce. The classics say, "Compress the body when rising and lengthen the body when landing." You need to find the real meaning behind this by feeling it inside. The pierce must be forceful, and the power launch done with an exhalation and sinking of the *qi* to the *dantian*. The power of the whole body is integrated and shows Xingyi sword's powerful flavour and unflinching demeanor.

Turn around: Cut horizontally around behind you, turning right, using the waist to turn around. Transfer power from the waist to the shoulder, from the shoulder to the arm, and from the arm to the sword, to draw a 370 degree circle with the sword tip. The point of focus of the cut is directly behind the body, so you should wait until the blade gets to the left side of the body before applying force. Then, once the blade has crossed the midline, don't use any more force – let momentum cut across to the right. Control the sword's direction to prepare for the following move.

BREATHING CYCLE FOR SWORD THRUST

- Inhale as you advance whether doing a hook or an entangle and draw.
- Exhale as you step forward and pierce, exhaling to launch power. Use a short and powerful exhalation, and settle the *qi* to the *dantian*.

PRACTICAL APPLICATIONS FOR SWORD THRUST

- The key element of sword thrust is the straight forward pierce. Its goal is to stab the opponent's chest, but of course you can stab the head or any other part. You should pierce to an area that can cause serious harm, to a key place that at least takes away his ability to fight. Of course, you pierce to an open area; tactics do not always allow you to choose your ideal target.

First method: The defensive move is *hook up and check*, which also sets up the attack. If the opponent stabs to your head or chest you can withdraw your lead foot and knock away his weapon so that it misses its target, and then advance to pierce his chest. If his weapon does not come in close you can hold your position, shifting back to prepare to attack. Similarly, you can adjust to the right or left as needed. You can also withdraw then advance, or withdraw and step forward, switching feet. You can also do exactly as in the practice, first advancing the lead foot and then stepping the other foot through. As long as your footwork is skillful, fast, and nimble you can adapt your technique to the situation. Effective defense also depends on the close coordination between your body and the sword, and the tight connection between the techniques. When attacking, your footwork must be quick and your attitude must be intimidating.

Second method: The defensive move is *entangle and draw back* to left or right. The use of this technique is to encircle and entrap a weapon coming towards you, then stick to it and draw it back out of the way, causing it to miss your body. Then you can advance and pierce to the opponent's chest. Adjust your footwork according to the situation. If the opponent stabs to your chest you can withdraw your lead foot or you can advance it a half-step. If the opponent comes in very strongly you can retreat your rear foot, also withdrawing your lead foot to get out of the way. Encircle his weapon with the front or middle section of your sword blade, then keep your blade stuck to his weapon and draw it back so that it misses your body. Then as he tries to take his weapon away, follow with a step forward and pierce to his chest. This movement must be quick and aggressive, and your intention must be to penetrate right through.

- Use one hand or two on the hilt to pierce. Two handed is stronger.

Sword thrust turn around horizontal cut is a method of dealing with an attack from behind. The horizontal cut can either cut the opponent or swing across to knock away the opponent's weapon. When thinking of connecting with the opponent's weapon, cut the tip across at waist height. When thinking of cutting the opponent, cut across with the hilt at shoulder height. If the opponent continues to come in, kick him with your right foot, then immediately advance and chop with a double handed hold. The chopping action also contains a sawing, or inward slicing action. Chop his weapon or body, whatever you can get.

- Just practising the techniques isn't enough to become skilled at using them. You must practise with a partner to develop the timing, strength, and speed needed for combat. Of course, skilled technique is important for combat, but just as important are well timed reactions, good judgment, the ability to adapt, and on overall feel for correct timing, spacing, and distance. You also need to develop combative awareness to develop and improve your courage and fighting ability.

THE POEM ABOUT SWORD THRUST

崩剑歌诀

崩剑技法气势雄，
步进身进向前冲。
左右上挂须坐腕，
摇身绞带刺其胸。

The bearing of the sword thrust is dauntless,

The footwork enters, the body enters, charging forward.

To hook up to left and right you must cock and press down the wrist,

Dodge the body, entangle and draw, pierce his chest.

4. SWORD SLASH

INTRODUCTION TO SWORD SLASH, *PAO JIAN*

Xingyi's sword slash is a slice on either side. The definition of slice is to use the under edge of the blade and slice up from below. A direct slice uses a normal grip and an inverted slice uses an inverted grip. Slice usually circles by one side of the body then continues forward and up. The wushu regulations define slice as: with a standing blade, slice forward and up from below, putting power to the forward section of the blade. A direct slice has the palm rotated towards the thumb, the palm up, and circles closely past the body before slicing out. An inverted slice is the same action, but with the palm rotated away from the thumb. Xingyi's left stance slash is a direct slice and right stance slash is an inverted slice. The footwork is the same as the empty hand pounding punch. The slicing action to left and right look similar to the pounding punch [*pao quan*], which is why this technique is called *pao jian*. here translated as slash. Xingyi's slash is not exactly like most slicing techniques – it contains a sculling and sawing action as well.

The key techniques for slash are: *advance, block up and draw* and *step forward slice*. Block up and draw is a combination of a block up and a draw back. Block up uses a standing blade that moves across to block up with the blade higher than the head, power reaching the body of the blade, palm in or out, depending on which side you are blocking. Draw back uses a standing blade or a flat blade and withdraws at the side, either straight back or back and up, the power reaching the body of the blade.

4a Right Stance Slash   yòubù pàojiàn   右步炮剑

Start from *on guard*. Continue with *left advance, left block up and draw; Right step forward, inverted slice*.

ACTION 1: Advance the left foot a half-step and follow in the right foot to beside the ankle. Place the left hand at the right wrist. Slice up to block up, then draw the sword back at the left side, rotating the right palm towards the thumb and bending the right elbow. The right hand, and thus the sword hilt, finishes near the left ear. The sword blade is standing, the tip slightly lower than the hilt and pointing directly forward. Use a full grip on the hilt. Turn the body a bit to the left, contain the chest and tuck in the belly. Look past the sword tip. (image 2.42)

ACTION 2: Take a long step diagonally forward and right with the right foot and follow in a half step with the left foot to take a *santi* stance. Bring the right hand left, down, and then right, diagonally forward, extending the arm to slice up. Keep the sword close to the left side then slice diagonally forward, rotating the right palm away from the thumb so that the palm turns out. Extend the right wrist and use a spiral grip on the hilt. Keep the right arm slightly bent and lift the elbow, finishing with the hand and sword hilt about ear height, the sword tip about chest height. Sit the body slightly down. Keep the left hand at the right wrist throughout. Put power to the forward section of the sword blade. Press the head up. Follow the movement of the sword with the eyes, then look forward past the tip. (image 2.43 and from the front)

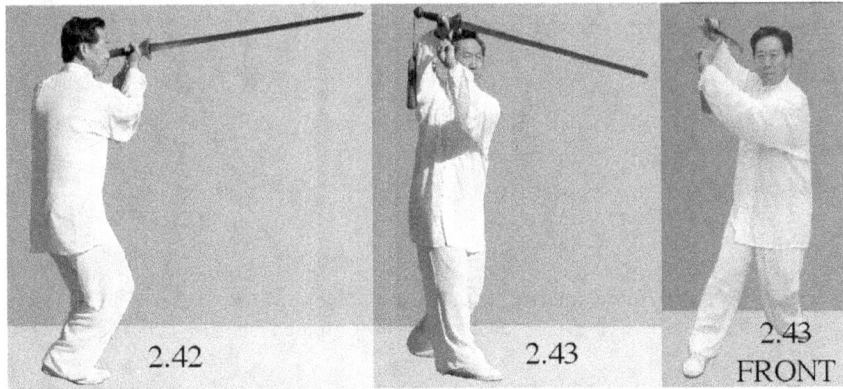

Pointers

- Complete the slicing block up on the left side as the left foot advances. Complete the inverted slice as the right foot steps forward. Complete all techniques as the leading foot lands.
- The right stance slash is one move; do not stop on *advance and block up*, but continue directly through to the *step forward slice*.

100   SWORD SLASH

4b Left Stance Slash   zuǒbù pàojiàn   左步炮剑

Right advance, right block up and draw; Left step forward, direct slice.

ACTION 1: Advance the right foot a half-step straight forward and follow in the left foot to beside the right ankle. Angle the sword tip to the left then swing it down, left, then right to block up. Do not stop here, but pull the hand back on the right side to the right ear. Keep the left hand on the right wrist throughout. The sword tip is angled towards the forward left, slightly lower than the hilt. Turn the body slightly to the right and look past the sword tip. (image 2.44)

ACTION 2: Take a long step to the forward left with the left foot and follow in a half-step with the right foot. Circle the sword back on the right side, around down to the waist. At this point release the left hand from the right wrist and swing it down then up past the chest to the forward left to above the left side of the head. Rotate the right palm towards the thumb to turn the palm up and slice diagonally to the forward left. Keep the right arm slightly bent, the hilt just above shoulder height, the sword tip angled to about chest height. Turn the body slightly left and reach the right shoulder forward. Press the head up. Follow the movement of the left hand at first, then look past the sword tip. (image 2.45)

2.44

2.45

Pointers

- o *Block up and draw back* must be completed as the lead foot advances a half- step. The *direct slice* must be completed as the stepping forward foot lands.
- o The body must be fully integrated with the sword, slashing right and left with complete power.
- • To continue on to *right stance slash* from *left stance slash*, first advance the left foot a half-step and follow in the right foot without touching down. Replace the left hand on the right wrist. Lower the sword tip and then circle it to the forward right, then up to block up, pulling it back by the left of the head. The rest of the action is the same as described above.

4c Slash Turn Around   pàojiàn zhuǎnshēn   炮剑转身

From the *right* stance slash. *Right hook-in step, hook; Left step forward, direct slice.*

ACTION 1: Hook-in the right foot in front of the left toes and shift onto the right leg. Lift the left foot by the right ankle and turn around 225 degrees to the left to face back in the way from which you came. Place the left hand on the right wrist. Pivot around the right wrist to circle the sword tip down, left, up, and then forward. Look at the sword tip. (image 2.46)

ACTION 2: Take a long step to the forward left with the left foot and follow in a half- step with the right foot. Circle the left hand from the right side down, then diagonally up to the forward left. Rotate the right palm towards the thumb and slice the sword snug at the right side of the body, then forward and up. The left hand finishes above the left side of the head. The sword slice is the same as the direct slice described above. Follow tthe left hand with the eyes, then look forward past the sword tip. (image 2.47)

From the *left* stance slash. *Left hook-in step, wrist cut; Turn around, right step forward, inverted slice.*

ACTION 1: Hook-in the left foot in front of the right toes and shift onto the left leg, lifting the right foot at the left ankle. Lower the left hand to the right wrist. Using the right wrist as pivot point, circle the sword tip down and back, keeping close to the right side of the body. Then circle the sword up and forward. Use a pincer grip. Look at the sword tip. (image 2.48)

ACTION 2: Turn the body 180 degrees to the right to face back in the way from which you came. Take a long step to the forward right with the right foot and follow in a half- step with the left foot. Bring the sword blade closely past the left side of the body to slice forward. (image 2.49)

SWORD SLASH

2.48   2.49

Pointers

- Complete a wrist cutting action during the hook-in step. Keep your wrist supple and use a pincer grip. Hook-in the foot considerably.
- Turn around, step forward, and slice up all as one integrated action, without a pause.
- Be sure not to lower the head or bend the waist when turning around. Keep the spine upright and straight and press the head up. Turn around quickly, step forward for distance, and slice aggressively.

4d Slash Closing Move   pàojiàn shōushì   炮剑收势

On arriving back at the starting point, do *turn around* to face the original direction. It doesn't matter which foot is forward, just step the right foot back and shift back to the right leg. Pull the sword straight back until the right hand is in front of the right shoulder, palm rotated out with the blade flat. Turn the left palm out and take the hilt with an inverted grip. Look at the sword tip.

- The rest of *closing move* is the same as *sword chop closing move*.

PROBLEMS OFTEN MET IN SWORD SLASH

PROBLEM 1: During the slice up to either side the student is inaccurate in direction, with no point of focus or poorly timed power launch. The blade wobbles. This is a common error for beginners.

CORRECTIONS: Firstly, the slice should be done so that the tip points in the same direction as the leading foot. That is, to a forty-five degree angle, as the combination advances in a zigzag pattern. The student must keep the head upright and look in the direction of the sword. If the eyes are looking in the correct direction then the sword will go there – the eyes follow the sword but they also lead it. The main reason for a lack of focus, poor power launch, and wobbly blade is that the body and weapon are not working as an integrated unit. The student must do some post standing in the final slash position until the requirements are drilled into the body. Then he should practise slowly, and add speed only when ready.

PROBLEM 2: When going into the block and draw on either side, the student doesn't control the sword tip. That is, he misses the first action of the movement.

CORRECTIONS: Start out from the final move of slash then do the block and draw to each side. Pay particular attention to the sword tip, first circling down then to the left or right to block up, and then drawing back. The sword tip must point in the direction of the right or left slice.

PROBLEM 3: The student holds the hilt too tightly while trying to bring the slice through, so that the blade cannot stay close to the body.

CORRECTIONS: While slicing, use a spiral grip and keep the wrist supple, remembering to rotate the forearm and to keep a bend in the arm. The student should concentrate on the hilt when doing the slice, controlling the sword from the hilt. The power reaches to the middle section of the blade. The sword must stay close to either side of the body.

POWER GENERATION FOR SWORD SLASH

- To find the proper power you must respect the following principle: the completion of each move is the origin of the following move. Every action is a preparatory gathering of power for the action that follows.

Draw back: The blade comes across and blocks up. When it gets in front of the head then pull it back. You must use the body for this – draw the hand back with the waist. The right hand draws a small elliptical circle to make the sword tip draw a large one. Rotate the right palm towards the thumb when blocking up and drawing back to the rear left. Rotate the right palm away from the thumb when blocking up and drawing back to the rear right. Adjust the grip on the hilt as needed while moving the sword.

Inverted grip slice: The height to which you slice must have a point of focus, you cannot randomly slice up. The sword must pass closely by the left side of the body and then slice up to the front. Gather power in the body and then launch – perform a countermovement to load back prior to moving forward, and to load right prior to moving left. Take the sword diagonally to the rear left to gather power for the slice diagonally to the forward right. This makes the power flow smoothly and gives a strong slice. First gather power in the lower back then lengthen it. First close the shoulders then open them. Send power to the middle portion of the blade.

Direct grip slice: The sword needs to pass closely by the right side of the body before slicing forward. The right hand rotates towards the thumb while slicing, taking the hilt with a spiral grip. First draw the hilt forward, making sure not to strike the ground with the sword tip. Reach the right shoulder forward and use the left hand to assist in launching power. When launching power, sit the torso down slightly.

- You can also slash with a double handed grip. The single handed grip allows for agile movement, but the double handed grip is stronger.

- In the final instant of launching power, pull the shoulder back slightly using the body core to create a short 'one inch power' to perform a backward sawing, slicing action in the sword blade. This is a unique characteristic of Xingyi sword. This kind of fine detail cannot be achieved without the instruction of a skilled teacher and considerable, careful and attentive practice.

- The path of movement of the slice follows the hand and wrist, but the origin is at the shoulder. The power of the slice follows the shoulder and elbow, but the origin is at the waist. The position of the hilt is due to the agility of the hand and fingers, but the origin is at the wrist.

When brandishing the sword or cutting the wrist, the hand and wrist must rotate as the sword moves, turning gradually and smoothly. The wrist and grip must adjust easily. The grip must change to a full grip when launching power, respecting the principle of hitting with a firm grasp. This is common to all weapons.

BREATHING CYCLE FOR SWORD SLASH

- Inhale as you advance, block and draw on either side.
- Exhale as you step forward and slice.

This is the general coordination of breathing with the techniques done at normal speed. You may also take a long breath in and a short breath out to assist the power launch.

PRACTICAL APPLICATIONS FOR SWORD SLASH

- The main attack of the slash combination is the slice. This can be a slice to deflect the opponent's weapon, a slice to his hand, arm, or leg, or, combined with a step, a move in to slice his torso. The slice can be used to attack or defend. As a defense, it knocks the opponent's weapon, and as an attack it slices directly to the body.

  > But, should the opponent come at you chopping down strongly with a long weapon such as a staff or spear, the slice is not going to be an effective defense. The oncoming weapon is heavy and long while the sword is light, sharp and thin, and thus can't be used to directly hit something. In this case you should follow the principle; "Avoid hard force, enter into the smallest crack and the sword will see blood red." That is to say, the sword should slice dierectly to the target in one strike, avoiding touching the opponent's weapon.

- The footwork for slash uses the lead foot to enter or retreat according to the situation. If the opponent comes in strongly then you should retreat. If the opponent keeps his distance then you should enter. When entering, you can either enter directly or advance a bit to the side, again, according to the situation. You can slice when you advance, retreat, or step to either side. You can also step the rear foot through to get the body in even closer as you slice. In this case, you must drive in strongly, confidently, and quickly.

Right stance slash combines *advance left block up, draw back* with *step forward inverted slice*. Looking at its form and technique, the right hand circles and blocks to knock aside an opponent's weapon, this action both defending and preparing the way for your attack. While blocking up you draw back to the left, sticking to the opponent's weapon and leading it back so that it is drawn off target. While you are drawing back to the left this also puts you into the position for stepping forward with the inverted slice. If you can get in close then slice to his body, if not, then slice his hand or arm. The key lies in being courageous and quick. *Left stance slash* uses the same principle, just using a direct slice instead of an inverted slice.

- Practise sword slash with large movements, but apply it with small movements. Smaller movements are quicker. They say that the only technique that has no counter is speed. Train with large movements to find the power. That is to say, once you have the correct power, then any technique that slices up and forward from below, using the under edge of the blade to slice up, is a slash. You can slide along the opponent's weapon to cut his hand, cut his arm, cut into his belly, or dig into his chest. Once you can use the moves freely then it is like ignoring the opponent in front of you – the highest level of skill in combat.

Slash can be used as a separate technique or combined with others. It combines well with chop, drill, and thrust. If you have just completed a chop, then you can rotate the right palm away from the thumb to bring the under edge of the blade forward and up to slice. After slicing up you can quickly circle the wrist to chop forward. If you tried and missed with an inverted grip low pierce (drill) then you can quickly advance with a rising slice. If the opponent stabs at your lower body you can hook down and back and then slide along his weapon to slice his hand and into his groin or whatever. As it says in the art of war; "There are no fixed tactics, just as water has no fixed form. The secret is to adapt to the enemy and wrest victory."

THE POEM ABOUT SWORD SLASH

炮剑歌诀

炮剑技法正反撩，
斜身拗步劲透梢。
架带身转随步走，
撩在肩肘劲在腰。

The sword slash is either a direct or an inverted slice.

Angle the body and use a reverse stance for penetrating power to the tip.

Block up and draw back, turning the body and following the footwork.

Slice from the shoulder and elbow, getting power from the body core.

5. SWORD CROSSCUT

INTRODUCTION TO SWORD CROSSCUT, *HENG JIAN*

Sword crosscut is a type of horizontal cutting, plastering technique across to left and right. The wushu competition regulations define 'cut' as a horizontal cut with a flat blade to left or right between head and shoulder height, with the power reaching the body of the blade and the arm straight. 'Plaster' is defined as to draw a flat blade back from the front in a circular action to right or left between chest and abdomen height with the power reaching the body of the blade. Xingyi's crosscut combines these two techniques – it cuts transversely across and draws back with a plastering action. This makes the technique more devastating and increases the integration of the sword blade with the whole body. The transverse cut is done more with the hand and arm, while the plastering is done more with the waist and torso. Combining the two brings out the characteristics and flavour of Xingyi.

The key techniques for crosscut are: *Advance check and hook to left and right* and *Step forward crossing cut to left and right*. The actions and footwork are similar to the empty hand crossing fist, advancing in a zigzag pattern.

5a Right Stance Crosscut　　　yòubù héngjiàn　　　右步横剑

Start from *on guard. Left advance, right block and hook; Step forward, crossing cut.*

ACTION 1: Advance the left foot a half-step and follow in the right foot to the left ankle. Place the left hand at the right wrist. With the right hand, bring the hilt across in front of the body to block across to the right with the sword tip, hooking back, and then circle across to the left in front of the face. The hands draw a small circle in front of the body. Once the right hand has circled to the left side, rotate it to turn the palm down, change it to a spiral grip to place the sword blade flat, the edges to right and left. Follow the sword movement with the eyes, watching the sword tip. (image 2.50)

ACTION 2: Take a long step forward with the right foot to the forward front and follow in a half-step with the left foot, putting most weight on the right leg to take a *santi* stance. Grip the hilt in firmly and bring the sword across the body from the left to the right in a flat cutting action, using the whole arm, until the tip points to the forward right. Then bend the right arm to pull back with a plastering action, keeping the palm down. The hand is slightly lower than the shoulder and the sword tip is slightly higher than the shoulder. Keep the left hand on the right wrist throughout. Press the head up and look past the sword tip. You may pull the right hand back as far as the right side to increase the final sideways sawing power, but be sure to press the head up. (image 2.51)

Pointers

- Complete the sword's circle in front of the body as the left foot advances. Pay attention to the positioning of the sword tip and hilt.
- Complete the transverse cut as the right foot steps forward, using fully integrated power between the feet and the hands.

5b Left Stance Crosscut   zuǒbù héngjiàn   左步横剑

Right advance, left block and hook; Step forward, left crossing cut.

ACTION 1: Advance the right foot a half-step and follow in the left foot to the right ankle. Circle the sword tip to the front, then block to the left, and then hook back. Finally rotate the right palm up and take the sword past the face to the right. Keep the left hand on the right wrist throughout. The hands draw a small circle in front of the body at the forward right, the arms finishing bent in front of the chest. Follow the movement of the sword tip with the eyes. (image 2.52)

108   SWORD CROSSCUT

ACTION 2: Take a long step to the forward left with the left foot and follow in the right foot a half-step to take a *santi* stance. Take the hilt in a full grip and turn the palm up. Cut across from right to left with the blade flat and the arm extended. When the blade arrives at the forward left, bend the right arm and tuck the elbow into the solar plexus and lift the left hand to above the head at the left. The sword tip is slightly higher than the shoulder. Send the power to the fore section of the blade. Press the head up and settle the *qi* to the *dantian*. Follow the movement of the sword tip, then look past it. (image 2.53 and from the front)

2.53   2.53 FRONT

Pointers

- o Coordinate the left and right block and hook with the half-step advance of the lead foot. Block to the right when the left foot advances. Block to the left when the right foot advances.
- o Coordinate the crossing cut with the forward step. Cut to the right when the right foot steps forward. Cut to the left when the left foot steps forward.
- o Each crosscut is one complete movement. Do not pause in the middle of the action. Keep the whole movement integrated.

• Continue on repeating right and left crosscut until you run out of space.

5c Crosscut Turn Around   héngjiàn zhuànshēn   横剑转身

Turn around is essentially the same no matter which foot is forward. The leading foot will do a hook-in step to turn the body around. From *left stance crosscut. Left hook-in step, turn around, left block and hook; Right step forward, crossing cut.*

ACTION 1: Hook-in the left foot in front of the right toes and shift to the left leg, lifting the right foot at the left ankle and pressing the knees together. Hook-in a considerable angle to turn around 270 degrees to face back in the way from which you came. Press the left hand on the right wrist and bring the sword around with the body as it turns right, so that it cuts across from left to right, then hooks back, circling in front of the face and across to the left. The right palm rotates away from the thumb to turn the palm down, to cut with the blade flat across to the left. Follow the movement of the sword with the eyes. (image 2.54)

ACTION 2: Take a long step to the forward right with the right foot and follow in a half-step with the left foot. Cut the sword across from left to right in an arcing horizontal cut, the tip angled to the forward right, extending the right arm with the elbow slightly bent. Hold the hilt with a full grip, palm down. Finish the cut with the hand slightly lower and the tip slightly higher than the shoulder. Keep the left hand on the right wrist throughout. Press the head up and look past the tip. (image 2.55)

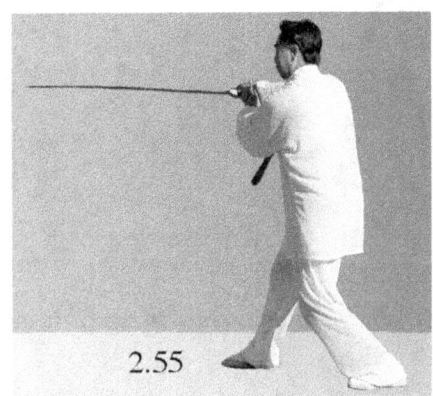

- From *right* stance crosscut, *turn around* is the same, just transpose right and left.

Pointers

- Be sure to first hook the foot in then turn the body around. Take a good hook-in step. The foot must hook-in at the outside of the rear foot, pointing to the toes. Do not step too far away from the rear foot, as this will make the weight shift too extreme, causing instability. Coordinate the cut around of the sword with the rotation of the body. Press the head up to keep the body upright, and be sure to shift the weight. Be careful to not look down or bend at the waist.
- The checking hook must be smooth, rounded, gentle, and well connected to the preceding move. Use the body to do the technique.
- Complete the crossing cut as the foot steps forward, as one integrated movement. Use the action of the body turning to put power into the sword. Transfer power from the lower back to the shoulder, from the shoulder to the arm, and from the arm to the hand and thus to the sword. The crossing cut conceals a sawing, slicing in power.

5d Crosscut Closing Move   héngjiàn shōushì   横剑收势

No matter which foot is forward, the closing is essentially the same. From *right stance crosscut*, do *right retreat chop*.

ACTION: Retreat the right foot and shift back to the right leg to take a *santi* stance. Rotate the right palm away from the thumb to circle the sword tip

110 SWORD CROSSCUT

forward, down, to the left side, to the right side, then up and forward to chop down in front. Keep the left hand on the right wrist throughout. (images 2.56, 2.57)

2.56

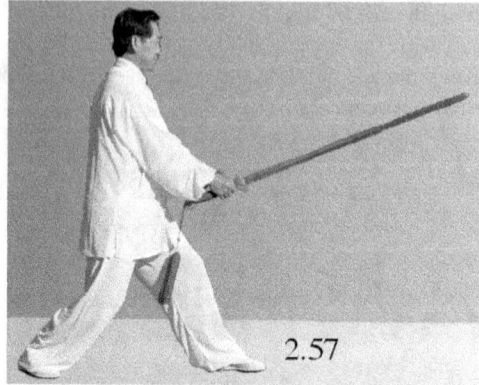
2.57

If from *left* stance *crosscut* the first action is slightly different to get into *santi* stance.

ACTION: Retreat the right foot a half-step then withdraw the left foot to in front of the right foot. Rotate the right hand to circle the sword tip forward, down, and to the right side, then up and forward to chop down. Advance the left foot a small step without moving the right foot, to sit into a *sant i* stance. (image 2.58, transitional)

2.58

- Complete *closing move* the same as described in *sword chop closing move*.

Pointers

- Complete the downward hook, upward circle, and forward chop by the time you complete the backward weight shift. Vary the grip to keep the action smooth as you do the internal or external rotation.
- Keep the spirit full while completing *closing move*. Keep the movements clean and accurate. Be sure to take the hilt cleanly with the left hand and to press the flat of the blade on the forearm.

PROBLEMS OFTEN MET IN SWORD CROSSCUT

PROBLEM 1: The student lifts his hand too high during the block and hook, so that the sword circles more like a brandish over the head.

CORRECTIONS: Explain the application of the move to help students understand the movement; this helps them to do a blocking and hooking action. The right hand should stay in front of the body, above the waist but below the shoulder, with the pivot point staying around the chest.

PROBLEM 2: The student holds the hilt too firmly during the block and hook so that his body is stiff and the sword's circle is uncoordinated.

CORRECTIONS: The student should grip the hilt firmly during the block to the right or left, but should loosen up during the circling action. In this way the wrist is supple, the action of the sword is fluid, and the power of the body can transfer to the sword. The student should work on the principle of setting up the left or right movement with a right or left countermovement, keeping the body relaxed. The only way to get the coordination is to practise repeatedly, and to apply some thought to the training – skill grows from thought.

PROBLEM 3: When doing the crossing cut, the student extends the arm too straight so that the sword is unstable or goes in the wrong direction.

CORRECTIONS: Remind the student to always keep a certain flexion in the arms, as this helps to launch power. The arm must keep a certain angle to maintain a good distance from the body so that you can use the full power of the waist and shoulder. The proper balance has spring. If the student is unstable when hitting the final posture, this is usually because he is trying to go too fast and using too much strength, so loses control. The incorrect direction is also often a case of too much momentum causing him to lose control over the blade. The student should first practise the action with a slow, quick, slow pattern. First gather power in the waist and shoulder with a slow action. Then extend the arm into the crossing cut with a quick action. Then sit the lower back, settle the shoulder, drop the elbow, and settle the buttocks with a controlling, stopping action so that the whole body is integrated with the sword – upper and lower, inner and outer. The sword tip should point in the direction that the lead foot points.

POWER GENERATION FOR SWORD CROSSCUT

Block and hook: The sword tip should draw a complete circle. The hands draw a small circle in front of the chest while the sword draws an elliptical circle with the top larger than the bottom. Draw a large circle when training, but a small circle if using the technique. Be sure to use the power from the body, transferring from the waist through to the hand, and from the hand to the sword. Use the principle of countermovement to get smooth power from the body – preload right to move left, pre-load left to move right. The movement should be coordinated and gentle, connected through the whole body, and with full spirit. Find the power and the technique by practising a large circle. Then find the application and speed by practising a small circle.

Right crosscut uses a spiral grip with the palm down, while *left crosscut* uses a full grip with the palm up. The final power launch comes after the halfway point. Wait until the sword tip has passed the midline, then accelerate. When launching power, coordinate the power of the torso and waist with the hand, transferring from the waist to the shoulder, shoulder to hand, and hand to sword.

- Power transfer uses the principle that each move is the preparation for the following move. The completion of a move always gathers power for the launching of the following move. You must put a lot of thought into your training to find this feeling.

- Crosscut contains a hidden pull back. In the last instant of the crossing cut, turn the waist to increase the reserve power in the sword body. This pulling power is integrally connected to the crossing cut – a continuation of the cut. To increase the pulling power, prepare ahead of time, during the cutting action – extend the right arm forward while cutting, sit the lower back and settle the shoulder, drop the elbow and pull. Keep your intent forward, press the head up. Pulling back during a crossing cut is a unique characteristic of Xingyi sword. It is a distinct type of power and technique – hidden and hard to judge. It is a very dangerous and effective technique, so is usually kept secret, not lightly taught.

- You may practise crosscut with a double handed grip. The single handed grip is agile, and good for performance. The double handed hold is strong, and good for combat. You can alter the final placement of the hands, pulling to the left and right in front, or pulling fully back to either side of the waist. Pulling further back makes the sawing, or inward slicing action, larger. You can do this with the double handed hold as well.

- The most important points about Xingyi sword are: move the sword and the body as one – the sword is an extension of the arm; emphasize the dignified bearing and integrated power; the techniques are simple and practical.

BREATHING CYCLE FOR SWORD CROSSCUT

- Inhale as you advance the lead foot a half-step, circling the sword in the checking hook. Breathe fully and evenly.

- Exhale as you step forward with the crossing cut. Exhale quickly.

Use natural, comfortable breathing during slow and easy practice.

PRACTICAL APPLICATIONS FOR SWORD CROSSCUT

- The main technique of the crosscut is the crossing cut with the under edge of the blade, targeting the neck. The neck is a weak link of the body, and vital, so you can gain considerable effect with little force.

Advance, block and hook is a defensive technique. In actual combat you can advance, retreat, or dodge to the side. If the opponent stabs towards your central area with a long or short weapon you follow along to whichever side is smoothest to block to right or left and hook back. The block takes him off target, and the hook draws his weapon further towards the rear. The masters of old could use this technique to take the weapon right out of the hands of the opponent. Of course, this sort of skill is not the work of a day.

Step forward crossing cut is the attack that follows your deflection. Step in quickly to get the body close, turn over the wrist to cut across the neck with the under edge of the blade. In combat, you don't aim too carefully when cutting across – cutting the head, neck, chest, abdomen, hand or arm will all work.

- One important point in applying the crosscut is that it must be applied in combination with other techniques. Take whatever opportunity presents to continue the attack, chopping, piercing or slicing up until you completely vanquish the opponent. Don't give your opponent any breathing space. If the opponent stabs with a long weapon you can do the crossing cut along his weapon to slice his hand and arm.

- The Xingyi sword is used mostly to counter attack. 'If the enemy does not move then I don't move. If the enemy moves slightly then I attack first. As the second person starts the first person has already arrived.' You must develop your confidence, you must not be shy in a fight. If you are shy then you are afraid and will certainly lose in a fight. You must develop a confident winning attitude. Of course, confidence comes from competence. If you have not developed the skills then confidence is just blind and you will most likely lose the fight. Thoroughly mastered skills come from long hours of daily intelligent training and frequent practical training.

THE POEM ABOUT SWORD CROSSCUT

横剑歌诀

横剑技法取敌项，
临敌不惧胆要壮。
左右格挂顺势折，
沉肘坐腰劲内藏。

Sword crosscut goes for the opponent's neck,

You cannot be afraid to you get close, you must be courageous.

Block and hook to right or left then go smoothly to cut,

Your power is hidden inside when you settle the elbows and sit the spine.

6. FIVE ELEMENTS LINKED SWORD FORM

INTRODUCTION TO THE FIVE ELEMENTS LINKED SWORD, WUXING LIANHUAN JIAN

The Five Elements Linked Sword is a short form that combines the sword's five element techniques with the basic structure of the five element hand form. It is quite widespread and popular among traditional Xingyi practitioners. The form varies by region and by branch of Xingyi, so there are quite a few Xingyi sword five element linked forms. Not all show the true characteristics of Xingyi. The form should show Xingyi footwork and power and the flavour and characteristics of Xingyi. The form is based on Xingyi principles, so if it doesn't have the flavour of Xingyi then it has lost the intrinsic nature that makes it Xingyi sword.

The form presented in this book has 16 movements that contain all five of the five element techniques. The movements are repeated out and back. It contains the techniques chop, pierce, cut, slice up, scull, entangle, hook, draw, lift, and check. The overall characteristics of the form are: the techniques are tightly connected, simple and practical; the power is integrated; stillness and movement alternate clearly; the rhythm is distinct; the form has a complete and full feeling; form and spirit are one; and hard and gentle blend together.

NAMES OF THE MOVEMENTS

1. Opening Move
2. Thrust: Advance, Draw and Pierce
3. Thrust: Hook Up, Right Stance Pierce Forward
4. Drill: Entangle and Lift, Right Stance Pierce Down
5. Chop: Hook Down, Right Stance Swinging Chop
6. Thrust: Lift Knee, Entangle, Flat Pierce
7. Turn Around Hide the Sword: Turn Around and Chop
8. Thrust: Step Forward, Hook Up, Right Stance Pierce
9. Chop: Wheel Around, Lift Knee and Chop
10. Slash: Step Forward, Right Stance Slice Up
11. Crosscut: Left Stance Crossing Cut
12. Crosscut: Right Stance Crossing Cut
13. Drill: Entangle, Draw Back, Left Stance Twisted Pierce
14. Pierce Behind: Cross-over Step, Turning Pierce Behind
15. Reaching Pierce: Step Forward, Reaching Pierce Forward
16. Chop: Hook Left, Right Stance Chop
17. Leopard Cat Turns Over Whilst Climbing a Tree: Turn Around, Crossing Cut, Heel Kick, Resting Stance Chop

(The following moves are repetition back in the returning direction)

18. Thrust

CHAPTER TWO: SWORD, *JIAN*   115

19. Thrust
20. Drill
21. Chop
22. Thrust
23. Turn Around and Hide the Sword
24. Thrust
25. Chop
26. Slash
27. Crosscut
28. Crosscut
29. Drill
30. Pierce Behind
31. Reaching Pierce
32. Chop
33. Leopard Cat Turns Over Whilst Climbing a Tree
(The following moves are the closing combination)
34. Thrust
35. Closing Move

Description of the Movements

1. **Opening Move**   qǐ shì   起势

The movement is the same as setting into *ready stance*. The actions are *Stand at attention holding the sword in the left hand; Transfer the hilt to the right hand; Right retreat and chop.*

ACTION 1: Stand at attention facing ninety degrees to the line of the form. Let the arms hang at the side. Nestle the sword guard in the left hand in an upside down hold. The sword tip points up, the flat of the blade nestles on the left forearm. Look straight forward. (image 2.59)

ACTION 2: Raise the hands at the sides until they arrive at shoulder height. Turn the torso ninety degrees to the left. Bring the right hand across to meet the left hand and change the hilt to the right hand. Release the left hand, taking the sword fingers shape. The left hand will remain in sword fingers shape throughout the form

116 FIVE ELEMENTS LINKED SWORD FORM

unless otherwise stated. Look forward. (image 2.60)

ACTION 3: Retreat the right foot and shift back, bending the right leg to sit into a *santi* stance. Circle the sword tip up, then chop forward and down, the blade standing, the tip pointing forward at nose height. Pull the right hand in towards the belly, about a forearm length away. Keep the left hand at the right wrist throughout. Press the head up and look past the tip. (images 2.61, 2.62)

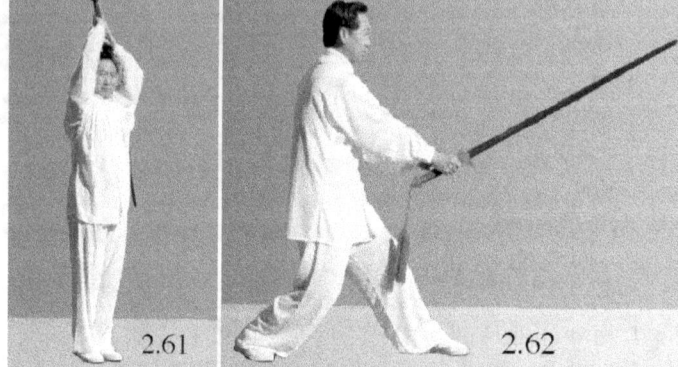

Pointers

- The left hand must hold the sword steady, not letting the blade wobble. The right hand must then take the sword accurately.
- Complete the sword chop as the right foot retreats. The power must be well anchored and weighty, the spirit full, with concentrated focus.

2. Thrust bēngjiàn 崩剑

Left advance, right draw; Right follow-in step, forward pierce.

ACTION 1: Advance the left foot a half-step without moving the right foot, shifting weight forward between the feet. Rotate the right palm away from the thumb and lift it, pulling the sword back on the right side of the body. Draw a small circle with the sword tip, keeping the tip pointing forward at all times. The right hand finishes a bit lower than shoulder height, the blade horizontal. Place the left hand at the right wrist. Turn the body slightly right and look past the sword tip. (image 2.63)

ACTION 2: Follow-in the right foot a half-step to land with a thump in the *crushing punch* stance. Rotate the right hand slightly to turn the blade to a standing blade and then pierce forward forcefully to chest height, sending power to the sword tip. Keep the right arm slightly bent and keep the left hand at the right wrist. Tuck in the jaw, press the head up, and look forward past the sword tip. (image 2.64)

CHAPTER TWO: SWORD, *JIAN*   117

Pointers

- o Complete the draw back as the left foot advances. Complete the pierce as the right foot lands with a shoveling thump.

3. **Thrust**   bēngjiàn   崩剑

Left advance, hook up; Right step forward, pierce forward.

ACTION 1: Advance the left foot a half-step and follow in the right foot to the left ankle. Take a full grip with the right hand and cock the wrist down, bending the arm to pull the hilt down to the right belly. The tip points up and hooks back in front of the right side of the body. Keep the blade about twenty centimetres from the body. Keep the left hand at the right wrist. Tuck in the elbows, contain the chest and tuck in the belly. Look forward. (image 2.65)

ACTION 2: Take a long step forward with the right foot and follow in the left foot to just behind the right foot, most weight on the left leg as with the *crushing punch* stance. Lift the right hand to chest height and use a spiral grip to bring the tip down to point straight forward. Extend the right hand forcefully forward to pierce to chest height, sending power out to the sword tip. Keep the left hand on the right wrist throughout. Press the head up, look past the sword tip. (image 2.66)

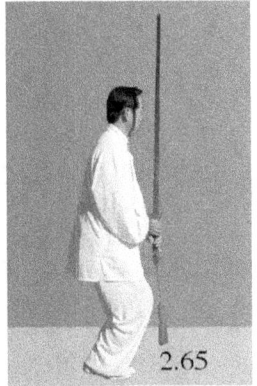

118 FIVE ELEMENTS LINKED SWORD FORM

Pointers

- Complete each sword technique as each foot lands. Complete the hook back as the left foot advances. Complete the pierce as the right foot steps forward.
- When hooking, take a firm grip and cock the wrist to hook up and pull back with the blade. Pull back and hook as one action, bending the elbow to gather power. Then extend the arm to pierce. Connect the hook and pierce smoothly, so that the whole movement is quick.

4. Drill   zuānjiàn   钻剑

Left retreat, entangle and lift; Right step forward, pierce down.

ACTION 1: Retreat the left foot and shift back towards the left leg, withdrawing the right foot a half-step and touching the toes down. Rotate the right palm away from the thumb and circle it right and down, then lift it to in front of the right shoulder, circling the sword tip down from the front, to entangle then draw back. The sword tip is angled down to chest height. Turn slightly to the right. Keep the left hand on the right wrist throughout. Look past the tip. (image 2.67)

ACTION 2: Advance the right foot a long step and follow in the left foot a half-step, keeping most weight on the left leg in a *s a n t i* stance. Pierce forward and down with the hand inverted (thumb web is forward and down) at chest height, the sword tip at knee height. Almost fully extend the right arm and reach the right shoulder forward. Swing the left hand up to the left to brace out, arm bent, above the head. Look past the sword tip. (image 2.68)

2.67   2.68

Pointers

- Circle and lift the sword as the left foot retreats, in a fully coordinated movement. Rotate the right hand to entangle with the sword, then lift the elbow to lift and draw with the sword. Use the body core to draw the shoulder, the shoulder to draw the elbow, the elbow to draw the hand, and the hand to draw the sword.
- Complete the pierce down as the right foot lands forward. Turn the waist, reach with the shoulder, and extend the arm to pierce forward.

Swing the left arm up to apply an equal and opposite force that balances and integrates the movement's power.

5. Chop pījiàn 劈剑

Left step forward, left hook down; Right step forward, swinging chop.

ACTION 1: Step the left foot forward in front of the right leg, landing hooked out. Don't move the right foot, but lift the heel and bend both legs to sit into an evenly weighted cross-over stance. Take a full grip on the hilt with the right hand and bring the sword tip down and back to the left rear of the body. Bring the left hand down to the right elbow. Turn the body left. Look at the sword tip. (image 2.69)

ACTION 2: Take a long step to the forward right with the right foot and follow in a half-step with the left foot to sit into a *s a n t i* stance. Rotate the right palm away from the thumb and lift it above the head to circle the sword tip back and up. Then take a full grip on the hilt and chop forward and down to waist height with a standing blade. Circle the left hand back and up to above the left side of the head. Look past the sword tip. (image 2.70)

Pointers

- Hook the sword down to the left as the left foot lands forward in the cross-over step. Circle and chop the sword and brace back with the left hand as the right foot lands forward. The chop needs equal and opposite forces acting upwards and downwards, forward and back. Start and complete the movement as a coordinated whole, and swing the arm with force, sending the power out to the leading edge of the blade.
- The entire movement is one coordinated action, with no pause midway. Take a long step forward, and take a quick follow-in step. The chop must have a point of focus. The final action of the chop is a sawing pull back. Settle the shoulder and elbow to pull the sword back.

6. Thrust bēngjiàn 崩剑

Right advance, entangle; Lift knee, flat pierce.

ACTION 1: Advance the right foot a half-step and shift the weight between the feet without moving the left foot. Lower the left hand to the right wrist. Use a spiral grip with the right hand to bring the sword tip right, down, and then left and up, completing a full circle. Then bend the arms and bring them together in front of the chest, the right hand rotated palm up, the blade flat, and the tip at chest height. Look past the sword tip. (image 2.71)

ACTION 2: Bend the right leg slightly for stability, shift to the right leg, and lift the left knee. Extend the arms forward to pierce with the flat blade, tip to shoulder height. Open the left hand and support the right hand with it. Press the head up, release tension in the shoulders, settle the *qi* to the *dantian*, and send the power out to the sword tip. Look past the sword tip. (image 2.72)

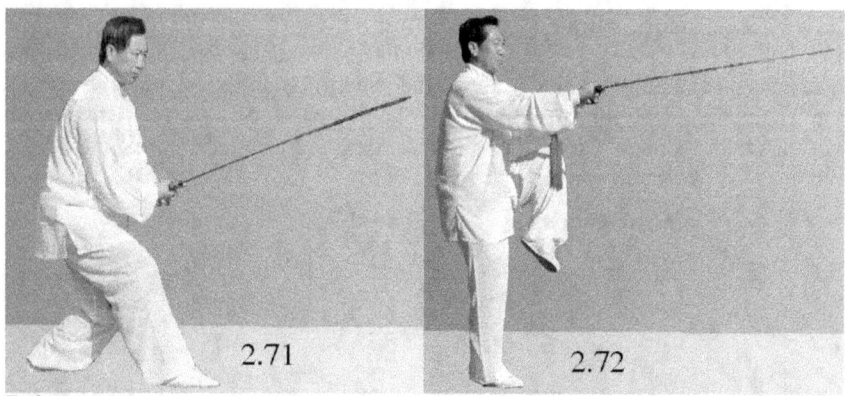

Pointers

- Complete the entangling action as the right foot advances. Complete the piercing action as the left knee lifts.
- The tip draws a clockwise circle about twenty centimetres in radius during the entangling action. The right wrist needs to be loose so that the movement is round and gentle, and the power reaches the tip of the sword.
- Shift forward as you settle the hands and bend the elbows and lift, putting the power out to the sword tip.

7. **Turn Around and Hide the Sword**   huíshēn cángjiàn   回身藏劍

Turn around, swinging chop; Left hook, chop and pull.

ACTION 1: Land the left foot behind and turn around 180 degrees to the left, rotating on both feet. Rotate the right palm towards the thumb and lift the elbow above the head. Once turned, shift forward to the left leg and chop the sword forward and down. Place the left hand, back in sword fingers shape, on the right wrist and extend both arms slightly. The sword tip is at chest height. Look past the sword tip. (image 2.73 transitional)

ACTION 2: After chopping down, pivot around the right wrist to bring the sword tip down, back past the left side of the body, then up and forward to chop down. Keep the left hand at the right wrist. Shift back to a *santi* stance on the right leg. Press the hilt down and pull back and down at the right side of the body, bringing the standing blade close to the right thigh with the tip pointing forward and up. Extend the left arm out at chest height. Look forward. (image 2.74)

2.73

2.74

Pointers

- o The movement is completed without hesitation. Be sure to shift the weight forward and back along with the movement of the sword.
- o The sword chops twice: a chop, a hook, and then another chop without a pause in between. Shift to the left leg during the first swinging chop, then shift back to the right leg during the second chop and pull.

8. Thrust   bēngjiàn   崩剑

Left advance, hook up; Right step forward, pierce.

ACTION 1: Advance the left foot a half-step and follow in the right foot to the left ankle. Extend the right arm to send the blade forward then take a full grip and cock the wrist down to bring the tip up. Then bring the right arm back, the hand in front of the belly, to bring the sword tip back to hook up about a foot away from the body, tip up. Keep the left hand on the right wrist throughout. Look forward. (image 2.75)

ACTION 2: Take a step forward with the right foot and follow in the left foot to behind the right, in the same short stance as *crushing punch*. Lift the sword hilt to in front of the chest to lower the tip to point straight forward, then pierce forcefully forward at chest height. The arms are almost straight. Keep the left hand on the right wrist throughout. Tuck in the jaw and press the head up. Look past the sword tip. (image 2.76)

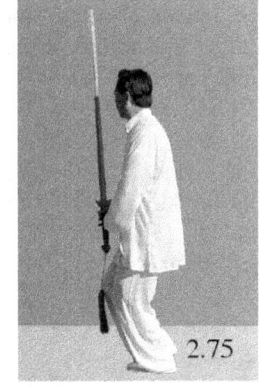
2.75

122   FIVE ELEMENTS LINKED SWORD FORM

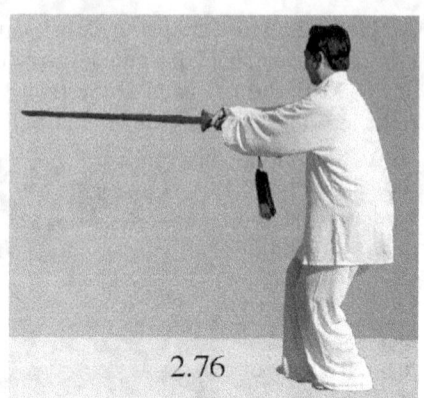

2.76

Pointers

- Movement 8 is the same as movement 2.

9. Chop   pījiàn   劈剑

Right hook-in and wheel around; Left lift knee, chop.

ACTION 1: Advance the right foot a half-step, landing hooked-in and shifting to the right leg, so that the body turns around to the left 180 degrees to face in the way in which you came. Turn the left foot to point forward. Rotate the right palm away from the thumb and lift the elbow so that the blade under edge is up. Circle the left hand up past the face to above the head while turning, then continue to circle forward and down to level with the left shoulder. Look past the left hand. (image 2.77)

ACTION 2: Stand steadily on the right leg, keeping the knee bent and lifting the left knee with the foot tucked in at the crotch. Circle the left hand down and back, then up to the upper left of the head to brace out with the arm. Use a full grip with the right hand and circle it from the back, up, forward, then down to chop at waist height. Finish with the arm bent and sword tip at chest height. Reach the right shoulder forward and reach the torso forward slightly. Send the power to the distal third of the blade. Look past the tip. (image 2.78)

Pointers

- The more you hook the foot in, the smoother the turn around will be. Do not step the hooking foot too far away, as this will destabilize the

turn.
- Three actions link without a pause: wheel around, lift the knee, and chop.
- Be sure to coordinate the hands in opposite actions to assist the power – the one forward and down and the other back and up. When launching power into the chop, turn the waist, extend the shoulder, reach the torso, swing the arm and lift the knee. The power transfer must be smooth.

10. Slash   pàojiàn   炮剑

Left step forward, crossing draw; Right step forward, inverted slice.

ACTION 1: Land the left foot forward and right, hooked-out. Bend the legs and shift between them equally. Rotate the right palm towards the thumb and bend and lift the elbow to bring the sword's under edge up. Lift the blade to draw across towards the left at eyebrow height, right hand at eyebrow height and sword tip pointing to the forward right. Turn the body slightly to the left. Keep the left hand inside the right wrist throughout. Look past the tip. (image 2.79)

ACTION 2: Take a long step forward with the right foot diagonally to the right and follow-in the left foot to take a *santi* stance. Using a spiral grip, circle the right hand to circle the sword tip up then back and down, staying close by the left side. Then continue forward and up to complete an inverted grip slice with the under edge of the blade up. The right palm is rotated away from the thumb above the shoulders with the arm bent, and the sword tip points forward at chest height. Send the power to the body of the blade. Keep the left hand at the right wrist. Look past the sword tip. (image 2.80)

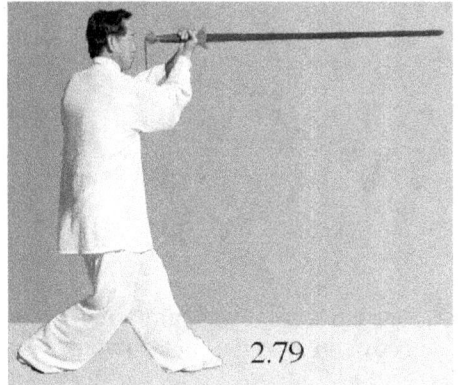
2.79

2.80

Pointers
- Rotate the right hand to lift the sword and draw back as the left foot steps forward. Turn the waist to draw the sword back, closing the shoulders and bending the elbow to take the sword across to the left. Use the power of the body core and keep the movement gentle and coordinated.
- Complete the inverted slice as the right foot steps forward, arriving

exactly at the same time. Keep the sword blade close to the body as it circles, and be sure to turn the wrist, keeping it supple. Transfer power from body core to shoulder, from shoulder to elbow, from elbow to hand, and from hand to sword.

11. Crosscut   héngjiàn   橫劍

Right advance, left brandishing entangle; Left step forward, crossing cut.

ACTION 1: Advance the left foot a half-step and follow in the right foot to the left ankle. With the left hand supporting the right wrist, extend the arms forward and up to bring the sword tip flat, encircling across from right to left, pointing forward. Then brandish in a circle back, passing by the face to circle to the right. To do this, the right hand rotates palm towards the thumb to bring the palm up and the sword tip across. Bend the arms in front of the chest. Follow the tip with the eyes during the movement. (image 2.81)

ACTION 2: Take a long step to the forward left with the left foot and follow in a half-step with the right foot. Take a full grip with the palm up and, with the right arm bent at about 120 degrees, cut the blade horizontally across to the left. When the sword arrives at the left side, bend the right arm and tuck the elbow towards the solar plexus. The sword tip is just above shoulder height, the power in the forward portion. Circle the left hand to above the left side of the head. Press the head up, settle the *qi* to the *dantian*. Look past the sword tip. (image 2.82)

 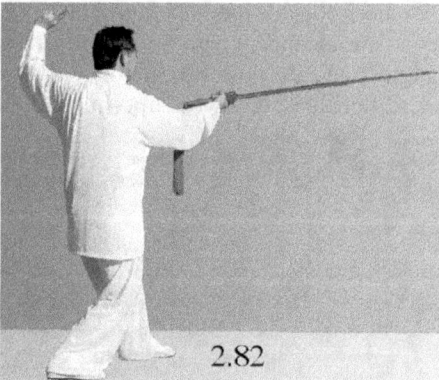

2.81   2.82

Pointers

- Circle the sword as the right foot advances, keeping the movement gentle. Draw the hand from the body core, and thus to the sword. Turn the wrist and adjust the grip as needed.
- Complete the leftward crossing cut as the left foot lands. Launch power with fully integrated strength.

12. Crosscut   héngjiàn   橫劍

Left advance, right brandishing entangle; Right step forward, crossing cut.

ACTION 1: Advance the left foot a half-step and follow in the right foot to the right ankle. With the left hand supporting the right wrist, lower them slightly to chest height, then swing them to the right, so that the sword tip circles from the front left to the front right, and then circles back in front of the face to the left. Rotate the right palm down to turn the blade flat. Close the shoulders towards the left. Follow the sword tip with the eyes during the movement. (image 2.83)

ACTION 2: Take a long step to the forward right with the right foot and follow in a half-step with the left foot, keeping most weight on the left leg. Take a full grip, turn the palm down, and almost fully extend the arm to cut to the right. Cut with the blade flat and the tip angled to the forward right at nose height. Keep the left hand on the right wrist. Press the head up. Look past the sword tip. (image 2.84)

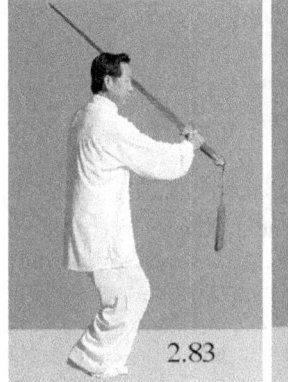

Pointers

o Left and right crosscut are similar actions, but because they go in different directions the rotation is slightly different. The right palm rotates up for the left crosscut and down for the right crosscut.

13. Drill zuānjiàn 钻剑

Right advance, entangle and draw back; Left step forward, twisted pierce.

ACTION 1: Advance the right foot a half-step and follow in the left foot to the right ankle. Keep the left hand at the right wrist. Lower the sword tip and circle it left then up, and then again to the right and pull to draw back. Once the hands are outside the right shoulder, bend the elbows to lower the hands to the right waist, rotating the right hand palm up so that the under edge of the blade is up and the tip points forward. Turn the body to the right, tuck in the belly and contain the chest, compressing the torso. Look past the tip. (image 2.85 transitional)

ACTION 2: Take a long step forward with the left foot and follow in a half-step with the right foot, keeping most weight on the right leg. Using a spiral grip, extend the right arm in front of the chest to pierce forward in an inverted grip, the under edge of the blade up and tip pointing forward. Finish with the arm slightly bent, the right shoulder extended and released, the elbow tucked in, and

the blade tip at eyebrow height. Send power to the sword tip. Swing the left hand forward and up by the head to brace out to the left side. Press the head up. Look past the sword tip. (image 2.86)

Pointers

- Circle and draw the sword to complete the action as the right foot advances. Transfer movement from the body core to the shoulder, from the shoulder to the elbow, from the elbow to the hands and from the hands to the sword. Keep the body action gentle and rounded, and keep the sword technique tight and well knit.
- Pierce with the sword as the left foot lands forward, sword and foot arriving simultaneously. As you first entangle, then draw back, and then twist and roll down, contain the chest and gather power in the lower back, turning the body as you move. When you then turn the blade over and pierce forward, turn the waist, reach the shoulder forward, and extend the arm. Extend the right shoulder forward and bring the left shoulder back, swinging the left hand up to assist the power launch.

14. Pierce Behind huí cì 回刺

Cross-over step, turning pierce behind.

ACTION: Shift forward without moving the left foot, and step the right foot across in front of the left foot, landing turned out. Bend the right leg and lift the left heel, turning the body to the right so that the legs are crossed, most weight on the right leg. Lower the left hand to support the right wrist. Tuck the right elbow in and extend the wrist, circling the sword tip down behind, pivoting around the wrist. The sword is now outside the right arm, pointing down behind the body. Look at the sword tip. Extend the right arm, almost straight, to the lower rear to pierce the sword tip to knee height with a standing blade. Extend the left hand forward to the upper left. Look at the sword tip. (images 2.87, 2.88)

Pointers

- Complete the whole action without hesitation.
- Adjust your grip on the hilt. First tuck in the elbow and extend the wrist. The left hand may push on the hilt to assist in pushing the sword tip down behind. Use a firm spiral grip for the pierce.
- Extend the left hand up to the front as the sword pierces down behind, perfectly timed together.

15. Reaching Pierce   tàn cì   探刺

Step forward, reach the body and pierce forward.

ACTION: Take a long step forward with the left foot and follow in the right foot a half-step, shifting forward to a *santi* stance. Rotate the right palm away from the thumb and extend the wrist, taking a firm grip on the hilt to cause the sword tip to rise, coming in towards the right side of the head to point forward. Turn the body left and turn the palm to face out, then extend the arm to pierce forward with a standing horizontal blade above head height. Place the left hand on the right wrist. Reach forward slightly with the torso. Keep the right arm snug to the right ear. Look past the sword tip. (image 2.89)

Pointers

- Pierce forward from above the head as the left foot lands. First sit the sword hilt up before piercing.

16. Chop   pījiàn   劈剑

Left advance, hook; Right step forward, chop.

ACTION 1: Advance the left foot a half-step and follow in the right foot lifted at the ankle. Lower the sword and hook back, passing closely by the left side of the body, then circle up to above and behind the head. Use a supple grip on the hilt, so that as the right hand draws a small circle the sword draws a large circle. Keep the left hand on the right wrist. Follow the sword with the eyes, then look forward. (image 2.90)

ACTION 2: Take a long step forward with the right foot and follow in the left foot a half-step, keeping most weight on the left leg. Chop the sword forward and down, then pull the right hand in to about a foot away from the abdomen. The sword tip is at shoulder height, the blade standing. Keep the left hand on the right wrist throughout. Press the head up and look forward. (image 2.91)

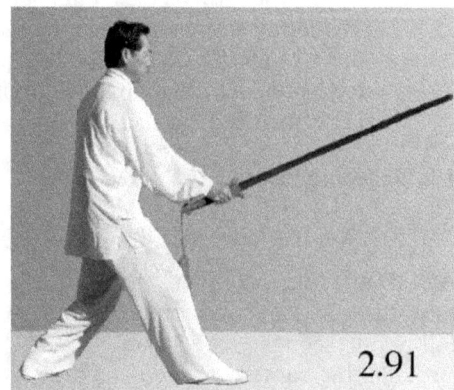

Pointers

- Hook back as the left foot advances, and chop as the right foot steps forward. The sword always acts in conjunction with the stepping. Complete the actions as one movement.
- First chop forward and down, then pull back, as one movement. When pulling back, settle the shoulders and elbows, keep the elbows tucked to the ribs, press the head up, and sit into the buttocks. The chop must have a point of focus.

17. Leopard Cat Turns Over Whilst Climbing a Tree

límāo dào shàng shù   狸猫倒上树

Turn around, crossing cut; Right heel kick; Resting stance chop.

ACTION 1: Step the left foot forward, landing hooked-in, and turn around 180 degrees to the right to face back in the direction from which you came. Shift onto the left leg. Keep the left hand on the right wrist, rotate the right palm down, and place the blade flat in front of the chest. As the body turns, open out both hands to either side, cutting flat across to the right with the blade at chest height and bracing the left hand out to the left. Look forward. (images 2.92)

ACTION 2: Bend the left leg slightly to stand firmly. Lift the right knee and then do a crossways heel hick forward and up to shoulder height. Look forward past the kick. (image 2.93)

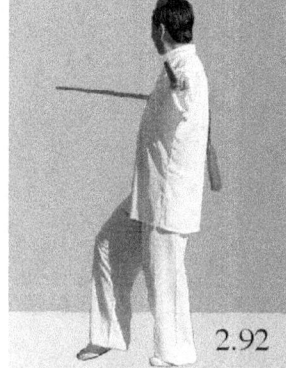

ACTION 3: Land the right foot forward, still crossways, and bring in the left foot a half-step, sitting down into a resting stance. Most weight is on the left leg, the left heel is raised, and the right leg is a bit straighter than the left. Rotate the right palm towards the thumb and lift the hand above the head and bring the left hand in to

the right wrist. As the body drops, chop forward and down, finishing with the blade standing, the tip between waist and knee height. Press the head up. Look past the sword tip. (image 2.94)

Pointers

- The turn must be completed smoothly in one move. Turn quickly, swing the arm forcefully to cut across with power. Kick with force. Sit and chop with stability.
- To do the crossing kick, tuck in the right hip. To land, drive forward to stomp forward and down.
- You must sit into the resting stance with stability. Chop down as the body lowers. Don't use too much force, but use a hidden power.

- The following moves, 18 through 33, are a repetition of the first section, moves 2 through 17, back in the returning direction.

18. Thrust see move 2.
19. Thrust see move 3.

130   FIVE ELEMENTS LINKED SWORD FORM

20. **Drill**   see move 4.
21. **Chop**   see move 5.
22. **Thrust**   see move 6. (image 2.95 with standing blade)

23. **Turn Around and Hide the Sword**   see move 7.
24. **Thrust**   see move 8.
25. **Chop**   see move 9. (image 2.96)

26. **Slash**   see move 10.
27. **Crosscut**   see move 11. (images 2.97, 2.98)

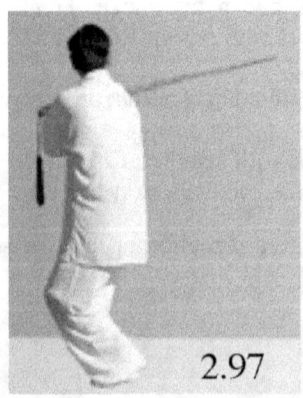

28. Crosscut	see move 12.
29. Drill	see move 13.
30. Pierce Behind	see move 14.
31. Reaching Pierce	see move 15.
32. Chop	see move 16.
33. Leopard Cat Turns Over Whilst Climbing a Tree	see move 17.

34. Thrust

See move 2, back in the same direction as at the beginning.

35. Closing Move　　　　　shōu shì　　　　收势

Starting from *thrust. Retreat and pull the sword; Stand and change hands; Stand at attention and hold the sword.*

ACTION 1: Retreat the right foot and shift back to the right leg, extending the left leg and hooking in the left foot on the spot. Pull the right hand back to in front of the right shoulder with a standing blade placed horizontally at shoulder height. Rotate the left palm away from the thumb to turn the palm out with the thumb down, and cradle the guard. Turn ninety degrees to the right. Look past the sword tip. (image 2.99)

ACTION 2: Withdraw the left foot in beside the right foot so that the feet are parallel. Hold the hilt with the left hand – thumb, little finger and ring finger cradling the guard, and index and middle finger along the hilt to keep the flat of the blade snug to the forearm. Circle the left hand up and left, then down to the left side. With the right hand in sword fingers shape, circle it down, right, then up to the right side above the head. Follow the movement of the right hand with the eyes, then look to the left. (image 2.100)

ACTION 3: Without moving the feet, bring the right hand down to the right side to stand to attention. Look forward. (image 2.101)

FIVE ELEMENTS LINKED SWORD FORM

Pointers

- The hand transfer must be smooth and accurate, taking the sword firmly in the left hand.
- Complete the hand actions as the feet come to attention.
- The movement must be well anchored and have full spirit. The *qi* must be settled and the attitude at peace.

FIVE ELEMENT SPEAR

五行枪

INTRODUCTION TO FIVE ELEMENT SPEAR, *WUXING QIANG*

The style of Xingyi is famous for its spear, Bagua for its sabre, Taiji for its sword, and Shaolin for its staff. In Xingyi, practising spear improves empty hand skills, and empty hand skills are the foundation of spear skills. The creator of Xinyi Liuhequan, Ji Longfeng, excelled at the spear. "He could hit a target from a galloping horse, when he raised his spear no one could escape. He was called the spear spirit. " He applied the principles of the spear to empty hand techniques when he created Xinyi Liuhequan, and spear practice retained its place of importance as *xin-yi* developed into *xing-yi quan*.

Previous generations of Xingyi masters examined many spear techniques and selected the most practical and strongest – those which most showed the flavour and characteristics of Xingyiquan. Xingyi spear emphasizes power and trained skill, and uses no flowery movements. It is simple and practical, and especially emphasizes spear and body moving as one with a full, integrated power and intimidating air. The power of the whole body connects through to the tip of the spear, so that the spear is truly an extension of the body. The five element techniques of the spear are the same as those of the five fists – chop, drill, thrust, slash, and crosscut. Although the moves are named simply spear chop, spear drill, spear thrust, spear slash, and spear crosscut, there are at least two moves contained in each short combination.[8]

The spear demands a high degree of deep skill and coordination. The spear is the king of the weapons. They say 'a year for the fist, a month for the staff, but day by day for the spear'. That is, it takes a year to master empty hand skills with hard training. With this foundation, a month is sufficient to learn staff. But the spear must be practised daily, year in and year out. There are no shortcuts in learning the spear, only hard practice. If you are not willing to work hard then you won't master the spear.

---

[8] Author's note: In the descriptions I use both the traditional and the modern names for each technique to make it easier to learn and teach.

SPEAR INTRODUCTION

If you want your spear technique to be familiar and refined then you must practise the techniques, the forms, and partner spear 'shaft sliding'. You must understand the application of all the techniques. If you think of the application and imagine an opponent, you will learn the techniques quicker. You should also study spear theory, learn from the experience of past masters, and study spear applications to improve your ability with the spear.

There are three lengths of spear – long, medium, and short. The long spear is about four meters, the medium spear about three meters, and the short spear about two meters. The long spear develops strength, the short spear develops agility, and the medium spear develops both strength and agility. Not many people practise the long spear, mostly because it is awkward to carry and store. Most Xingyi players like to use something between the medium and short spears – about 2.5 meters.

In choosing the wood for a spear shaft, you need a good quality white waxwood. It should be supple and smooth skinned with no knots or kinks. The base should be the size of your own thumb and forefinger held in a circle. A short spear can be a bit thinner, and a long spear a bit thicker. The circumference of the tip should be the natural thickness of the wood as it has grown. You should not shave down the wood as this reduces its natural suppleness and can lead to breakage.

A spear is comprised of three parts, the wooden shaft, the metal head, and the horsehair tassel. The spear shaft is divided into thirds – the third of the shaft at the tip is the fore-section, the third of the shaft at the base is the aft-section, and the third in the middle is the midsection. During spear practice, the hands often slide up and down the shaft to best carry out the different techniques. The very end of the spearhead is called the tip, and the other end of the shaft is called the base or butt.

FIVE ELEMENT SPEAR TECHNIQUES

On Guard yùbèishì 预备势

On guard position is the opening of any Xingyi weapon form or practice session, and is the ready position for many techniques. *On guard* is the *santi* stance with both hands holding the spear, ready to do any technique. *On guard* is the foundation for spear training, so you need to do post standing, similar to *santishi* post standing, in this position to establish the correct posture in the body and prepare the way for further spear study.

The actions are: *Stand the spear; Left bow stance send out the spear; Left on guard position.*

ACTION 1: Stand at attention with the right hand holding the spear vertical at the right side with the base on the ground. Let the left hand hang naturally, press the head up, and look forward. (image 3.1)

CHAPTER THREE: SPEAR, *QIANG* 135

ACTION 2: Turn ninety degrees to the left to face the way in which the stance will face. Step the left foot forward and bend the knee while straightening the right leg, shifting forward into a bow stance. Lift the spear horizontally with the right hand, pointing the tip forward [to the side, in the new direction], extending

the right arm with the spear shaft at chest height. Bring the left hand to the right armpit with the palm up to support the shaft. Look past the spear tip. (images 3.2)

ACTION 3: Shift back, extending the left leg more and bending the right leg to shift back into a *santi* stance. Extend the left arm to send the spear out and slide the right hand back to the base, pulling the base to the right waist. Keep the left arm almost straight, and hold the shaft with the palm down. Keep the spear on the midline of the body, the shaft almost horizontal, but the tip at chest height. (image 3.3 and from the front)

Pointers

- Complete the three actions smoothly as one move.
- When moving into the bow stance and sending the spear forward, be sure to send the tip directly forward without wobbling around. Slide the

right hand smoothly, maintaining contact with the shaft.
- Complete the placement of the spear as you sit into the *santi* stance. This is the final posture of the ready stance.
- This is the spear's equivalent to the *santishi*, and the posture is adjusted to suit the spear. In the empty hand *santishi*, the trunk is angled forty-five degrees to the front. With the spear, however, the trunk should turn more, about sixty to seventy degrees. The rear foot is also turned out more — about seventy degrees. The spear shaft must be held snug to the trunk, with the right hand holding the base at waist height on the right side. The left hand is in front, pointing the spear in the correct direction. Three points serve to stabilize the spear – the lead hand, the rear hand, and the waist – so that the spear and body are joined as one. Practice post standing in this posture. Post standing might seem like a waste of time, but it builds a strong foundation for future mastery of the techniques and proper performance of the movements. Post standing sets the basic posture into the ideal shape so that movements can become correct. During post standing you should seek kinesthetic awareness, get a feel for the power lines, and master the requirements of the spear.

1. SPEAR CHOP

INTRODUCTION TO SPEAR CHOP, *PI QIANG*

The chop is the most basic of the spear techniques. The definition of a spear chop in the wushu dictionary is 'holding the spear in both hands, strike downward from above with power and speed, sending power to the tip'. In the competition regulations it is 'holding the spear in both hands, chop down from above, sending power to the fore-section. ' This is simply for the actual chop. In Xingyi, spear chop is practised as a number of combinations that contain hook, scoop, swinging chop, and stab. The spear chop combinations contain both defensive and attacking techniques. The movements are simple but very practical, taking care of defense and attack in one move.

There are five different footwork or stances: step forward, retreat, roundabout steps, left stance, and right stance. Any technique that brings the spear down in a chopping action from above is considered a chop. There are three different hand methods: left handed, right handed, and changeover. There is also a chop with the base.

METHOD ONE: CHECK, HOOK, AND CHOP

1a Right Stance Chop   yòubù pīqiāng   右步劈枪

Start from *on guard*. Continue with *Advance, right checking hook; Right step forward, chop*.

ACTION 1: Advance the left foot a half-step and follow in the right foot to the

CHAPTER THREE: SPEAR, *QIANG*   137

left ankle without touching down. Bend the left elbow slightly and rotate the palm to face in, to turn the shaft counterclockwise, lifting the tip above head height. At the right waist, rotate the right palm away from the thumb. These actions cause the fore-section of the spear to check to the right. Look past the spear tip. (image 3.4)

ACTION 2: Take a long step forward with the right foot and follow in the left foot a half-step. Rotate the left palm towards the thumb and tuck in the left elbow so that the thumb to forefinger web presses down. Chop the spear forward and down forcefully with the left hand, the spear tip finishing at waist height. Keep the right hand at the waist and assist the left hand with a small turning and lifting action. Press the head up and look past the spear tip. (image 3.5 and from the front)

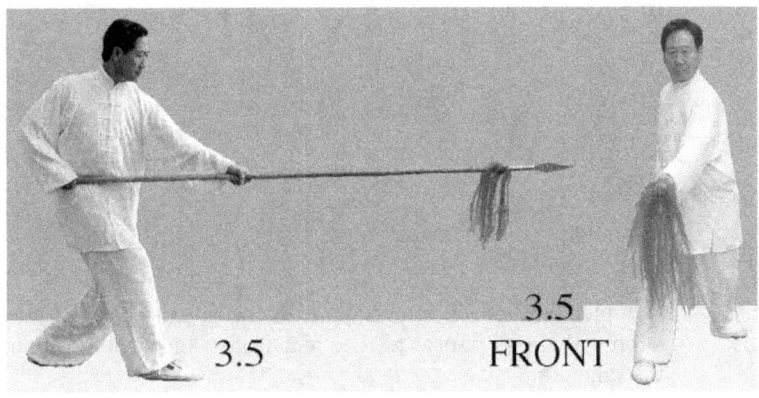

1b Left Stance Chop   zuǒbù pīqiāng   左步劈枪

Advance, left hooking check; Left step forward, chop.

ACTION 1: Advance the right foot a half-step and follow in the left foot to the right ankle without touching down. Place the left hand near the aft-section of the shaft and rotate the palm towards the thumb while bending the elbow, so that the palm turns in – lifting and turning the spear tip above head height. Bend the left elbow so that the left hand is in front of the left shoulder. Keep the right hand at the waist and assist the left hand with a turning action. These actions cause the fore-section of the shaft to check to the left and hook back as the feet advance. Look forward. (image 3.6)

138   SPEAR CHOP

ACTION 2: Take a long step forward with the left foot and follow in a half-step with the right foot to tale a *santi* stance. Rotate the left palm away from the thumb to press down with the thumb/forefinger web, and extend the arm forward and down forcefully to chop the spear tip down to waist height. Hold the base with the right hand at the waist.

Send the power to the fore-section of the spear. Press the head up and look forward. (image 3.7 and from the front)

Pointers

- Complete the check and hook with the advance step. Complete the chop with the step forward. The feet, hands, and spear must all arrive at the same time.
- The spear points straight forward when it chops. To assist the action, when advancing, step the lead foot about fifteen degrees to the side. This helps to keep the spear on the midline.
- Always send the left shoulder forward into the spear chop, whether in right stance or left stance.

• Continue on with right and left chop as space permits.

METHOD TWO: CHOP AND STAB

1c Right Stance Chop and Stab yòubù pīzhā qiāng   右步劈扎枪

Start from *on guard*. *Left advance, scoop; Right step forward, chop; Stab.*

ACTION 1: Advance the left foot a half-step and follow in the right foot without touching down. Lower the spear tip to knee height, then, as the left foot lands, bend the left elbow and pull the spear back. Push the base forward and down slightly with the right hand. These actions cause the spear tip to scoop up above the head. Look forward. (image 3.8)

ACTION 2: Step the right foot a long step forward and follow in the left foot a half-step. Push the left hand forward and down on the shaft, and pull the right hand back to the right waist on the base. This causes the fore-section of the spear to chop strongly down, the tip arriving at waist height, the power in the fore-section. Press the head up and look past the spear tip. (image 3.9)

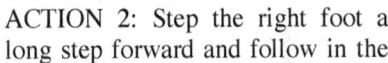

ACTION 3: Without moving the feet, push the base forcefully forward with the right hand to send the spear forward. Loosen the left hand to guide the shaft. Accelerate the right hand as it approaches the left hand to send power forward to the spear tip so that it quivers. The shaft is horizontal at chest height. Shift the weight forward. The right hand is nestled in the left hand. Look past the spear tip. (image 3.10)

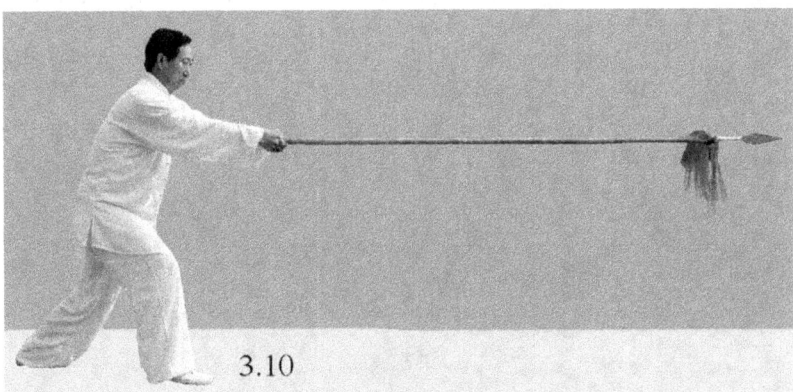

140 SPEAR CHOP

1d Left Stance Chop and Stab   zuǒbù pīzhā qiāng   左步劈扎枪

Right advance, scoop; Left step forward, chop: Stab.

ACTION 1: Lower the spear tip to knee height. Advance the right foot a half-step and follow in the left foot to beside the right ankle without touching down. Loosen the left hand and pull the right hand with the spear base back to the right side, pressing down slightly. Slide the left hand forward and bend the elbow. These actions cause the spear to scoop up, the tip finishing above the head. Look forward. (image 3.11)

ACTION 2: Take a long step forward with the left foot and follow in a half-step with the right foot. Push the left hand forward and down and pull the right hand slightly upwards, using both hands to chop the spear tip forcefully forward and down. Send the power to the spear tip, at waist height. Press the head up and look forward. (image 3.12)

ACTION 3: Without moving the feet, extend the right arm forcefully to send the spear forward. Loosen the left hand to allow the spear to slide through. As the right hand approaches the left hand, abruptly accelerate to

send the power to the spear tip, causing it to quiver. The spear is level at chest height. Shift the weight slightly forward. Nestle the right hand in the left hand. Press the head up and look forward. (image 3.13)

Pointers

- o Although described as three actions, this is one unbroken movement. Complete the scoop up as the lead foot advances. Complete the chop as the rear foot steps through. Follow closely and quickly with a forceful stab.

• Continue on to repeat right and left, limited only by the space available.

1e Chop Turn Around   pīqiāng zhuànshēn   劈枪转身

Using the <u>left</u> stance chop or stab as example. *Left step forward, lift and punt; Turn around, retreat, chop.*

ACTION 1: Advance the left foot hooked in without moving the right foot, straightening the legs to stand up. (From *left stance <u>stab</u>* hook the left foot in on the spot.) Rotate the right palm away from the thumb and lift it to turn and bring the spear base above the head at the right side with the palm up and the arm rounded. Loosen the left hand and slide it forward, rotating the palm away from the thumb to face out and bending the arm. This brings the spear tip in an arc to the left and down to in front of the body, the tip at knee height. Look past the spear tip. (image 3.14)

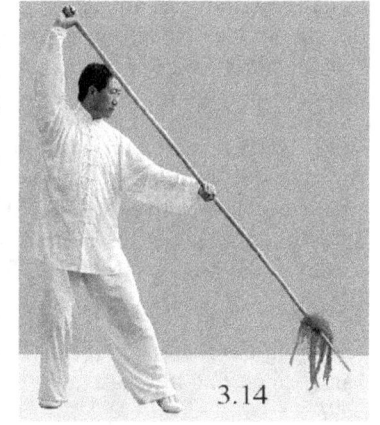

ACTION 2: Turn around 180 degrees to the right to face back behind, pivoting both feet on the spot. Shift back and retreat the right foot, then settle the body down and shift back some more to sit mostly on the right leg, in a *santi* stance. Swing the spear forward and down from above the head to chop forcefully. Pull the right hand, holding the base, to the right waist. Finish with the left hand in front of the body, the spear tip at waist height. Press the head up and look past the spear tip. (image 3.15)

142   SPEAR CHOP

From <u>right</u> *stance chop* step the left foot forward hooked in. Do the *lift and punt* then *turn and retreat*, the same as described above.

Pointers

- Hook in, turn around, and retreat smoothly – link the steps together closely.
- Rotate the hands to do the punting and lifting action. Turn the right palm away from the thumb and the left palm towards the thumb. This action of '*yin* and *yang* mutually rotate' goes through the whole body.
- Complete the chop as the retreating foot lands. Settle the trunk down slightly. The spear must have a focal point in the chop, and the tip must not hit the ground.

1f   Chop Closing Move   pīqiāng shōushì   劈枪收势

On arriving back at the starting point, do a *turn around* to face the original direction. Once you are in *left stance chop* or *stab* then do *closing move*: *Right retreat, snap the spear; Close the feet and put the spear at attention; Stand at attention with the spear.*

ACTION 1: Retreat the right foot a half-step then withdraw the left foot a half-step and shift back mostly to the right leg. Pull the spear base back to the right side between the hip and waist. Slide the left hand forward and tighten the grip abruptly to snap the spear up. The spear tip should quiver up and down. The spear tip is at head height. Look forward. (image 3.16)

ACTION 2: Turn and shift to the right leg. Hold the spear shaft in the left hand and bring the shaft to vertical at the right of the right shoulder. Slide the right hand, supporting the shaft at the right of the body. Look at the left hand. (image 3.17)

ACTION 3: Bring the left foot in beside the right foot and stand up to attention. Release the left hand and lower it across the body to the left side, then lift it at the side, and then bend the elbow to press down in front of the body, finishing

with the arm vertical at the left side. Follow the movement of the left hand with the eyes, and once the left hand has pressed down, look forward. Keep the right hand holding the spear. The closing is now completed. (image 3.18)

3.18

- If the right foot is forward then retreat the right foot behind the left and shift back, withdrawing the left foot slightly.

Pointers

- Each of the five elemental techniques uses the same closing move.
- The power must reach the tip of the spear in *retreat and snap the spear*. The tip must quiver up and down.
- The closing move must be done continuously and be well coordinated between the upper and lower segments. It must be stable. The eyes and spirit must be bright and focused to the completion of the movement.

POWER GENERATION FOR SPEAR CHOP

Chop: the hands work together as a unit on the shaft of the spear. The left hand uses a downward and forward pushing and pressing power while the right hand grips tightly with a backward pulling and slightly lifting power. Be sure to use the waist, torso and shoulders to move the hands. The actual hand movements are slight, relatively hidden. The chop must have a focal point at waist height. As the left hand arrives at the focal point it must stop sharply. At this time tighten its grip with an upward pulling power and press the spear base down with the right hand. The spear momentum is stopped abruptly, and a snap is developed, the power reaching to the tip, which is the chopping power.

- The power in the hands comes from the body core, the shoulders, and the arms. The trunk compresses then lengthens while the chest closes then opens and the shoulders close then open. Turn the waist, reach with the shoulders, extend the arms, sit into the hips, and press the head up to create a whole body coordinated power.
- The classics say, "Chop depends on sitting the knee." Sitting the knee means that the front leg must maintain a certain flexion. Because the spear chops down with considerable force the lead knee must absorb more force than usual. To lengthen the time of power application the knee bends with a springing action. This springing flexion is what 'sitting' means – it is not

just a static sitting or flexion of the knee. Pushing into the lead foot creates it. The momentum of the body will cause the knee to flex with a springing action.

Check and hook: Both hands must twist simultaneously. When checking and hooking to the right, close the left shoulder a bit to the right by using the waist. Hook up by twisting and bending the arms, check by using the right or left turn of the trunk. The power of the check is in the body core, while the power of the hook is in the hands.

Scoop: The power comes from the shoulders, shoulder girdle and arms. Release and settle the shoulders, put a sharp checking action into the shoulder girdle, and move the arms in a turning action. Keep the hands firm on the spear so that the power of the body transfers through to the spear fore-section or tip to complete the scoop. Do not use too large an action when practising the scoop on its own. When practising the scoop with the chop you may use a bigger action to gather more power for the chop.

Turn around: *Lift and punt* is a low defensive action. The hands work in opposite directions, rotating in opposite directions. The right hand rotates and pulls as it lifts the spear, using a bracing out power. The left hand uses a carrying power. Transfer power from the body core to the arms. During the *retreat and chop* action, slide the left hand. Turn around, retreat, turn the waist, and reach the shoulder, to send power through to the fore-section of the spear.

Closing: During the retreat and snap action pull and snap the right hand quickly, pressing down at the last instant. Brace the right arm and keep the body solid. Slide the left hand then abruptly tighten the grip to stop the spear. The left arm also has a bracing power, so that it moves as one with the body. The hands must coordinate these two actions together, and with the retreating footwork.

BREATHING CYCLE FOR SPEAR CHOP

- Inhale during defensive actions.

- Exhale as you step forward and chop. Settle the *qi* to the *dantian*.

PRACTICAL APPLICATIONS FOR SPEAR CHOP

Each of the upward actions is an effective defense that also serves to place the spear tip in position for the downward chop. Chop should always be followed up with a stab – the spear has a straight sharp tip, so the stab is its most effective technique.

Checking hook and chop and *upward scoop* are defensive actions, knocking the opponent's weapon either aside or up. With a scoop you can knock the opponent's weapon up or knock his lead hand or arm. With a check and hook you can lead his weapon back as you knock it aside. If the opponent is chopping towards you, use a checking hook to take him off target then slide along his weapon's shaft to chop, sliding directly along to his lead hand or arm. If he retreats, then stab his chest.

With either technique, use the fore-section of your spear shaft to contact halfway along the opponent's long weapon as he stabs towards you. You then must chop instantly, moving smoothly into the chop, and then stab to his chest.

Chop can be used either as an attack or a defense. You can use the chop directly, knocking the opponent's weapon out of his hands to create an attacking opportunity. You can attack by chopping the opponent's arm or body. You can defend by chopping his weapon. The classics say, "use the clockwise trap for inside, use the counterclockwise trap for outside, use the lift for low attacks, and use the seize for high attacks. Only the chop can be used for either right or left." You can see that the chop is a very practical and strong technique.

- The footwork must be agile to use chop. Step to either side when defending so that the opponent has difficulty taking his aim. Stepping to the side also sets up your spear to cross his weapon. The spear must be at a certain angle to the opponent's weapon to be used to block or knock aside effectively. Step straight in to attack, sending the spear tip directly to the target.
- The head, chest, belly, hips, knees, and feet and the lead hand are the targets of the spear. They are the seven spots that the spear 'sees'. Attack quickly, fiercely, and accurately, and don't take any pity on the opponent.

THE POEM ABOUT SPEAR CHOP

劈枪歌诀

劈枪技法最平常，
劈开敌械扎胸膛。
左右挂挑枪上起，
劈手劈械把敌伤。

The most common technique of the spear is a chop.

Chop aside the opponent's weapon and stab to his chest.

Lift the spear to hook or scoop his weapon to the side,

Chop the opponent's hand or weapon to injure him.

2. SPEAR DRILL

INTRODUCTION TO SPEAR DRILL, *ZUAN QIANG*

The spear drill takes its name from the empty hand drilling punch of the five element fists. The drilling punch is a punch up and forward from below, so as long as you are doing this type of technique, then you are within the category of drilling. So what sort of technique should a spear drill be? Different sources answer this question differently. Some classics say that the spear drill is a low outer trap to left or right combined with a step forward and stab to the head. The Shang style Xingyi book says that the spear drill is a back step with an inverted hand stab to the top of the head. Some books say it is an outer trap, inner trap, and then high stab to the head. Others say that it is a block to left or right, then step forward to stab to the head. Each source has its own way of looking at the technique, and each has reason.

After many years of practice and thought on spear drill, and analysis of the five element techniques of the spear, I feel that spear drill combination should have a stab to the head – coming from below to attack high – but should also have an inverted hand low stab. The low stab uses a lift and punt to defend and then advances with an inverted hand stab to the knee or foot. "Lift and punt to control below " is an important traditional technique, and its inclusion here ensures it will be practised. If the opponent blocks the low attack, then you can cover and press down, and then stab his face. This keeps the traditional view of spear drill as a stab to the head, while also adding a low stab to the knee or foot into the spear's repertoire. Including both upper and lower stabs in the drill combination enriches spear drill practice.

The spear drill combinations include *Lift and punt, stab to the knee; Cover and press, stab to the face; Spear drill turn around;* and *Spear drill closing move.*

2a Right Stance Drill: Lift, Punt and Low Stab

yòubù zuānqiāng   右步钻枪

Start from *on guard*. Continue with *Advance, lift, punt; Step forward, stab to knee*.

ACTION 1: Advance the left foot a half-step and follow in the right foot to the left ankle without touching down. Lift the spear base to above the right of the head, rotating the right palm away from the thumb to turn the palm up, and bracing out with the arm bent. Let the shaft slide

3.19

CHAPTER THREE: SPEAR, *QIANG*   147

through the left hand to bring the hand forward and rotate the palm towards the thumb to turn the palm angled forward. Bend the left arm and hold the shaft tightly with the left hand at waist height, pushing the hand forward slightly. This makes the spear tip circle left, down, and right, finishing at knee height. Follow the movement of the spear tip with the eyes. (image 3.19)

ACTION 2: Step the right foot forward and follow in the left foot a half-step to take a sixty/forty stance. Hold the base tightly with the right hand and thrust it forward and down. Let the shaft slide through the left hand, keeping the left hand extended to aim. Push the right hand forward and down until it meets the left hand. The hands will be a bit higher than the shoulders and the spear tip will be at knee height. Send the power to the spear tip. Look at the spear tip. (image 3.20 and from the front)

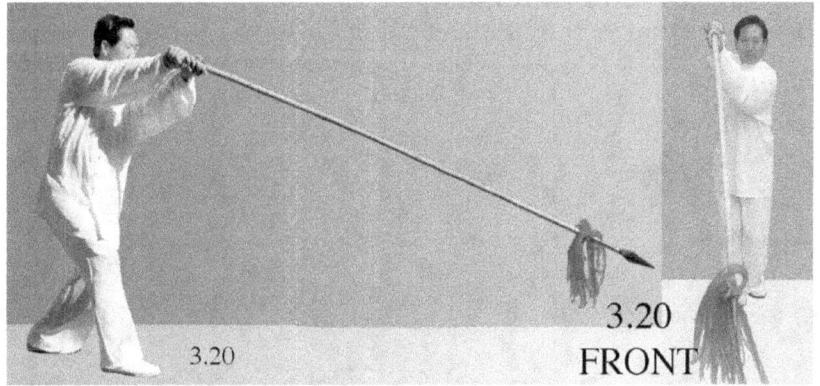

Pointers

- Coordinate the action of the hands to do the lifting scull as the left foot advances.
- Complete the stab as the right foot lands. To do the inverted grip low stab close the chest, open the upper back, and bring the shoulders in together.
- Although you learn the techniques as two actions, they should be done continuously as one move.

2b Left Stance Drill: Cover, Press and Stab   zuǒbù zuānqiāng   左步钻枪

Advance, cover and press; Step forward, stab up.

ACTION 1: Advance the right foot a half-step and follow in the left foot to by the right ankle without touching down. Bend the elbows and set down slightly. Pull the spear base back with the right hand, lowering the hand to the right waist. Rotate the right palm towards the thumb to turn the palm up. Slide the shaft through the left hand, rotating the left palm away from the thumb to turn the palm down. Bend the left elbow and press down with the thumb/forefinger web. The spear tip circles left, up, and then right with the shaft remaining level at

148 SPEAR DRILL

waist height. Look at the spear tip. (image 3.21)

ACTION 2: Step the left foot forward and follow in the right foot a half-step. Lift the left hand slightly to aim the spear to head height and release slightly to allow the spear to

slide through. Push the spear forcefully with the right hand, accelerating until the right hand arrives at the left hand. Open the left hand to support the right hand. The spear stabs to head height while the hands are at chest height. Send power out to the spear tip so that it quivers. Look past the tip. (image 3.22 and from the front)

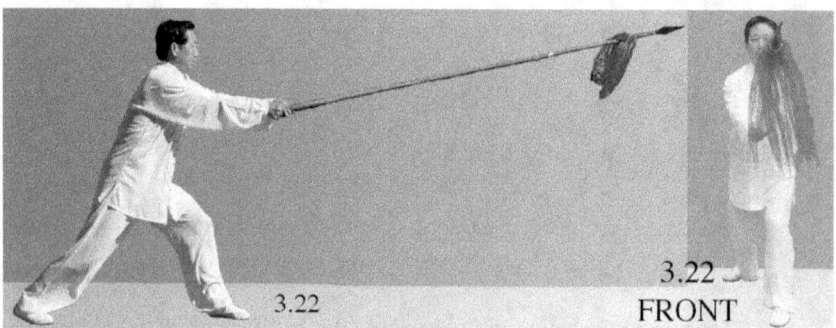

Pointers

- Complete the circle and press down with the hands as the right foot advances, coordinating everything together. Remember to open and close the body.
- Stab forward as the left foot steps. The whole movement should be completed as one action, without pause.

• Connect to *right stance drill*, and continue. The number of repetitions is limited only by the size of your training space.

2c Drill Turn Around   zuānqiāng zhuànshēn   钻枪转身

Using the <u>*left*</u> *stance upper drill* as example. *Hook-in lift, scull; Turn around, retreat and chop.*

ACTION 1: Hook-in the left foot on the spot and shift to the left leg, standing up. Rotate the right hand and pull the spear while lifting and rotating. Lift the base above the head. Slide the spear through the left hand to bring the left hand forward on the shaft. The spear tip is forward, pointing down at knee height. Look at the spear tip. (image 3.23)

ACTION 2: Turn around 180 degrees to the right to face back in the way from which you came. Retreat the right foot and shift back mostly onto the right leg. Pull the spear base forward and down to the right side with the right hand. Bring the left hand up and forward, then chop down with the shaft, so that the spear tip has drawn a circle up, then forward and down. The spear finishes horizontal at waist height. Send the power to the fore-section of the spear shaft. Press the head up and look past the spear tip. (image 3.24)

Pointers

- Lift the spear as the left foot hooks in, chop the spear as the right foot retreats. Complete both moves without hesitation.

2d Drill Closing Move   zuānqiāng shōushì   钻枪收势

- The *closing move* is the same as described above in *chop closing move*.

POWER GENERATION FOR SPEAR DRILL

Lift: The hands must alternate between *yin* and *yang*. That is, as the right palm rotates away from the thumb, the left palm rotates towards the thumb, working together and gaining power from the body. Transfer the power of the body to both shoulders, both arms, and through them to the fore-section of the spear shaft. The right hand combines pulling, bracing, and rotating while the left hand combines bracing and presenting. The power of the body, together with the flexibility of the shaft, makes the spear tip quiver.

Step forward low stab: The right hand starts out above the head and stabs down with an inverted grip, so this naturally is not as strong as a straight thrust. To put as much power as possible to the inverted grip, raise the elbow, close the shoulders together, send the arms forward, and reach forward slightly with the torso, opening the upper back and closing the chest, while tucking in the lower back. Stab down quickly and pull the spear back quickly.

Advance cover and press: This technique emphasizes body technique. Shift the body back slightly as the right hand pulls the spear base back. Shift the body forward as the hands rotate to trap, closing the shoulders and chest and pressing the head up. Put all of the body's power to the spear's fore-section as the right hand sets the base at the waist and the left hand presses down the shaft. Skilled spear technique can only be achieved when the spear becomes one with the body.

Stab up: The key to the high stab is the left hand – it is used like the sight of a rifle to determine the direction and placement of the tip. The left hand must control the spear shaft, not allowing any swaying at all. The right hand puts the force into the stab, the left hand aims the spear. When the spear stabs, turn the waist, release the shoulders forward, and extend the arms.

Turn around: The turning move is expansive and in a high stance. Then settle down into the retreat and chop, collecting the body together. Press the head up. Breathe out to give more power. Be sure to set the base of the spear firmly to gain power for the chop. Remember to bring the shaft past the halfway point before accelerating the power, and to have a focal point.

PRACTICAL APPLICATIONS FOR SPEAR DRILL

Lift and punt is a defensive move, what is called 'lift and punt to remove something underneath '. If an opponent comes at you with a low stab, just as he is fully extended but not quite in contact, that is, just before his right hand reaches his left hand, lift your right hand above your head and snap your spear head down in a semi-circle. Your spear shaft will hit his and knock it off target.

Inverted grip low stab is a stab to the lead leg, knee or foot. This is not a strong stab since it uses an inverted grip, so it must be fast. Whether or not you hit your target, you must also pull it back quickly because your inverted grip is relatively easily knocked out of your hands should the opponent have time to knock your spear.

Advance press down contains a stir, a knock away, a trap and a press down, all of which protect the central or lower areas of your body. If your opponent stabs at you from out of reach you can knock his spear with your tip and then slide along his spear with a stirring action to trap and press down. Snap the spear at the end to knock his spear down. Then stab to his face.

> Always wait for the crucial moment before defending. The crucial moment is just as the opponent has committed to the attack but not yet reached the target. You must react neither early nor late. If you react too early the opponent can easily change his technique. If you react too late you will get hit. This is a question of training the timing and recognition of the crucial moment. The crucial moment is something that many masters know but don 't teach. As they say, 'rather teach ten

techniques than the skill of timing.' Mastery of a technique is really a question of knowing the timing and how to gain the crucial moment.

You need instruction and practice with sliding spears together. General Qi Jiguang described this in his book: "Face each other with two spears, one chops and the other presses, trapping with a large or small circle. Lining up the spears counts as one repetition. After 10,000 repetitions without losing contact, each lining up perfectly, then skill is perfected." This precious theory should be pondered until understanding comes, be repeated until the technique comes, and be practised until the application comes.

THE POEM ABOUT SPEAR DRILL

钻枪歌诀

钻枪习练过万遍，
提撸防下阴阳转。
上步反手扎膝脚，
绞拨盖压扎其面。

The spear drill must be practised more than ten thousand times.
Lift and punt to protect below, alternating *yin* and *yang*.
Step forward and invert the grip to stab the opponent's knee or foot,
Stir, knock, cover and press to stab his face.

3. SPEAR THRUST

INTRODUCTION TO SPEAR THRUST, *BENG QIANG*

What is traditionally called '*bengqiang*' in Xingyi is the spear technique of outer trap, inner trap, and stab. The final stab is similar to the '*beng*' driving punch of the five elements – a half step advance with a straight attack.[9]

Traditionally the spear thrust is done with a half step advance and following step. I have added a cover step, a back step, and a circling step to make the footwork more agile, train the connection between the spear and body more effectively, and make the spear technique more applicable.

---

[9] Author's note: In most styles, '*beng qiang*' is defined as an upwards or sideways snap of the fore-section, with the power shaking the tip. Only in Xingyi is the thrust called a '*beng*'. So when in Xingyi you perform a normal, snapping '*bengqiang*', it is called a '*bibeng qiang*', or, 'the other *beng*' to differentiate the two.

152   SPEAR THRUST

Spear thrust includes *stationary thrust, back-cross step thrust, cross-over step thrust, roundabout step thrust, turn around thrust,* and *closing move.*

3a   Stationary Thrust   yuánbù bēngqiāng   原步崩枪

Start from *on guard* (image 3.25). *Stationary outer trap; Stationary inner trap; Stationary stab.*

3.25

ACTION 1: Without moving the feet, rotate the left palm towards the thumb to circle the palm up while rotating the right palm away from the thumb at the side. Work the hands together so that the spear tip circles up, left, and down in a counter clockwise half-circle about thirty centimetres in diameter. Look past the spear tip. (image 3.26)

3.26

ACTION 2: Close the left arm a bit forwards and rotate to press down with the thumb/ forefinger web. Rotate the right palm towards the thumb. Work the hands together so that the spear tip circles clockwise down, left, and up, and then right and down. Send power out to the spear tip. Look past the spear tip. (image 3.27)

3.27

ACTION 3: Shift forward, pushing into the right leg and bending the left leg to shift about sixty percent of the weight forward on the left leg. Allow the shaft to slide through the left hand, using it to aim forward. Send the spear out forcefully with the right hand, accelerating into the stab. Cup the right hand in the left hand. Send power to the tip of the spear so that it quivers. Almost fully straighten the arms, and hold the spear horizontal at chest height. Look past the spear tip. (image 3.28)

Pointers

- The hands must rotate at the same time to turn the spear. The spear must be held tight to the body while trapping inward and outward. The spear tip must draw two half circles.
- When stabbing, the spear must go in a straight line and the power must go out to the tip. It must be sent out like an arrow, and be brought back in a straight line.

3b Back-cross Step Thrust   bēibù bēngqiāng   背步崩枪

Back-cross step outer trap; Step forward inner trap; Stab.

ACTION 1: After stabbing, pull the spear back in a straight line to the right side of the body with the right hand, letting the spear slide through the left hand. Without moving the left foot, step the right foot forward behind the left foot and shift into a cross step. Rotate the hands to circle the spear up, left and then down to complete an outer trap. Look forward. (image 3.29)

154 SPEAR THRUST

ACTION 2: Step the left foot forward and shift mostly onto the right leg. Rotate both hands to circle the spear tip down, left, up, and then right and down to complete an inner trap. (image 3.30)

ACTION 3: Without moving the feet, shift forward, straightening the right leg and bending the left leg with most weight on the left leg.[10] Stab forward forcefully with the spear, sliding it through the left hand. Finish with the spear tip at chest height and the shaft level. Send power to the spear tip so that it quivers. Support the right hand in the left hand. Keep the arms slightly bent. Look past the spear tip. (image 3.31)

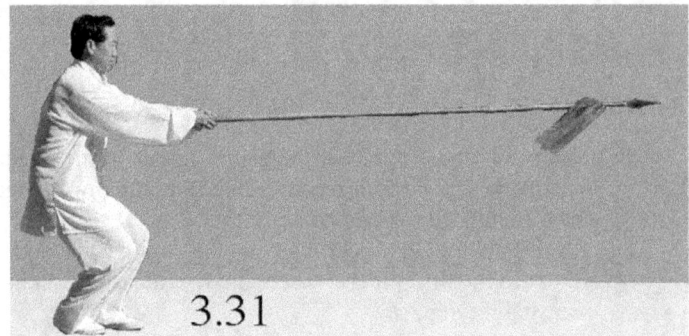

Pointers

- Complete the outer trap while the right foot steps through behind the left leg.
- Complete the inner trap while the left foot is stepping forward.
- Be sure to transfer your power through to the spear tip so that it quivers.

3c Cross-over Step Thrust   gàibù bēngqiāng   盖步崩枪

Right cross-over step, outer trap; Left step forward, inner trap; Stab.

ACTION 1: Without moving the left foot, step the right foot forward in front of the left foot, turning the foot out to land with a hooked out foot. Shift weight forward between the feet to take a cross step with the legs slightly bent. Rotate

---

[10] Translator's note: The stab may be done shifting into a forward stance or bringing the right foot forward to a closed stance. Either way is correct. I have translated the text as is throughout, even when the author has done the alternate stance in the photo.

the left palm towards the thumb to turn the palm up. Rotate the right hand at the waist, palm away from thumb. Rotate both hands simultaneously to cause the spear tip to draw a counter clockwise half-circle up, left, and down. Keep the spear shaft tight to the belly. Look past the spear tip. (image 3.32)

ACTION 2: Step the left foot forward without moving the right foot, keeping most weight on the right leg. Rotate and press down on the shaft with the thumb/forefinger web of the left hand. Rotate the right palm towards the thumb, so that both hands work together to draw a clockwise circle down, left, up, right and down with the spear tip. Keep the spear shaft tight to the belly. Send the power to the spear tip. Press the head up and look past the spear tip. (image 3.33)

ACTION 3: Without moving the feet, shift the weight forward by pushing the right leg straight and bending the left leg to take a sixty/forty stance weighted to the left leg. Push the spear straight forward forcefully with the right hand, letting it slide through the left hand. Stab to chest height with tthe spear shaft level. Open the left hand to support the right hand. Keep the arms almost straight. Send power to the spear tip so that it quivers. Look past the spear tip. (image 3.34)

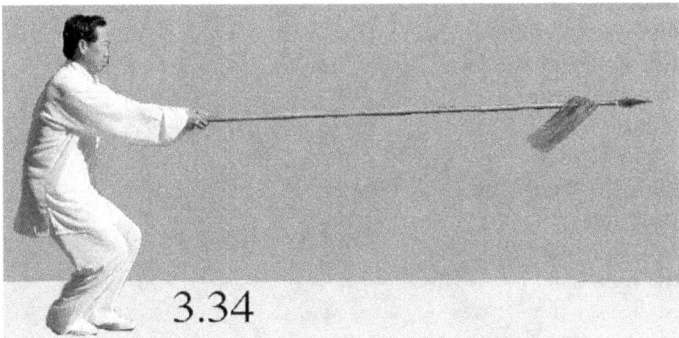

156 SPEAR THRUST

Pointers

- ○ Complete the outer trap as the right foot does the cross-over step.
- ○ Complete the inner trap as the left foot steps forward.

3d Roundabout Step Thrust   ràobù bēngqiāng   绕步崩枪

Left roundabout step, outer trap; Right step forward inner trap; Stab.

ACTION 1: Pull the spear base back to the right side with the right hand, letting the shaft slide through the left hand. This forms a ready stance. Advance the left foot with a circular step, landing to the forward right with the foot hooked out. Rotate the left hand palm towards the thumb to complete an outer trap with the spear tip. Rotate the right palm away from the thumb, keeping the spear shaft tight to the waist. The spear tip draws a counter clockwise half-circle up, left and down. Look past the spear tip. (image 3.35)

ACTION 2: Step the right foot forward without moving the left foot, shifting most weight to the left leg. Rotate both hands to complete a clockwise inner trap with the spear. (image 3.36)

ACTION 3: Shift forward towards the right leg, extending the left leg almost straight and bending the right leg to take a right bow stance.

Slide the spear through the left hand, releasing just enough to let it slide while aiming. Holding the spear base in the right hand, push forward forcefully, finishing with the right arm almost straight. Slide the left hand back until it snugs onto the right hand. Stab the spear straight

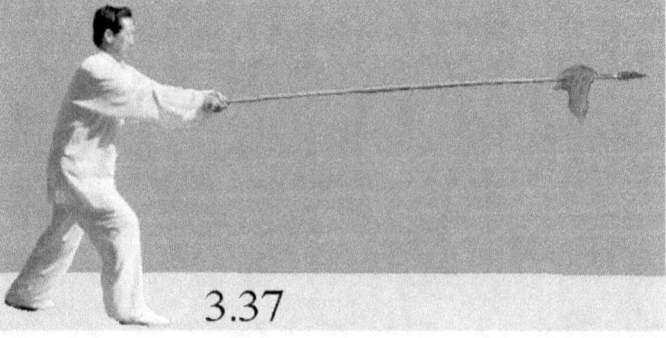

forward at chest height with the shaft level. Press the head up and send the power to the spear tip. Look forward. (image 3.37)

Pointers

- o Use a circular pathway to complete the roundabout step. Use both hands to complete the outer trap.
- o Complete the inner trap as the right foot steps forward. Complete the stab as the body shifts forward.
- o Do three clear movements – outer trap, inner trap, and stab – but complete them without hesitation.

• Do another stationary thrust by bringing the left foot forward while pulling the spear base back to the waist to take a ready stance. Then continue on.

3e Thrust Turn Around bēngqiāng zhuànshēn 崩枪转身

When you run out of space, if the <u>left</u> foot is forward, hook-in in front of the right foot. If the <u>right</u> foot is forward, then step the left foot through to hook-in in front of the right foot. *Hook-in step, lift and punt; Turn around, heel kick; Rotate, spear chop.*

ACTION 1: Hook-in the left foot and stand up. Lift the spear base with the right hand as you rotate the palm away from the thumb. As the right hand arrives above the head, the palm should face out. Slide the spear in the left hand to bring the hand closer to the right hand. As the right hand arrives above the head, rotate the left palm towards the thumb and bend the arm. This makes the spear shaft snap towards the left side. The tip should be slanted downward to knee height. Look at the spear tip. (image 3.38)

ACTION 2: Turn around to the 180 degrees to the right, shifting to the left leg and bending it. You are now facing back in the way from which you came. Bend the right knee and lift it with the foot turned out, then kick with the heel at least to waist height, keeping the foot turned. Do not move the hands or the spear. Look ahead of the kicking foot. (image 3.39)

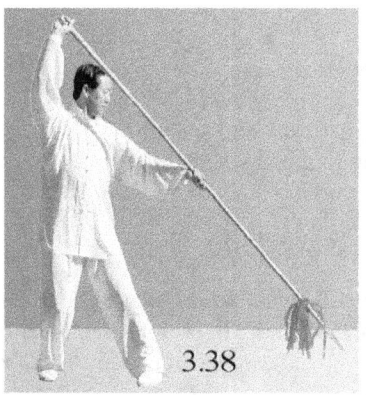

158 SPEAR THRUST

ACTION 3: Quickly land the right foot forward and down with the foot still turned out. Rotate the body rightward and land with the legs crossed, dropping down and bending the legs in a scissors stance. Bring the spear base forward, down, and then pull back with the right hand to the side of the waist. Bring the left hand down and back then slide it up the spear shaft, and then chop forward and down from above. Tighten the left hand as it arrives, pressing down with the thumb/forefinger web, palm down. The spear is level, just below the waist. Send power to the fore-section of the spear. Press the head up and look forward. (images 3.40 transitional and 3.40)

3.40 transitional   3.40

- Continue on, stepping the left foot forward to move into *outer trap, inner trap, and stab*.

Pointers

- *Turn around* is one move and should be completed without hesitation. Hook- in well to get the body turned around. Turn around quickly and kick as high as you can. Land firmly. Coordinate the action of the hands and spear with that of the feet and body.
- *Lift and punt* uses a rotation of the hands. To chop, first slide the left hand and then tighten it to put force into the chop. Be sure to lower the body to chop.

3f Thrust Closing Move   bēngqiāng shōushì   崩枪收势

Closing move is always the same. See the description in *spear chop*. First complete a stab, then retreat the right foot a half-step and withdraw the left foot slightly, shifting back. Pull the spear back and snap it up. The tip should quiver up and down. This will place you in a ready stance. From there, continue on to finish as usual.

POWER GENERATION FOR SPEAR THRUST

Thrust is the most characteristic and fundamental technique of the spear, as it combines outer trap, inner trap, and stab. It is done with various footwork patterns – stationary, back-cross step, cross-over step, and roundabout step. The primary technique is the stab, but first you must circle. This structure of the spear determines this defensive circling. The spear must first control and cross an oncoming weapon before it can stab. Thus, inner trap and outer trap are the most fundamental of spear techniques, and the most important skills. This fundamental combination is traditionally called 'circle spear' or 'circle spear mother technique'.

There are four main principles to the outer trap, inner trap.

- First, outer trap and inner trap draw two half circles to left and right, completing a full circle. The aft-section of the spear shaft must be held tight to the belly, it must not leave the body.

- Second, the hands must alternate *yin* and *yang*, rotating together in opposite directions. As the left hand turns out the right hand turns in, when the left hand closes in the right hand turns out. This is called 'twist the spear, twist the pole'.

- Third, the radius of the circle should be thirty cm. When learning, the spear tip may move in a large circle, but not over head height or under hip height.

- Fourth, the power of the circles comes from the body, transferring directly from the body to the spear. The spear is flexible, so the tip circles from the power transfer. Hold the spear with the left hand neither too loosely nor too tightly. If the left hand is too tight the technique is stiff, and if it is too loose the technique is flaccid. Keep the wrist supple and the grip just right, firm but supple. The right hand should hold firmly with a supple wrist.

To do the outer trap, turn the left hand out, draw back and open the left shoulder, settling it down. The belly should have a very slight power pressing forward, turning rightward. To do the inner trap the left hand rotates in and presses forward and down with the thumb/forefinger web, closing the left shoulder and turning the body slightly rightward. In this way the power of the body core transfers to the spear shaft, giving it more power than just the arms. The spear flexes as the body's power reaches it, completing the circle.

> To stab, the spear should shoot out like an arrow and come back like pulling in a line. The spear absolutely must go in and out in a straight line. The power must reach the tip, making it quiver.
>
> The left hand controls the direction and height of the spear tip, sending it accurately to its target. Stab quickly and bring the spear back quickly. When stabbing, release the left hand's grip enough to slide the spear through, using the left hand to aim.
>
> The right hand sends the spear forward, accelerating gradually, releasing power sharply. As the right hand arrives near the left hand, apply one inch power to complete the stab. Turn the hips and waist, close the shoulders, extend the arms and send the

hands out to transfer power to the spear tip.

The spear shaft and arms form one straight line. The spear must stab accurately with a focal point. The tip must not wobble.

The bodywork and waist action must be coordinated with the footwork. The footwork must be agile. The bodywork should work together with the footwork to combine with the spear.

Turn around is made up of three actions: *hook-in step and lift, turn heel kick,* and *rotate chop*. When the right hand lifts and pulls the spear, the spear tip should draw a circle left and down while being pulled back. The right hand must rotate and put a bracing power into the spear while the left hand stabilizes the spear with a carrying power. The turn and kick is the same as the thrusting punch turn and kick, and uses the same trampling power on landing. When rotating and chopping, rotate the waist, settle in the belly, reach the left shoulder forward, tuck in the left elbow, and put the body's power into the chop. Press up into the head while sitting down.

PRACTICAL APPLICATIONS FOR SPEAR THRUST

The essence of spear techniques, and the most representative, is the outer trap, inner trap and stab combination, normally called 'middle level spear,' which in Xingyi is called *spear thrust*.

Outer trap and inner trap are used to defend against a straight attack from another long weapon. If a long weapon is coming towards your left side – your 'outside' – use the outer trap. If a long weapon is coming towards your right side – your 'inside' – use the inner trap.

Because of the spear's shape, the stab is the most important of all spear techniques, and all other techniques are based on setting up for this technique. The spear stabs out quickly in a straight line with its sharp tip. If it reaches its target it can inflict serious damage or death. Its main targets are high, middle, and low – the head, chest, and abdomen. Other effective targets are the opponent's leading hand or arm. The opponent's leading hand and arm are close, so easily reached; you just need to extend your arm to get them with the spear. So if you are good with a spear you should go for your opponent's lead hand first. Once the opponent's lead hand is injured he will lose his grip and drop his weapon, and then you can attack at will.

> Using different footwork – back-cross step, cross-over step, roundabout step, advance, retreat, and shifting to right and left – has two purposes. One is to keep moving so that the opponent cannot fix on you. The other is to use footwork to get your spear shaft to cross your opponent's weapon. Your spear can be used for defense much more effectively once it crosses your opponent's weapon. You attack to the centre,

getting inside, and defend by crossing, to take your opponent offline.

The spear's 'middle stab' is the spear's strongest attack and the hardest to defend against. There are many descriptions of this in the classics. "The spear is the king of the centre." "The spear stabs out in a straight line." "The spear goes out like an arrow and comes back like (pulling) a rope." These are all attempts to describe the directness, speed, and ferocity of the spear stab. You must take care to keep your spear aligned straight with your opponent's weapon when stabbing, as his position is very hard to defend. There is another way to use the stab, and that is as a direct counter attack. As the opponent stabs towards you, stab back without any defensive action, just sitting back to get your body out of the way. Once the opponent fully extends the spear without hitting the target, he will pull it back. You then follow his spear back to stab. This is called 'eating a spear and returning a spear', also known as 'don't defend or block, just use one strike.' And, once your opponent goes on the defensive, you can follow up with continuous multiple stabs – high, middle and low – without giving any breathing space. This is called 'responding to an attack with ten.'

For the spear you need to remember: 'cross weapons to defend, straight line to attack.'

As well as practising the outer trap, inner trap, and stab combination, you should be able to stab directly from the outer trap or just the inner trap. You should always, however, start the outer trap action when doing the drawing back action after a stab. And you should always start to stab forward as you do an inner trap. These actions set up the habits that will enable you to take advantage of situations with the spear. This is what the classics mean by "going out is a circle, coming back is also a circle, there is a straight line within the circle, and there is a circle within the straight line, the original spirit of the spear is in the circle". Circling the spear is its defensive technique, and is the means to the end, which is to attack. The best attacking technique of the spear is the stab.

You must practise the basics diligently if you hope to ever be able to use the spear in a fighting situation. Just training the techniques and forms is not enough, you must do partner 'shaft sliding' training. You need to master the techniques on your own. Partner training is to gain feeling and the ability to slide and stab, finding the distancing, timing, and ability to attack. It is hard to find a partner who understands the 'shaft sliding' practise, they are 'as scarce as phoenix feathers and unicorn horns'. Most people now just practise forms.

THE POEM ABOUT SPEAR THRUST

崩枪歌诀

崩枪技法强中强，
拦拿圆中找其枪。
背盖绕步随身走，
中平一点是枪王。

Spear thrust's strength lies in attacking the midline.

Use the circles of the outer trap and inner trap to control the opponent's weapon.

The footwork follows the body work – back-cross step, crossover step, and roundabout step.

One touch with the middle level stab shows why the spear is the king of weapons.

4. SPEAR SLASH

INTRODUCTION TO SPEAR SLASH, *PAO QIANG*

The spear slash uses the footwork and the same directional power of the empty hand pounding fist. With both hands on the spear, it strikes diagonally forward with an action that combines blocking, slicing, dragging, and scooping. There is also a traditional technique that blocks with the base, switching the hand grip and applying power similar to the pounding fist, stepping in a diagonal pattern. This technique is good because it uses the base and puts the circular movement of the spear to good use. The first method is more practical since it sets the tip up for a stab. The two methods show the technique and flavour of the pounding technique. You should practise both to develop your abilities more fully.

The first slash method includes *right back-cross step inner coil; left advance outer coil; step forward block up and push with a sculling slice up; retreat pound with the base; hook with the base; wheel and trap,* and *step in and stab.* The second slash method includes *right stance slash, left stance slash,* a continuation to *right stance slash,* and *slash turn around.*

METHOD ONE: COIL, SLASH, POUND, TRAP, STAB

4a Right Back-cross Step, Inner Coil

yòu bēibù lǐchán qiāng　　右背步里缠枪

Start from *on guard. Back-cross step inner coil; Left advance outer coil; Step forward, high block and push with a sculling slice up; Retreat, pound with the base; Hook with the base, sheel and inner trap; Step in and stab.*

CHAPTER THREE: SPEAR, *QIANG* 163

ACTION 1: Shift forward without stepping the left foot, stepping the right foot behind the left to advance in a back-cross step. The legs are crossed with the weight between them. The right hand always grips the spear base. Slide the left hand forward along the spear shaft and lower the tip, keeping the shaft tight to the body, to circle the tip down to the left. Turn the waist slightly left. Look at the spear tip. (image 3.41)

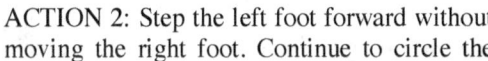

ACTION 2: Step the left foot forward without moving the right foot. Continue to circle the spear with the left hand, moving the tip up and right. Finish with the left thumb/forefinger web down, pressing the spear tip at waist height. The right hand, on the spear base, draws opposite circles to the left hand, keeping the shaft on the body. Look at the spear tip. (image 3.42)

3.41

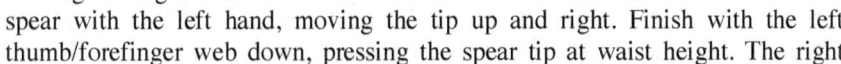

3.42

Pointers

o   Complete the right back-cross step as the spear tip circles down to the left. Complete the left step forward as the spear tip circles in. The spear should not stop between circles, so the stepping needs to be quick.
o   The left hand controls the height of the spear tip, which should not go above the shoulders or below the hips. Transfer power from the waist to the spear, keeping the power gentle and connected.

4b   Left Advance, Outer Coil

zuǒ jìnbù wàichán qiāng   左进步外缠枪

ACTION: Advance the left foot a half-step and follow in the right foot to beside the left ankle, bending the left leg slightly to stand firmly. Control the spear tip with the left hand to draw it up, left, and then down with an outward coiling action. Keep the right hand at the right waist, then move in the opposite direction as the left hand and keep the shaft tight to the body. Draw a circle with the spear tip, no higher than the shoulders and no lower than the knees. Look at the spear tip. (image 3.43)

3.43

164   SPEAR SLASH

Pointers

- Step the left foot forward as the spear tip draws a circle up to the left.
- Slide the left hand forward along the shaft. Press the right hand firmly to keep the shaft tight to the body.
- *Right back-cross inner coil* connects immediately to *left advance outer coil*. The spear tip should draw two circles in two opposite directions in front of the body.

4c   Step Forward, High Block and Push with a Sculling Slice Up

shàngbù jiàtuī huōliāo   上步架推擓撩

ACTION: Take a long step to the forward right with the right foot and follow in a half-step with the left foot, to take a sixty/forty stance with the weight back. Bring the right hand from the waist to brace out above the head with the arm almost straight, rotating the palm to face out. Rotate the left palm towards the thumb slightly and bring the spear tip from the lower left to the upper right to slice up with the palm facing obliquely to the right front. Bend the left arm and push diagonally forward and right, finishing at chest height. The spear tip is pointing to the forward right at waist height with the power in the fore-section. Look past the spear tip. (images 3.44 and 3.44 from the front)

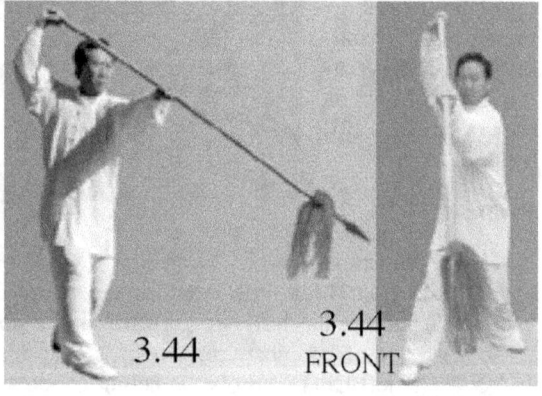
3.44   3.44 FRONT

Pointers

- Step the right foot a long step forward, landing when the left hand slices up and the right hand blocks up. High and low, left and right actions must all coordinate together.
- This move is connected directly to *left advance outer coil*, without a pause.

4d   Retreat, Pound with the Base   tuìbù zábà   退步砸把

ACTION: Retreat the left foot a half-step and shift back, withdrawing the right foot a half-step to sit mostly onto the left leg. Slide the left hand up the spear shaft and tighten it at the one third mark. Pull the left hand to the left waist with the palm turned out. Slide the right hand to about fifty centimetres from the spear base and press down with the thumb/forefinger web so that the spear base covers and presses forward and down. Pound the spear base down at waist height. Turn the body left and tuck in the right shoulder. Press the head up. Look past the spear base. (image 3.45)

CHAPTER THREE: SPEAR, *QIANG*

3.45

Pointers

- Retreat and withdraw the feet quickly. First slide the left hand along the spear. Then slide the right hand and pound down with the base. The covering pound must be done forcefully.
- The hand slide must be coordinated, and the movement quick. The length of shaft extended to pound should be the length of your own arm.

4e Hook with the Base, Wheel and Inner Trap

guàbà fānshēn náqiāng   挂把翻身拿枪

ACTION 1: Hold the shaft with the right hand and bend the arm to hook the base up and back. As the base arrives above the head, slide the right hand back to the base. Push forward with the left hand. Shift back to the left leg. Look forward. (image 3.46)

3.46

ACTION 2: Wheel the body 180 degrees to the right, landing with the right foot hooked out, then stepping the left foot forward. Most weight is on the right leg. Pull the spear base back to the right waist with the right hand, drawing a small circle. Slide the left hand back along the shaft to a placement conducive to the trapping action. Circle the spear tip left, up, and then right, finishing at waist height. Look past the spear tip. (image 3.47, left foot not yet landed)

3.47

166 SPEAR SLASH

Pointers

- The right hand first completes the backward hook. It slides back to the base after it gets to shoulder height. When the right hand is at the base it should always be completely at the end. If it does not make it fully back during the wheeling action, it must be placed at the end by the time you do the trapping action.
- You may jump when you do the body wheel. The inner trap should be done quickly with a forceful snap.

4f Step in and Stab   gēnbù zhāqiāng   跟步扎枪

ACTION: Do a follow-in step with the right foot to bring it up behind the left foot, keeping the weight back on the right foot similar to the stepping pattern of the driving punch footwork. Loosen the left hand to allow the spear to slide through it, and use it to aim. Push forcefully forward with the right hand until it meets the left hand and stops with the left hand supporting it. The spear must remain level with the tip at chest height. The arms are straight, the head up. Look past the spear tip. (image 3.48)

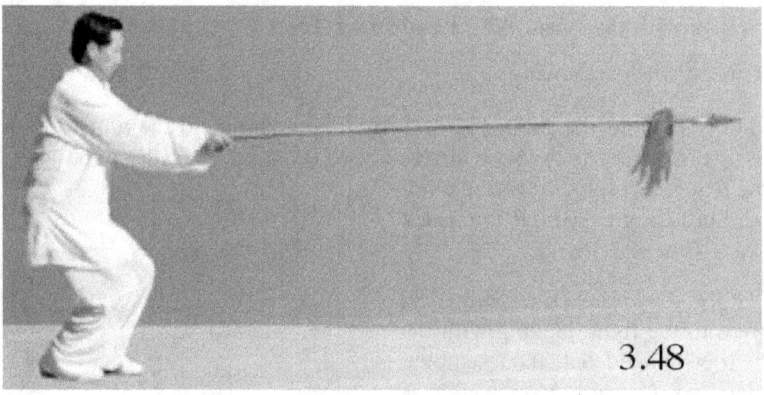

Pointers

- Send the spear out as the right foot lands. Send power to the tip so that it quivers.
- Connect *hook and wheel* immediately to *step in and stab*.

4g Right Back-cross Step Inner Coil

yòu bēibù lǐchán qiāng   右背步里缠枪

ACTION 1: Advance the left foot a half-step without moving the right foot, keeping most weight on the right leg in the same stance as *on guard*. Release the left hand enough to slide the spear shaft through, and pull the spear back with the right hand to the right side. Keep the spear shaft snug to the body. Look past the spear tip. (image 3.49)

CHAPTER THREE: SPEAR, *QIANG* 167

ACTION 2: Shift forward and step the right foot behind the left foot, shifting onto the left leg without moving the left foot, to take a back-cross stance with the legs bent. Slide the left hand forward along the shaft a bit without moving the right hand.

Use the waist and left hand to circle the spear tip down and to the left. Look at the spear tip. (image 3.50)

ACTION 3: Step the left foot forward without moving the right foot. Continue to circle the spear up and right until the left thumb/forefinger web presses down, holding the spear at waist height. Circle the right hand in a small circle in opposite direction to the left hand, keeping the spear shaft tight to the

body. Look past the spear tip. (image 3.51)

Pointers

- Actions '4a' through '4f' are the full combination, then action '4g' starts a repetition of the combination. The combination should be done without a break in movement. The spear technique must be clear and completed. Never allow any technique to become messy just because you are trying to make the movement continuous.

METHOD TWO: RIGHT AND LEFT SLASH

4h Right Stance Slash   yòubù pàoqiāng   右步炮枪

Start from *on guard*. Continue with *Left advance, outer coil; Right step forward, scull and slice up*.

168 SPEAR SLASH

ACTION 1: Advance the left foot a half-step and follow-in with the right foot to beside the left ankle. Pull the spear base back with the right hand and slide the left hand forward along the shaft. Lift the left hand, bringing it to the rear left, circling the spear tip up, left, and then back. Follow this action with the right hand, pushing forward. Look at the spear tip. (image 3.52)

3.52

ACTION 2: Take a long step diagonally forward with the right foot and follow in the left foot a half-step. Lift the right hand up from the waist to above and to the right of the head, rotated palm up and with the arm rounded to brace. Push the left hand forcefully to the forward right as the right foot lands, palm facing in that direction. The spear tip circles from below, diagonally forward, the spear tip finishing at waist height. Send power to the fore-section so that it quivers. The left arm is almost straight, the left hand at chest height. Look past the spear tip. (image 3.53)

3.53

Pointers

- Coil the spear as the left foot advances. Make a large circle with the spear.
- As the right foot steps forward, lift the base with the right hand and slide the left hand on the shaft to scull and slice. The spear must arrive as the foot arrives.

4i Left Stance Slash

zuǒbù pàoqiāng   左步炮枪

Right advance, slice and changeover the hands; Left step forward, sculling slice.

ACTION 1: Advance the right foot a half-step and follow in the left foot to beside the right ankle. Swing the left hand to the left to circle the spear tip from the forward left up and back to the right. When the spear tip is up and the spear base is above the head, switch the position of the hands

3.54

on the shaft. Lower the left hand, sliding it along the shaft to the base. Slide the right hand along the shaft to the midsection. Pull the spear back to the rear right with the right hand. Watch the spear as it moves. (image 3.54)

ACTION 2: Take a long step to the forward left with the left foot and follow in the right foot a half-step, keeping most weight on the right leg. Lift the left hand, holding the spear base, to above and to the side of the head, rotating it palm out. With the right palm facing the left front, push it forcefully to the forward left. The spear tip finishes at waist height. Almost fully extend the right arm, the hand at chest height, and send power to the fore-section of the spear. Press the head up. Look past the spear tip. (image 3.55)

Pointers

- Circle the spear up as the right foot advances. Switch positions quickly and smoothly, in a well coordinated way. The hands should switch over as the spear is lifted, when it is above the head. Keep the palms facing each other as they change over.
- Lift the spear base with the left hand and slide the right hand to push the shaft as the left foot steps forward. The spear must arrive as the foot lands.

4j Right Stance Slash   yòubù pàoqiāng   右步炮枪

Left advance, slice and changeover the hands; Right step forward, sculling slice.

ACTION 1: Advance the left foot a half-step and follow in the right foot to beside the left ankle. Swing the right hand to the right to circle the spear tip to the forward right. Lower the left hand to the left waist. Push the spear base forward with the left hand and slice up with the right hand to circle the spear tip up. When the spear tip is above the head, switch the position of the hands on the shaft. Lower the right hand, sliding it along the shaft to the base. As the spear circles down, slide the left hand along the shaft to the midsection. Watch the spear as it moves, and watch the hands as they switch over. (image 3.56)

170   SPEAR SLASH

ACTION 2: Take a long step to the forward right with the right foot and follow in the left foot a half-step. Lift the right hand, holding the spear base, to block above and to the side of the head, rotating it palm out with the arm bent. With the left palm facing the right front, push it forcefully to the forward right, palm forward and arm bent. The spear tip completes a scull and slice, finishing at waist height. Send power to the fore- section of the spear. Look past the spear tip. (image 3.57)

Pointers

- Advance the half-step and switchover the hands in front of the head at the same time. Make the switch quickly.
- When alternating left and right slash, first swing the spear into position, then push to the direction, whether right or left. Complete the slice up as the lead foot lands.

• Continue on with left and right slash, as space permits.

4k   Slash Turn Around   pàoqiāng zhuànshēn   炮枪转身

From the _right_ stance slash. Right hook-in step, slice, change over the hands; Left step forward, sculling slice. If the _left_ foot is forward, do the same thing, just reversing right and left.

ACTION 1: Hook-in the right foot to the outside of the left foot and shift onto the right leg to turn around 270 degrees to the left. Lift the left foot to the right ankle, bending both legs and keeping them together. You have now turned around to face back. Bring the spear around as you turn, circling the tip left and up. Switch hands when the spear tip is up and the base is in front. Slide the left hand along the shaft back to the base and slide the right hand up to the middle. Continue to circle the spear tip to the right and down, bringing it down at the right side of the body. Watch the movement of the spear, and watch the hands as they switch over. (image 3.58)

ACTION 2: Take a long step forward with the left foot and follow in a half-step with the right foot. Gripping the spear base with the left hand, rotate it palm away from thumb and lift it above the head. Rotate the right palm towards the thumb so that the palm faces diagonally to the forward left and push it forcefully forward. Send power to the fore-section of the spear shaft, causing it to quiver. The spear tip finishes at waist height. Look past the tip. (image 3.59)

3.59

Pointers

- Turn around quickly. To do this, hook-in the foot considerably. Be sure to bring the spear around with the body, then slice up and switch hands after the turn.
- The action is the same as a normal slash, with the same points to remember.

41 Slash Closing Move   pàoqiāng shōushì   炮枪收势

On arriving back at the starting point, do a *turn around* to face the original direction. If you are doing the first method, go until you are have the right foot forward in the stabbing posture, then close the same as from spear chop. If you are doing the second method, turn and go until you are in *right stance slash*. Then do *left step forward inner trap, right follow step stab*. The rest of the closing move is the same as usual: *Right follow in step, stab; Right retreat, snap the spear; Close the feet and put the spear at attention; Stand at attention with the spear.*

ACTION: Shift forward without moving the right foot, and take a step forward with the left foot, keeping most weight on the right leg. Rotate the right palm towards the thumb and control the spear with the left hand so that the tip circles left, up, and right to do an inner trap. Rotate the left palm away from the thumb so that the palm is down, pressing down with the thumb/ forefinger web. The spear shaft is horizontal with the

3.60

tip at waist height. Press the head up and look past the spear tip. (image 3.60)

POWER GENERATION FOR SPEAR SLASH

Sculling slice: Spear slash applies the structure of the empty hand cannon, or pounding punch, to the characteristics of the spear. The posture and character of the pounding punch work well applied to the sculling slice technique of the spear. The main technique of the spear slash combination is the sculling slice, which applies power to the fore-section of the spear. The power application must be smooth and forceful and coordinated with an exhalation to increase strength. The upper hand first lifts and pulls to above the head, then braces out. When the lower hand launches power to push forward strongly the arm must stay tight to the body so that the power comes from the body. The lower back uses a straightening power. Use full body power, connecting fully into the spear.

Coiling: This is a circular technique, taking the tip around to the inside or outside, also called left or right coiling. A clockwise coil is an inner coil, and a counter clockwise coil is an outer coil. To do the coil the spear shaft must stay connected to the body, otherwise the movement of the body will not control it. The arms move from the body, the left hand circling the spear, transferring the power completely to the tip. The inner coil is the same power as the inner trapping press, and the outer coil is the same power as a scooping hook. You must feel as if you are controlling an opponent's weapon, circling and sticking to it. You should feel as if you cannot be made to lose contact with his weapon. Be sure to use the hands in opposite directions, acting as 'yin ' and 'yang'. The circle should keep the spear tip no higher than the head and no lower than the knees.

Pound with the base: The power of the whole body presses down into the base of the spear. Be sure to slide the hands quickly to get into position. Tuck in the belly and contain the chest when pounding down. When retreating the foot, first retreat the rear foot then withdraw the lead foot. Make sure you turn your body to pound.

- The overall principle of the body technique is to pre-load in the opposite direction to gain power for the weapon technique. You should examine this principle in each and every technique. Once you can apply it then your bodywork will be correct and you can be fully connected and strong.

PRACTICAL APPLICATIONS FOR SPEAR SLASH

Block up and slice: The main technique of slash is the upper block with a slice. An upper block normally blocks up over the head, but because the spear slash's upper block is angled, it does more than this. The action of blocking across and up with the base brings the tip through to slice up. The slice up brings the tip forward and up from below. This can also be called a scull and scoop. Scull is a power used to bring the spear through from the rear. Scoop is any technique that strikes up and forward with the fore-section of the shaft. So this technique blocks up to protect the head, but the action contains a low attack. Attack and defense are completely integrated.

Scull and slice: If someone comes at you using a sweeping action with a long weapon, you lift the base of your weapon to protect your midline and head and push your spear through with the other hand to attack his leg, groin, or stomach. Combined with a charging step, this technique protects and attacks at the same time – one of the characteristics of Xingyi. You must step in quickly and attack forcefully with full intent and spirit. Try to completely uproot your opponent.

Coil: The main idea is to coil around an incoming long weapon to control it. You must stick to his weapon, not allowing him to pull it away. This is not as simple as is sounds – this skill takes years to develop. You need to practise coiling with a partner. You need to develop the same sensitivity as Taiji push hands so that you can stick with the shaft of your spear. Once you can stick to and control another weapon then you can create opportunities to get in with a stab. While coiling, get the fore-section of your spear on the mid-section of your partner's spear. Coiling is just the means to the end, which is the stab. Inner (clockwise) coiling, contains a hidden inner trap and press down. Outer (counter clockwise) coiling, contains a hidden scoop and hook.

Pound the base: This technique uses a long weapon as if is a short one, using a short technique to control the attack of a long weapon. Retreat and withdraw to dodge the attack and strike the oncoming weapon or your opponent's body with the base of the spear. If the opponent pulls his weapon back to try to stab your head, then bring the butt with your right hand to slide the base of your spear along to hook and knock his weapon away to the right. Quickly wheel your body and do an inner trap with your spear, then step in and stab to his heart. These are the theoretical applications of the technique, to give you an idea of how it could be used. Of course you need to respond freely in a real situation.

THE POEM ABOUT SPEAR SLASH

炮枪歌诀

炮枪技法气势雄，
架撩攉挑劲要冲。
里外缠绞粘敌械，
砸把翻拿扎其胸。

The spear slash is a fierce technique.
Block up and slice, scull and scoop while charging in.
Coil in or out to stick to the opponent's weapon.
Pound the base of the spear, wheel, trap and stab his chest.

5. SPEAR CROSSCUT

INTRODUCTION TO SPEAR CROSSCUT, *HENG QIANG*

The spear crosscut takes its name from the empty hand crosscut technique. This is the traditional name, and what everyone calls it from habit. Crosscut is a technique that moves horizontally from side to side. It always moves flatly from left to right, or from right to left, as opposed to moving vertically or straight forward. It is a method of training to utilize a sideways strike with the spear.[11] It uses a full body, evenly balanced power that starts from the body core and utilizes the flexibility of the spear to reach and snap the fore-section of the shaft. The sudden stop at the end of the movement causes the spear to quiver. You need to practise crosscut with attention to detail over a long time to get a feel for the technique and to learn how to transfer power out to the spear tip.

The techniques in spear crosscut are *Left stance crosscut* and *Right stance crosscut*. Left stance crosscut contains a *Right advance encircle* and *Left step forward crossing snap*, while *Right stance crosscut* contains a *Left stance encircle* and a *Right stance crossing snap*.

5a Right Stance Crosscut   yòubù héngqiāng   右步横枪

Start from *on guard*. *Left stance encircle; Right stance crossing snap*.

ACTION 1: Advance the left foot a half-step and follow in the right foot to the left ankle. Lift the right hand to the chest and extend the left hand forward. The palms face each other. Draw a counter clockwise circle with the spear tip. The spear tip should not go above the head or below the waist. The right hand makes the spear base draw a small circle in front of the chest. Look past the spear tip. (image 3.61)

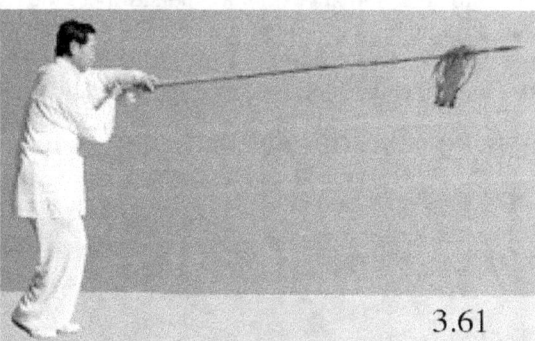

ACTION 2: Take a long step to the forward right with the right foot and follow in a half-step with the left foot, keeping most weight on the left leg. Pull the right hand across to the right, stopping in front of the right shoulder with the arm bent to ninety degrees. While doing this, rotate the right palm away from the thumb so that the palm faces out. Slide the left hand along the shaft and push it horizontally to the right, abruptly stopping so that the fore-section snaps to the right. Keep the left arm slightly bent. The spear shaft is almost horizontal, with

---

[11] Translator's note: In Xingyi this sideways snapping action is traditionally named the same as the empty hand crosscut that is resembles – *heng*. This snap is normally called a sideways *beng* in other styles.

CHAPTER THREE: SPEAR, *QIANG*   175

the tip slightly higher than the shoulders. Turn the body slightly to the right. Look past the spear tip. (image 3.62)

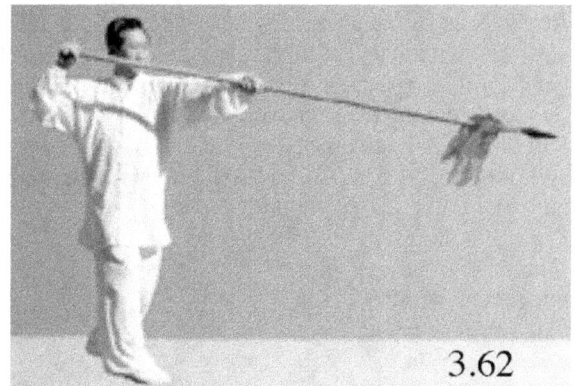

Pointers

- Circle with the spear while advancing the left foot. Be sure to send the spear forward. Both hands must be in front of the body.
- Snap the spear when the right foot steps forward. Coordinate the upper and lower movements so that the power impulse is all together. Transfer power to the spear tip. Be sure to control the hand's slide along the shaft.
- The actions must be completed as one movement. The encircling action is gentle, while the snapping action is strong.

5b Left Stance Crosscut   zuǒbù héngqiāng   左步横枪

Right advance, encircle; Left stance crossing snap.

ACTION 1: Advance the right foot a half-step and follow in the left foot to beside the right ankle. Send the spear forward, keeping the right hand on the base and sliding the left hand along the shaft. Turn the body a bit to the left. Circle the spear tip down, left, and then up and right in a clockwise circle. The right hand should draw a small circle in front of the body, under the left armpit. The spear tip circles between head height and waist height. Follow the action of the spear tip with the eyes. (image 3.63)

176 SPEAR CROSSCUT

ACTION 2: Take a long step to the forward left with the left foot and follow in a half- step with the right foot, keeping the weight evenly balanced with both legs bent. Pull the spear base back from beneath the left armpit towards the right shoulder, rotating the right palm away from the thumb so that the palm faces out. Pull the elbow back at shoulder height. Slide the left hand along the spear shaft and bring it across to the left, abruptly stopping it and gripping firmly, making the spear quiver. The spear should be horizontal with the tip slightly above the shoulder. Turn the body slightly to the right. Look past the spear tip. (image 3.64 and from the front)

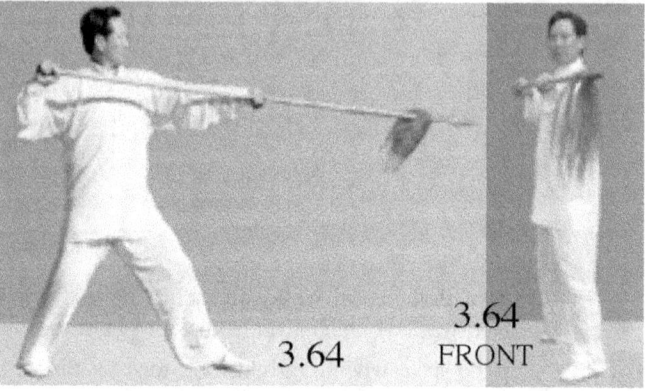

3.64

3.64 FRONT

Pointers

- The hands must work together to draw the circle with the spear. The right hand draws a small circle while the spear tip draws a large circle. The hands operate in opposite directions, and snap forcefully at the end.
- Do not stop midway through the movement.

5c Crosscut Turn Around   héngqiāng zhuànshēn   横枪转身

Starting from a *Left stance crosscut*. *Left hook-in turn around and sweep; Right advance and encircle; Left step forward and crossing snap.*

ACTION 1: Hook-in the left foot towards the right foot, turning the body around 180 degrees to the right to face back in the way from which you came. Advance the right foot a half-step without moving the left foot, keeping most weight on the left leg. Lower the right hand to the waist and slide the left hand a bit forward along the spear shaft, turning the palm forward. Bring the spear around as the body turns sweeping it horizontally around to point forward at shoulder height. Follow the movement of the spear with the eyes, looking past the spear tip at the end of the

3.65

action. (image 3.65)

- The rest of the turn continues on the same as usual for *left stance crosscut*.

Pointers
- o Hook-in the left foot well and turn around quickly. Sweep the spear using the power from the body core. Make sure to move the body and spear as one, launching power from the waist.

From a <u>right</u> *stance crosscut*, do *Left hook-in lift and scull; Right retreat and chop; Crosscut.*

ACTION 1: Step the left foot forward, landing it hooked-in in front of the right foot and shifting onto the left leg. Lift the right hand above the head, turning it palm away from thumb so that the palm faces out. Lower the left hand and swing it a bit to the right so that the spear tip circles left, down and then right. The spear tip is at ankle height. Look at the spear tip. (image 3.66)

ACTION 2: Turn the body around 180 degrees to face back in the way from which you came. Retreat the right foot and shift back so that a bit more weight is on the right leg. Bring the spear through so that the tip moves back, up and then forward to chop down. Pull the right hand back to the waist and extend the left arm. The spear is near horizontal at chest height. Look past the spear tip. (image 3.67)

3.66

3.67

- The rest of the turn continues on with *crosscut*.

Pointers
- o Lift the spear base to cut down as the left foot hooks in. Be sure to rotate both hands.
- o Wheel the body around as the right foot retreats so that the full power goes to the spear chop.

178 SPEAR CROSSCUT

5d Crosscut Closing Move   héngqiāng shōushì   横枪收势

Continue on and turn when you are back where you started. From a *right* stance crosscut, do *Left step forward inner trap; Follow-in stab; Retreat snap up*. Then complete the closing as described in *spear chop*.

ACTION 1: Step the left foot forward without moving the right foot, keeping the weight on the right leg. Press the spear base down at the right waist, rotating both hands to do an inward trap. The spear shaft should be relatively level with the tip at waist height. Look past the spear tip. (image 3.68)

ACTION 2: Shift forward and follow in the right foot a half-step to behind the left foot. Push the spear base forward forcefully with the right hand, allowing the spear to slide through the left hand, using it as a guide. The spear is level and moves straight forward to chest height, the power reaching the tip. Look past the spear tip. (image 3.69)

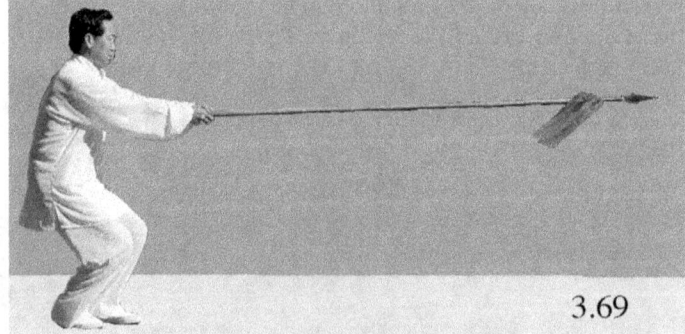

ACTION 3: Retreat the right foot a half-step and shift back to the right leg without moving the left foot. Pull the right hand back to beside the waist and slide the left hand up the spear shaft. Use both hands to snap the spear up so that the tip quivers at head height. Look past the spear tip. (image 3.70)

- The rest of the closing is the same as described in *spear chop*.

Pointers

- o Rotate the hands to perform the inner trap as the left foot steps forward. Stab as the right foot steps up. The spear must arrive as the foot lands.
- o Snap the spear up as the foot retreats. The left hand must slide and then grip strongly, and the timing must be perfect in order to send the power to the tip of the spear.

POWER GENERATION FOR SPEAR CROSSCUT

- Spear crosscut is made up two techniques – circling and sideways snap. Circling means to circle the spear tip in front of the body. The snap is a sudden acceleration and braking action coming from within the circle, to snap the spear tip to the side. Use the momentum of the spear tip to snap it to either side.

Circle: The action should be soft and fully rounded. Close the shoulders and chest in slightly, and gather power in the lower back area. Use the left hand in front as the pivot point and draw a small circle with the right hand in front of the chest. The spear tip will thus draw a large circle as the hands use power in opposite directions. That is, as the right hand goes down the left hand goes up, and as the right hand goes left the left hand goes right. The power in the hands is entirely due to the action of the waist and shoulders. The left hand should have a light grip, neither too tight nor too loose. If it grips too tightly then the action will be stiff. If it grips too loosely then the action will be weak. Work to find the principle of loading within the body to create power in the opposite direction.

Snap: The left arm drives across to the left or pushes across to the right. The right hand pulls back and braces out. Both hands rotate in opposite directions. At the point of power application, turn the body slightly right, straighten the lower back slightly, spread the chest and open the shoulders, and put a bracing and pulling power in the hands. The left hand braces forward while the right hand pulls back. Use power in the shoulders and arms, but that power is transferred from the lower back to the shoulders and from the shoulders to the arms. In this way the power will transfer through to the spear. Breathe out to gain more power, and send all your power to the fore-section of the spear. The left hand is the key in controlling the snap. Coordinate the upper and lower, forward and back, inner and outer elements of the movement so that the backward and forward movement of the arms and the pulling and bracing action of the hands results in a strong snap of the spear shaft.

Turn around: This is a crossing sweep that uses the power from the waist as the body turns. You need to sit down into the buttocks and rotate the waist. Shift back to help the power release, and rotate both hands. Move the spear as one with the body.

- When doing the crosscut, the left hand's slide and the arm's flexion adjust. The slide and degree of flexion determines how far you take the spear across to either side and how large the circle is. This is coordinated with the right hand's placement and amount of pull. And all this is coordinated with the body's action. Respect the principle of 'every single posture and action of all parts of the body must assist actively in the power launch.' The body must be comfortable and natural at all times. In addition, and most importantly, the structure and action must conform to the principles of defense and attack. So when you are training for the feeling of the spear, you must most of all find 'complete power'. That is – how do you gather the power of the entire body and send it to the end of the spear?

PRACTICAL APPLICATIONS FOR SPEAR CROSSCUT

- The crosscut is a snap that cuts to the side from within circling. Circling is not simply a fully rounded and even circle of the spear tip. The circle is actually a partial circle that is constantly adjusting the extent of its curve to control an opponent. The circle is one of the most important of spear techniques. They say that it is the 'primary basic' of all spear techniques.

Circle: The application of the circle is mostly to defend. As one classic[12] says most clearly,

> "To use a spear, the key lies in circling. With a circle you can defend to right and left, up and down. It is as if you have a shield three feet in front of you. Also, used to attack, who can defend against it? Go out with a circle and you will win. Come back with a circle and you can turn defeat into success."

Circling can be done clockwise (called inner circling) and counter clockwise (called outer circling). If an opponent comes on your right side, this is your inside, so you use an inner circle to protect against him. If an opponent comes on your left side, this is your outside, so you use an outer circle to defend.

If the opponent stabs to your head then lift your left hand slightly to cross the fore-section of your spear with the midsection of his spear. If he stabs to your waist, lift your right hand to your left armpit and rise slightly so that you can easily cross your spear with his, once again crossing the fore-section of your spear with the midsection of his. Crossing the shank of the spear is the main principle of defense. Your spear tip comes closer to the opponent, so that you have a quick and direct route and have the advantage over him. Crossing at the midsection of his spear puts him at a disadvantage, as it is difficult for him to pull his spear back or adjust the line of action. This is the main defensive principle of 'using the front to control the middle'. It uses the technique of the circle to trap. The circle has the inner trap and outer trap techniques contained within it.

---

[12] Wu Shu, "Record of hand techniques"

Snap: The snap attacks mainly the opponent's head, neck, or chest, though of course his lead hand or arm is also a prime target. You could also knock his weapon out of the way. If the opponent attacks with a short weapon, once the blade touches your spear then a well timed and well placed snap will knock it out of his hands.

Used as an attack, crosscut strikes the opponent's head, body or hands. Used as a defense it knocks the opponent's weapon away. This is also really an attack. Attack and defense are done together and can quickly change from one to the other. Once you have knocked the opponent's weapon then you should quickly snap to his body. This is really one action.

- Your footwork must be agile. You must be able to advance, retreat, and dodge to the side. You must take control of the distance between you and the opponent. The distance that you want is the distance that is optimal for the spear. That is, it is not the distance sought when you are fighting empty handed – 'hit as if you are giving a kiss'. That is too close for a spear. The distance you want is one that will kiss the opponent with your spear tip – that is, you want to be at a distance that the spear will be on him when it is extended.

- The essence of the spear lies in mastering the circle. You must train hard and long so that it becomes 'more natural than natural', 'more perfect than perfect'. Only then can you be considered a true spear player.

THE POEM ABOUT SPEAR CROSSCUT

横枪歌诀

横枪技法是圈崩，

圈枪久练德其精。

横崩两膀腰身力，

勤学苦练日日功。

The technique of the crosscut combines a circle and a snap.

You must train the circle long and hard to master its essence.

Use the strength of the body and shoulders to snap.

Study diligently and train hard day after day to gain skill.

6. FIVE ELEMENTS LINKED SPEAR FORM

Introduction To The Five Elements Linked Spear, *Wuxing Lianhuan Qiang*

The Five Elements Linked Spear form is a short traditional form that combines the foundation of the five element techniques of the spear. Forms that share this name vary by region and by branch of Xingyi. The common thread is that the form must show the flavour and characteristics of Xingyi spear. The characteristics of Xingyi spear are: the techniques must be refined, they are succinct and practical, the power is hard and strong, the spirit is imposing, all moves can be directly applied, and the body and weapon must move as one.

The overall characteristics of the form are: the movements connect smoothly, the power is unimpeded, the actions connect well, the attitude is fierce, the power is hard, the spear technique is clean, the intent and spirit are focused. The footwork is based on the *santi* stance. The power is whole body power that transfers to the spear, the body and spear acting as one.

The Xingyi world respects the spear immensely. Training the spear is a vital part of Xingyi training. This is why they say, ' Taiji sword, Bagua sabre, Xingyi spear, and Shaolin staff. ' Every Xingyi player should practise the spear often to learn how to become one with it, and improve power in Xingyi. As they say, 'the deeper your spear skills, the deeper your fist skills. ' Training the Xingyi spear improves your overall body skills and deepens your fist skills, strengthens your body and improves your self defense ability.

NAMES OF THE MOVEMENTS

1. Opening Move (On Guard)
2. Thrust: Stationary Outer Trap, Inner Trap, Stab
3. Thrust: Back Cross Step, Outer Trap, Inner Trap, Stab
4. Thrust: Roundabout Step, Outer Trap, Inner Trap, Stab
5. Chop: Step Forward, Swinging Chop
6. Slash: Coil, Step Forward, Block, Slice, Sculling Scoop
7. White Crane Flashes its Wings: Retreat, Circle, Poke, Wheel, Cover and Stab
8. Chop: Step Forward, Scoop the Base, Chop, Stab
9. Drill: Lift, Punt, Right Stance Inverted Grip Low Stab
10. Drill: Step Forward Covering Inner Trap, Left Stance High Stab
11. Thrust: Back Step, Entangle, Inner Trap and Stab
12. Crosscut: Right Step Forward, Circle, Right Stance Crossing Snap

CHAPTER THREE: SPEAR, *QIANG* 183

13. Crosscut: Left Step Forward, Circle, Left Stance Crossing Snap
14. Spear Thrust Turn Around: Turn Around, Heel Kick, Twist the Body, Swinging Chop

(the following moves are repetition back in the returning direction)

15. Thrust: Step Forward, Outer Trap, Inner Trap, Stab
16. Thrust
17. Thrust
18. Chop
19. Slash
20. White Crane Flashes its Wings
21. Chop
22. Drill
23. Drill
24. Thrust
25. Crosscut
26. Crosscut
27. Thrust Turn Around

(The following moves are the closing combination)

28. Thrust
29. Closing Move

Description of the Movements

1. Opening Move   qǐ shì   起势

This is the same as setting into *ready stance*. The movements are *Stand at attention with the spear; Left aligned spear; Left santi stance hold the spear.*

ACTION 1: Stand to attention with the right hand holding the spear vertical at the right side with the base on the ground. Hold the spear with the thumb and index finger circling the shaft, the arm naturally straight with the spear shaft snug to the right shoulder. Let the left hand hang naturally with the palm on the left thigh. Press the head up and look straight ahead. (image 3.71)

3.71

ACTION 2: Turn the body ninety degrees to the left to face the direction in which the form will go. Step the left foot forward and straighten the right leg, bending the left leg to sit into a left bow stance. Extend the spear out flat with the right hand, the spear tip pointing forward. Extend the right arm so that the spear shaft is at chest height. Place the left hand under the right armpit with the palm up to support the spear shaft. Look past the spear tip. (image 3.72)

3.72

ACTION 3: Shift back so that most weight is on the right leg, bending the legs to take a *santi* stance. Extend the left hand forward, holding the spear shaft. Release the right hand to slide the spear through, bringing it back to the base. Hold the spear base at the right side of the waist. Keep the left arm almost straight with the elbow tucked in, palm down, pressing firmly on the shaft. The spear is on the midline of the body, level, with the tip at chest height. Press the head up and look past the spear tip. (image 3.73)

3.73

Pointers

- The opening move must be stable and smoothly connected without any breaks.
- Place the legs, body, hands, and spear into the *santi* stance as one. Do not allow any portion of the body or spear to finish separately.

2. **Thrust: Stationary Outer Trap, Inner Trap, Stab** bēngqiāng 崩枪

Stationary outer trap; Stationary inner trap; Stationary stab.

ACTION 1: Without moving the feet, rotate the left palm up and the right palm down. This makes the spear tip draw a half-circle up, left, and down. Keep the shaft snug to the abdomen. Press the head up and look at the spear tip. (image 3.74)

ACTION 2: Rotate the left palm down to press down with the thumb/forefinger web. Rotate the right palm in, keeping it at the waist. Use the power of the waist combined with the flexibility of the spear shaft to draw a half-circle the spear tip up, right, and down. Keep the shaft snug to the abdomen. Press the head up and look past the spear tip. (image 3.75)

3.74

ACTION 3: Bend the left leg slightly and extend the right leg slightly, shifting forward into a slightly

3.75

forward stance. Release the left hand to direct the spear shaft through it and extend the right hand quickly and forcefully forward. When the right hand arrives at the left hand, settle it into the left hand. The right arm is almost fully extended. The spear is level with the tip stabbing to chest height. The body is turned to face forward. Press the head up and look at the spear tip. (image 3.76)

3.76

Pointers

- These three actions must be smoothly and integrally connected.
- Send power to the spear tip for the stab. The tip should quiver.
- Use the body to do the outer and inner traps. First shift back slightly, then shift forward. The body turns slightly right to do the out trap, then turns slightly left for the inner trap. Keep the spear shaft snug to the abdomen so that the body's actions transfer to it.

3. Thrust: Cross-over Step, Outer Trap, Inner Trap, Stab
bēngqiāng 崩枪

Cross-over step, outer trap; Step forward inner trap; Stab.

ACTION 1: Do not move the left foot, and step the right foot across in front of it with the foot turned out. This forms a cross-step with the legs bent and weight between them. Pull the spear base back to the right waist, sliding the shaft through the left hand. Do the outer trap action. Look past the spear tip. (image 3.77)

ACTION 2:. Step the left foot forward without moving the right foot, shifting mostly onto the right leg. Rotate the hands to do an inner trap action. (image 3.78)

ACTION 3: Shift forward and stab, sliding the shaft through the left hand. (image 3.79)

Pointers
- Complete the outer trap as the right foot steps across.
- Complete the inner trap as the left foot steps forward.

CHAPTER THREE: SPEAR, *QIANG* 187

4. Thrust: Roundabout Step, Outer Trap, Inner Trap, Stab
bēngqiāng 崩枪

Roundabout step, outer trap; Step forward inner trap; Stab.

ACTION 1: Advance the left foot diagonally to the right with the foot turned out. Do not move the right foot but shift weight forward between the feet. Pull the right hand back to the right side, sliding the shaft through the left hand. Complete the outer trap as the left foot steps. Look at the spear tip. (image 3.80)

3.80

ACTION 2: Step the right foot in front of the left foot. Land with the foot hooked in slightly and turn the body slightly left so that the stance is facing straight forward. Do the inner trap at the same time. Look at the spear tip. (image 3.81)

3.81

ACTION 3: Shift forward a bit towards the right leg. Push the right hand forward forcefully, sliding the spear through the left hand to stab forward. Support the right hand in the left when it arrives. The spear shaft is level with the tip at chest height. Send power to the spear tip. Look past the spear tip. (image 3.82)

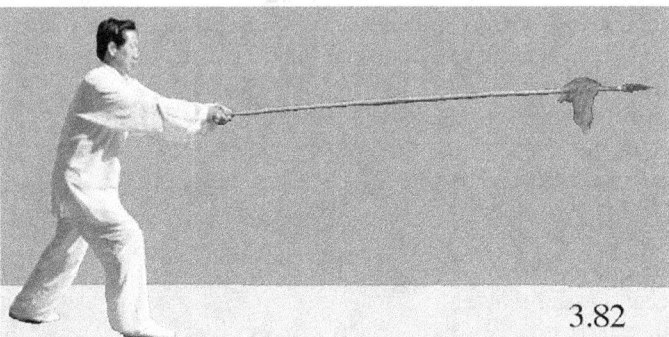
3.82

Pointers

- o   Pay attention to the direction and angle of the stepping. The feet step in a roundabout way, drawing a curved line. The stepping must be agile

and quick and coordinated well with the spear traps.
- As you step, the left hand must control the direction in which the spear points – to the front. The spear must not wobble. The spear tip must point accurately to its forward target during the outer trap, inner trap, and stab.

5. Chop: Step Forward, Swinging Chop   pīqiāng   劈枪

Advance and vertical circle; Step forward and chop.

ACTION 1: Advance the right foot a half-step and bring the left foot in to the right ankle. Pull the spear base back with the right hand then lift it up above the head at the right side with the arm almost fully extended. Slide the left hand forward along the spear, reaching it down to the front, pointing the spear tip down. Circle the spear tip back at the left side of the body. Lift the body slightly. Watch the spear tip as it moves. (image 3.83)

ACTION 2: Take a long step forward with the left foot and follow in the right foot a half-step, sitting between the legs. Circle the left hand back then lift it, and then chop the spear down to the front. The right hand brings the spear base forward, then down, then pulls back to the right side. Finish with the spear shaft level, the tip at waist height. The left arm is almost straight. Press the head up and look past the spear tip. (images 3.84 and 3.85)

Pointers

- The swinging chop is a continuous move, and must be practised as such.

CHAPTER THREE: SPEAR, *QIANG* 189

The final chop must be completed as the left foot lands.
- o The left hand slides along the spear. Slide forward as you bring the spear tip down. Slide back as you bring the spear through to chop. Tighten the grip at exactly the right time and in the optimal position to send power to chop strongly with the spear's fore-section.

6. Slash: Coil, Step Forward, Block, Slice, Sculling Scoop

pàoqiāng   炮枪

Advance and coil; Step forward, block, slice, sculling scoop.

ACTION 1: Advance the left foot a half-step and follow in the right foot to beside the left ankle. Slide the left hand forward along the spear and circle the spear tip up, left, then down. Move the right hand in the opposite direction, bringing the spear base up. Keep the spear shaft snug to the body. The spear tip should circle no higher than the eyebrows and no lower than the knees. Watch the tip as it moves. (image 3.86)

ACTION 2: Take a long step diagonally to the forward right with the right foot and follow in the left foot a half-step to take a *santi* stance. Bring the right hand forward and then lift it up, rotating the palm to face out – brace out above the head with the arm rounded. Rotate the left palm towards the thumb so that the spear tip circles diagonally forward and to the right, to slice up with the left palm angled to the forward right. Push the spear shaft forward forcefully with the left hand, keeping the arm slightly bent. Finish with the left hand at chest height and the spear tip at waist height. Send the power to the fore-section of the spear. Look past the spear tip. (image 3.87)

Pointers
- o Coil the spear with the left hand as the left foot advances. Be sure to slide the left hand fluidly along the shaft. The coiling action should be large and smooth, and use bodywork. Draw the body with the arm and lead the arm with the body, moving the spear along.
- o The slash must be completed all at once – the right foot lands forward, the right hand lifts to block and the left hand pushes with a sculling

190 FIVE ELEMENTS LINKED SPEAR FORM

scoop. The feet and hands must arrive together. The left hand must have a focal point. Using the power from the body core, slide the hand until the right moment then tighten the grip to strike.

7. White Crane Flashes its Wings: Retreat, Circle, Poke, Wheel, Cover and Stab   báihé liàngchì   白鹤亮翅

Retreat, circle and poke; Wheel and block; Cover and stab.

ACTION 1: Retreat the left foot and withdraw the right foot, touching down and shifting onto the left leg. Bend the left leg to squat down and turn left to bring the right shoulder on line with the front. Slide the left hand along the shaft and bring it left, up, and then down to in front of the right shoulder with the palm pressing down. Bring the right hand down and then push under the left armpit. The right hand under the left armpit makes the spear tip poke with a dotting action, moving in a circular motion from the forward lower right, up, and then forward and down. The spear shaft is level with the tip around chest height or lower. Look at the spear tip. (image 3.88)

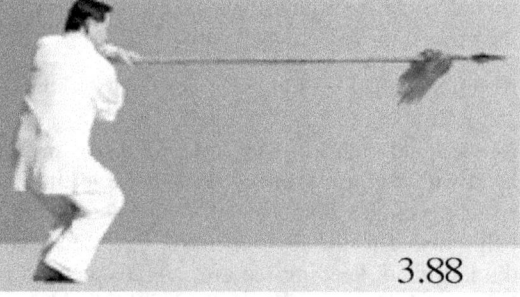

3.88

ACTION 2: Lift the right knee and push off the left leg, turning rightward and landing on the right foot, foot turned out. Then land the left foot forward and sit into a half-horse stance with most weight on the right leg. Rotate the right palm away from the thumb and pull it up in front of the right shoulder, palm out. Slide the left hand along the spear shaft and control the tip with the left hand to circle the spear tip up, left, and then down. The spear tip is at waist height. Look past the spear tip. (image 3.89 transitional)

3.89

ACTION 3: Keep the hands in motion without moving the feet. Bring the spear base down to the right waist and rotate the

3.90

right palm up. Circle the spear with the left hand to bring the tip left, up, then down, to complete a cover and inner trap. Keep the left arm bent and press down with the palm. Press the head up and look past the spear tip. (image 3.90)

ACTION 4: Bring the right foot up behind the left foot. Push the spear base forward forcefully with the right hand, controlling the shaft by sliding it through the left hand to stab forward. Support the right hand with the left when it arrives beside the left. Stab with the spear shaft level at chest height, sending power forward to make the tip quiver. Look past the spear tip. (image 3.91)

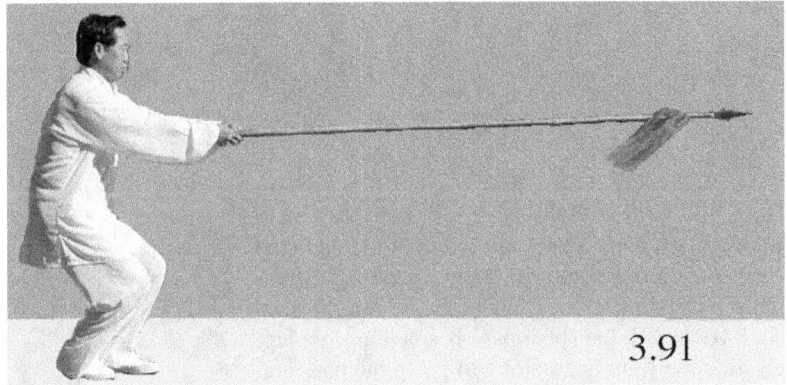

Pointers

- Take a considerable retreating step and withdraw the other foot quickly to do the 'dotting' action. The footwork must be coordinated with the hand action moving the spear. Be sure to circle the spear tip – it draws quite a large circle while the hands move in a small circle. Turn the body left when the spear tip pokes down. The movement is soft and the strike does not use a lot of strength – just a touch is enough.
- During the jumping wheel both hands rotate and both arms open so that the spear tip circles. In this way, the shaft blocks up with quite a large movement. All elements of this move must be completed together.
- Complete the covering inner trap as the feet land. Stab forward with a shift in weight.

8. **Chop: Step Forward, Scoop the Base, Chop, Stab**   pīqiāng   劈枪

Step forward, scoop the base: Step forward, chop; Stab.

ACTION 1: Advance the left foot a half-step and follow in the right foot to the left ankle. Pull the spear base back with the right hand, sliding the left hand forward along the shaft. Extend the left arm forward to reach the spear tip forward, keeping the shaft on the body. Look past the spear tip. (image 3.92)

ACTION 2: Step the right foot forward and advance the left foot a half-step, shifting forward towards the right leg. Slide the left hand forward along the spear shaft and scoop up the tip, then hook it down to the rear, the left hand finishing at the left hip, palm out. Slide the right hand along the shaft until about fifty centimetres of shaft is showing, and bring it forward and up to scoop up. The right hand is at chest height with the thumb/forefinger web up. The spear base is at head height. Keep the shaft snug to the left hip. Look past the spear base. (image 3.93)

ACTION 3: Withdraw the right foot and place it in front of the left foot. Shift onto the right leg and step the left foot forward without stepping the right foot, to settle into a *santi* stance. First lower the right hand to hook back with the spear base beside the right leg. Then slide the right hand along to grasp the base and pull it to the right waist. Lift the left hand to above the head then swing the spear forward and down. The spear tip comes up, forward, then down in a swinging chop until the shaft is level at waist height. Send power to the fore-section of the spear. Look past the spear tip. (images 3.94, 3.95)

ACTION 4: Shift forward to the left leg. Send the spear forward forcefully with the right hand to stab. Slide the spear through the left hand, lifting the hand slightly to guide the spear tip to chest height. The right arm is almost straight, the hands connected. The spear shaft is level at chest height, power in the tip. Look past the spear tip. (image 3.96)

3.96

Pointers

- Scoop the base up as the right foot steps forward. The hands must slide along the shaft quickly and smoothly. Use the body to scoop into the spear base. Keep the right hand tight to the body with the elbow tucked in and the shoulder settled to put power into the elbow. Settle the left shoulder back and down.
- *Step forward and chop* connects immediately to *withdraw and hook down* without hesitation. The whole body must be coordinated. The chop must be strong, and land as the foot lands. The hands work together to chop – the left hand pushes while the right hand pulls.
- Turn the waist, release the shoulders, and extend the arms to stab. The stab must be strong and quick, and the power must be in the tip.

9. Drill: Lift, Punt, Right Stance Inverted Grip Low Stab

zuānqiāng   钻枪

Lift and punt; Right stance inverted grip low stab.

ACTION 1: Advance the left foot a half-step and follow in the right foot to the left ankle. Pull the spear base back to the chest, then lift it above the head at the right side, rotating the right palm up and bracing out with the arm. Slide the left hand forward along the shaft. When the right hand lifts, rotate the left palm towards the thumb to turn the palm forward, so that the spear tip draws a half-circle left, down, and then right, pointing to knee height. Tuck in the left elbow. Look at the spear tip. (image 3.97)

3.97

ACTION 2: Step the right foot forward and follow in a half-step with the left foot to take a *santi* stance. Keep the left arm extended to aim the spear to the

lower left. Push forward and down with the right hand inverted. Slide the spear shaft through the left hand. Lift the left hand slightly and stab with the right until it meets the left. The right hand and spear base are at shoulder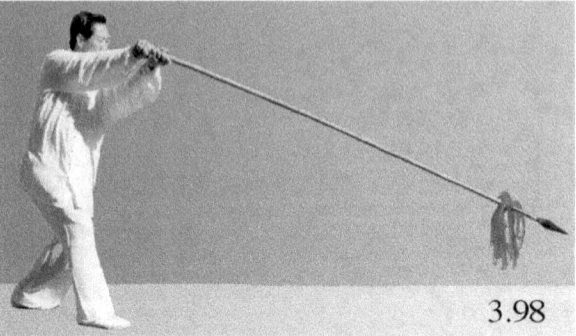
height, the arms are almost straight, and the spear tip is twenty to thirty centimetres above the ground. Lean forward slightly and look at the spear tip. (image 3.98)

Pointers

- Lift the spear base as the left foot advances. Stab the spear down as the right foot steps forward. The spear should always arrive as the foot lands, so that hands and feet work together in an action that is fully connected through the whole body.
- Rotate the right palm away from the thumb as you lift to block. Rotate the left palm towards the thumb as you slide it forward along the shaft to pull and check. The inverted grip stab is not as strong as the regular grip stab, so you must send the power to the tip and control the action cleanly.

10. Drill: Step Forward Covering Inner Trap, Left Stance High Stab

zuānqiāng　　　　　　　　　　　　钻枪

Step forward covering inner trap; Left stance high stab.

ACTION 1: Step the left foot forward without moving the right foot, keeping most weight on the right leg. Pull the spear base back to the right waist, rotating the right hand to press down. Slide the left hand forward along the shaft, circling and rotating it to press palm down, so that the spear tip draws a circle left and up, then right and down – do an inner trap. The spear shaft remains level with the tip at waist height. Look at the spear tip. (image 3.99)

CHAPTER THREE: SPEAR, *QIANG*   195

ACTION 2: Shift slightly forward without moving the feet. Push the spear base forcefully forward with the right hand, sliding the shaft through the left hand. Angle the tip to stab up to nose height with the hands together at chest height. Send power to the tip so that it quivers. Press the head up and look past the spear tip. (image 3.100)

Pointers

- Complete the inner trap as the left foot steps forward. Press the trunk slightly forward as you do the inner trap. Press the head up. The hands must rotate simultaneously in opposite directions. Press down with the left hand.
- Send power to the spear tip when you stab. Accelerate the right hand as it pushes the spear forward, reaching peak acceleration at the end of the stab.

11. Thrust: Back-cross Step, Entangle, Inner Trap and Stab

bēngqiāng　　　　　　　　　　　　崩枪

Back-cross step, entangle; Inner trap; Back-cross step, entangle; Inner trap; Stab.

ACTION 1: Cross the right foot back behind the left foot and shift forward onto the left leg without moving the left foot. The legs are bent and crossed. Pull the spear base back to the right side, sliding the shaft through the left hand, keeping the left arm almost straight. Circle the spear tip down, left, then up. The tip should circle no higher than the head and no lower than the knees. The right and left hands work in opposite circles, keeping the spear shaft snug to the trunk throughout the action. Look at the spear tip. (image 3.101)

ACTION 2: Step the left foot forward and continue to circle the spear with the hands so that the tip goes up, right, and then down. Keep the shaft on the torso throughout. The hands do not slide on the spear. Look at the spear tip. (image 3.102)

ACTION 3: Cross the right foot back behind the left foot. Continue to circle the spear tip left, then up, keeping the spear shaft snug to the trunk throughout. The right hand circles at the right side of the body as the spear circles. Watch the spear tip. (image 3.103)

3.102

3.103

ACTION 4: Step the left foot forward without moving the right foot. Rotate the right hand and bring the spear base in to the right waist. Continue to circle the spear with the left hand so that the tip goes right and then down – a covering inner trap. The spear is level with the tip at waist height. (image 3.104)

3.104

ACTION 5: Shift forward towards the left leg without moving the feet. Stab the spear forward level to chest height with the right hand, sliding the shaft through the left hand. Look past the spear tip. (image 3.105)

3.105

Pointers

- o The back-cross step coil is repeated twice in an unbroken movement. The stepping should be small and quick.
- o The spear coil is a soft movement, with full, nicely rounded circles. The

CHAPTER THREE: SPEAR, *QIANG*   197

hands work together. Be sure to keep the spear shaft snug to the trunk of the body, using it as the pivot point. The circling of the hands uses the action of the body. Coordinated with the footwork, the whole body works in an integrated whole, strong but soft, containing a certain hardness within.

12. Crosscut: Right Step Forward, Circle, Right Stance Crossing Snap
héngqiāng   横枪

Right step forward, circle; Right stance crossing snap.

ACTION 1: Advance the left foot a half-step and follow in the right foot to the left ankle. Pull the right hand back to in front of the chest and slide the left hand forward along the spear shaft. Turn the right palm up, rotating the spear, and draw a small circle with the base to the left and down. Control the spear shaft with the left hand, using it as the pivot point, so that the spear tip draws one circle right and up. Look past the spear tip. (image 3.106)

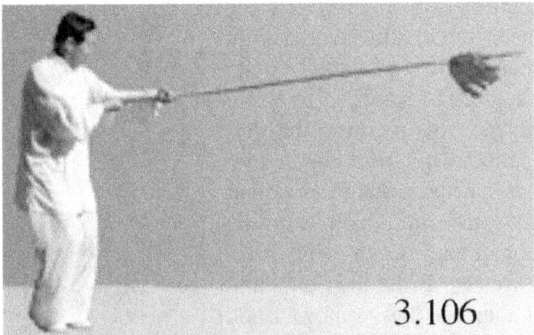

3.106

ACTION 2: Take a long step to the forward right with the right foot and follow in the left foot a half-step, keeping most weight on the left leg. Slide the left hand forward along the spear shaft and push it towards the forward right with the palm facing right. Then tighten the grip and stop abruptly. Rotate the right palm away from the thumb and pull back to the right strongly, palm turning out. Bend the right arm and pull the spear base back to in front of the right shoulder. Send power to the fore-section of the spear so that the spear tip snaps toward the right. The spear is level at about shoulder height. Look past the spear tip. (image 3.107)

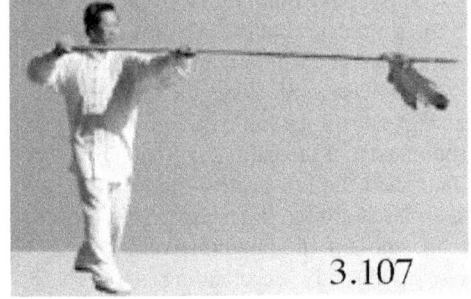

3.107

Pointers

o The movement must be continuous without a break. Neither the footwork nor the handwork should hesitate, and they must integrate fully together.

o The circle is counter-clockwise, and the tip should circle between head and knee height. Contain the chest during the circling so that the body gathers energy. Pull back and rotate to snap the spear, launching power with the whole body connected through to the hands. The key is the controlling action of the left hand. You must practise this carefully to find how to do it.

13. Crosscut: Left Step Forward, Circle, Left Stance Crossing Snap

héngqiāng   横枪

Left step forward, circle; Left stance crossing snap.

ACTION 1: Advance the left foot a short step forward without moving the right foot, shifting evenly between the feet. Loosen the left grip to allow the spear to slide and rotate within it. Send the right hand forward in front of the chest. Work with both hands to circle the spear tip clockwise, the right hand drawing a small circle. Rotate the hands in opposite directions, rotating the left palm away from the thumb so that the palm faces down, and the right palm towards the thumb so that the palm faces up. Bring the right hand under the left armpit. Look past the spear tip. (image 3.108)

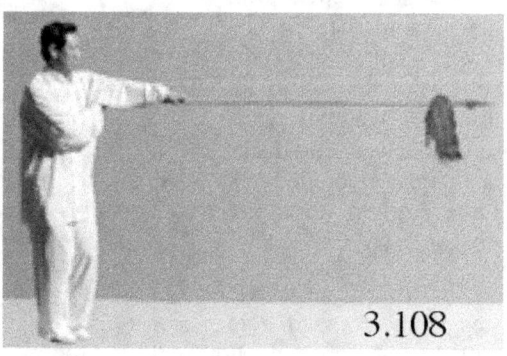

ACTION 2: Step the left foot forward and follow in the right foot a half-step, keeping most weight on the right leg. Pull the right hand back to in front of the right shoulder, rotating it palm away from thumb so that the palm faces out. Bend the right arm to hold the spear base in front of the right shoulder. Slide the left hand forward along the shaft and rotate it palm away from thumb so that the palm faces back, then snap the left arm to the left, sharply stopping the spear. This stops the tip in the midst of its circle, abruptly accelerating and snapping left with an oscillation. The spear tip is at shoulder height. Turn the body a bit to the right. Look past the spear tip. (image 3.109)

Pointers

o   The circling is soft, gathering power in the hands and body.

o The snap is sudden and sharp. The hands rotate – the right hand pulls back while the left hand stops the spear. Coordinate the spear snap with a snap from the waist, timing the slide and stop of the left hand.

14. Spear Thrust Turn Around: Turn Around, Heel Kick, Twist the Body, Swinging Chop bēngqiāng huíshēn 崩枪回身

Turn around, heel kick; Twist the body, swinging chop.

ACTION 1: Hook-in the left foot towards the right foot. Bend the legs and shift onto the left leg. Rotate the right palm away from the thumb and lift it above the head with the palm facing out. Slide the left hand forward along the shaft and bring the hand down and a bit towards the right. This circles the spear tip left, down, and right to point down at knee height. Look at the spear tip. (image 3.110)

ACTION 2: Turn a full 180 degrees, holding the spear motionless. Lift the right knee then do a heel kick forward to waist height with the foot turned out. Look forward. (image 3.111)

ACTION 3: Land with a trampling action forward and down, keeping the foot turned out. Follow in the left foot slightly, turn the body to the right, cross the legs into a scissors stance, and sit down. Bring the spear base forward, down, and then pull back to the right waist. Lift the left hand, then bring it forward and down to chop forcefully. Tighten the grip and press down with the thumb/forefinger web. The spear chops level with the tip

200 FIVE ELEMENTS LINKED SPEAR FORM

at about waist height, power in the fore-section. Press the head up and look forward. (image 3.112)

Pointers

- o The turn around should be smooth, well balanced, quick, and stable without hesitation in the movement.
- o Hook-in the left foot as you lift the spear. Turn around and kick quickly and strongly, but keep balanced. Land, turn the body, and chop the spear all at the same time.
- o The chop is low and well rooted. Control the slide of the left hand along the shaft and stop it under control with focus so that the spear does not hit the ground.

- The following moves, 15 through 27, are a repetition of the first section, moves 2 through 14, back in the returning direction.

15. Thrust: Step Forward, Outer Trap, Inner Trap, Stab bēngqiāng 崩枪

Step forward, outer trap; Inner trap; Stab.

ACTION: Step the left foot forward without moving the right foot. Pull the right hand back to the right waist and perform the outer trap, inner trap and stab the same as described in movement 2. (outer trap image 3.113)

16. Thrust	see move 3.
17. Thrust	see move 4.
18. Chop	see move 5.
19. Slash	see move 6.
20. White Crane Flashes its Wings	see move 7.
21. Chop	see move 8.
22. Drill	see move 9.

23. Drill   see move 10. (image 3.114)

24. Thrust	see move 11.
25. Crosscut	see move 12.
26. Crosscut	see move 13.
27. Thrust Turn Around	see move 14.

28. Thrust

See moves 2 and 15. This move is now facing the original direction.

29. Closing Move   shōu shì   收势

Starting from *thrust. Snap up the spear; Stand the spear to attention; Stand to attention.*

ACTION 1: Shift back towards the right leg without moving the feet. Pull the right hand back to the right side and slide the left hand forward along the spear shaft. Stop the left hand abruptly to snap the spear tip upward, sending power to the fore-section of the shaft. The spear tip should be no higher than the head. Press the head up and look past the spear tip. (image 3.115)

202 FIVE ELEMENTS LINKED SPEAR FORM

ACTION 2: Stand up, bringing the left foot in beside the right foot and turning ninety degrees to face front. Bring the left hand to the side to stand the spear vertically beside the right shoulder. Slide the right hand along the shaft and bring the hand to the waist to put the spear base on the ground. Look at the left hand. (image 3.116)

ACTION 3: Release the left hand and circle it down and to the left, then up to shoulder height. Look at the left hand. (image 3.117)

ACTION 4: Bend the elbow and press down in front of the face. Then let the left hand hang naturally at the side. Turn the head to look straight ahead. Stand to attention, and the form is completed. (image 3.118)

3.116

3.117

3.118

Pointers

- The eyes must remain bright and attentive throughout the closing move. The spirit and feeling must remain full. The facial expression must remain dignified through to the final completion of the form.

FIVE ELEMENT STAFF

五行棍

Introduction To Five Element Staff, *Wuxing Gun*

As with the sabre, sword, and spear, the names of the staff techniques are taken from the five element hand techniques. Xingyi masters of old selected the most straightforward and practical staff techniques and blended them with the characteristics of Xingyi. In this way we have a set of five elemental techniques that fit the theories and methods of Xingyi.

The five element staff techniques are simple and easy to learn. All Xingyi staff techniques are clear, powerful, full of spirit, and show obvious applications. Just like the five fist techniques, the emphasis is placed on full power, body core power, and improving deep skills. Power is applied with the body, leading from the lower back and waist with a fully integrated strength. There are no dazzling or entertaining moves.

The five staff techniques are more than just five different techniques, but are five different ways of applying power. Although the movements appear simple, they have rich techniques hidden within. The combinations for the five element techniques actually involve over ten techniques, and include: chop, cover, scoop, hook, poke, slice, block up, brandish, sweep, and check. Each of the five element combinations includes at least two techniques. For example, the chop combination includes a hook up and chop, a hook down and chop, and hook right or left and chop. The drill combination has a hook and a scoop. The thrust combination includes an outer trap, a press down, and a poke. The slash combination includes entangle, cover, block up, and slice. The crosscut combination includes a brandish, a check and a crosscut strike. Each technique must be clear and distinct, and you must clearly understand the movement, power use, and application of each. If you do, it will help you to learn and master the techniques quickly.

Although the five element technique combinations are not widely practised, the Five Elements Staff form is popular. The form differs in different regions, but only in small ways. The five element techniques that I present here combine the traditional techniques with what I have learned from different masters and my own training and teaching experiences over the years. I have of course kept the traditional characteristics. I have included the standard names for the staff techniques in addition to the old names, as name standardization makes it easier to spread and popularize.

The length of the staff in Xingyi should be slightly longer than the height of the player. An overly long staff is awkward, while a shorter staff lacks power. The thickness at the base is that of the circle made by the player's thumb and index finger. The tip will then be the natural circumference of the staff. You must not shave it down, as this destroys its natural suppleness and risks breakage. When choosing a staff, pick the best quality white wax wood that you can – clean and shiny with as few kinks and knots as possible, and with good spring.

The narrow end is called the tip, the thick end is called the base or butt. The shaft is divided into three parts to better explain the actions. The third at the tip is called the fore-section, the third at the base is called the aft-section, and the third in the middle is called the midsection.

FIVE ELEMENT STAFF TECHNIQUES

On Guard yùbèishì 预备势

Before training the staff techniques you must first do post standing, similar to when you learned the five element hand techniques. *On guard* position is similar to *santishi,* and similarly serves as a foundation for all techniques to come. All techniques come from this posture, so it must be perfected.

On guard standing develops an understanding of the position and sets the proper feeling of each part of the body and its relation to the staff – the placement, direction, angles, and height. While post standing you find the power in each part of the body, and the proper requirements of the posture. This sets the posture so that the movements can become regulation and the techniques will be correct. This is the foundation for all of the five element techniques. You must not only do post standing in the *on guard* position, but in every single basic posture. In this way you will find the posture, requirements, and power for every technique. Post standing takes time but it is time well spent. Setting the postures well will speed up your mastery of the movements.

The actions of *on guard* are: *Stand with the staff; Raise the staff in both hands; Left advance and chop.*

ACTION 1: Stand to attention with the feet together, angled forty-five degrees to the line that the form will take. Hold the staff vertically at the right side with the base on the ground. Extend the right arm and hold the midsection of the shaft with the thumb/forefinger web. Extend the left arm at the left side. Press the head up slightly and look forward. (image 4.1)

ACTION 2: Grip with the right hand and raise the staff vertically. Bring the left hand to the right armpit and grasp the staff about ten centimetres from the base. Turn the head to look to the left. (image 4.2)

ACTION 3: Turn to the left and step the left foot forward, following in the right step slightly to take a *santi* stance – the weight sixty percent on the rear leg. Grip the staff with both hands and chop down and forward. Pull the left hand back to the left, midway between the waist and hip socket. Push the right hand out to chest height. Extend the right shoulder forward, keep the right arm slightly bent with the elbow rolled inward, and press down on the staff with the thumb/forefinger web. The tip of the staff is at nose height. Press the head up and look past the tip. (image 4.3)

Pointers

- Focus your mind during *stand with the staff*.
- During *raise the staff in both hands*, when the head turns to the left, tuck the jaw in and show spirit in the eyes. Raise the right hand and take the staff in the left hand slowly. Start an intention of turning the body to the left.
- Complete the chop when the left foot lands. Before stepping the left foot forward, turn the body to the left and sit down. Put power to the staff tip. The distance between the hands should be the length of the player's forearm. The chop must have a focal point, and that is when the right hand stops its action. Turn the waist, reach the shoulder forward, and breathe out to launch power.

1. STAFF CHOP

INTRODUCTION TO STAFF CHOP, *PI GUN*

Chop is a strike that moves forward and down. The wushu regulations definition of chop is "the staff chops down from above with power and speed. Power is applied with the tip of the staff." The Xingyi staff chop should be strong, focusing the power of the whole body into the tip of the staff. Xingyi particularly emphasizes that weapons are extensions of the body. This means that the power of the whole body must transfer to the weapon so that the weapon and body become one.

Because the chop comes down from above, it must first be placed in the optimal position for this – this includes the position of the staff and the placement of the body for power application. The tip must be above horizontal, aligned on the circle of the strike, with the optimal placement being above the head. You must pay particular attention to getting a feel for this during practice.

There are two methods for staff chop. The chop is set up with a hook up or a hook down. The techniques involved are: *hook up to left or right and chop, hook down to left or right and chop, swinging chop, covering chop with the butt, reverse grip chop, wheeling around chop*.

METHOD ONE: HOOK UP AND CHOP

1a Left Stance Chop   yòubù pīgùn   右步劈棍

Start from *on guard*. Continue with *Right step forward, hook up; Left step forward, chop*.

ACTION 1: Shift forward without moving the left foot. Then step the right foot forward a long step, landing firmly with the knee bent, and bring the left foot up to the right ankle, keeping the thighs together. With the right hand, first lower the staff tip to waist height, then pull it to hook up and back. The right arm pulls to the chest, the right hand to in front of the right shoulder. Push forward with the left hand to waist height. Tuck in the abdomen and move the right shoulder back slightly. Look forward. (image 4.4)

ACTION 2: Take a long step forward with the left foot and follow in a half-step with the right foot to sit into a *santi* stance. Hold the staff firmly with the right hand and chop forcefully down directly to the front, the tip at chest height. With the left hand pull back to the side, sticking tightly to the body at a height between the waist and hip crease. Reach the right shoulder forward, keep the

right arm slightly bent with the elbow tucked in, and press down with the thumb/forefinger web just below chest height. Press the head up and look past the staff tip. (image 4.5)

Pointers

- o The combination is made up of a hook up and a chop down – these actions must connect without hesitation to develop the power transfer. Step forward for distance, and follow in the rear foot quickly.
- o Lower the staff tip as the weight shifts forward, then raise the tip to hook up as the right foot steps forward.
- o Complete the chop as the left foot lands. The staff must always arrive simultaneously with the foot, so that the movement is fully connected from top to bottom.

• Continue on, repeating as space permits.

1b Turn Around for Hook Up and Chop

shàngguà pīgùn zhuànshēn　　　　　　　　　上挂劈棍转身

Right hook-in, lift the staff; Turn around, retreat, chop.

ACTION 1: Take a step forward with the right foot, hooking it in. Lift the base of the staff above the head with the left hand, rotating the left palm away from the thumb to turn it out away from the body. Slide the right hand forward along the shaft and turn the palm forward. The staff is angled in front of the body with the tip just below knee height. Look at the fore-section of the staff. (image 4.6)

ACTION 2: Turn around 180 degrees to the left to face back in the way from which you came. Shift onto the right leg and retreat the left leg behind. Then shift back to a *santi* stance weighted to the left leg – putting a trampling power forward and down into the right foot. Use both hands to bring the staff up, forward, then down in a swinging chop, finishing with the staff tip at chest height. Pull the left hand back to stick tightly to the body between the hips and waist. Press the head up, tuck the jaw in, and look past the staff tip. (image 4.7)

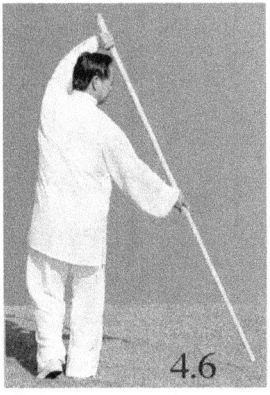

Pointers

- o Do not hesitate between the hook-in turn and the sit back and chop. The power must continue between the actions to develop the power transfer.
- o Land the retreating left foot, grab with the right foot, and chop with the staff all at the same time. Use the turning of the waist and tucking in of the abdomen to send power to the staff

• Continue on with *right advance hook up, left step forward chop*. Repeat as space and energy permit.

METHOD TWO: HOOK DOWN AND CHOP

1c Hook Down to the Right, Covering Chop

yòu xiàguà gàipī gùn   右下挂盖劈棍

Start from *on guard. Left advance, hook down to the right; Right step forward, covering chop.*

ACTION 1: Advance the left foot a half-step and follow in the right foot to the left ankle. Raise the base of the staff with the left hand, pushing forward and up in front of the left shoulder. Hold the right hand at mid-shaft and circle down and back so that the tip circles down and back to the right, then swings up. Turn to the right. Press the head up and follow the staff tip with the eyes. (image 4.8)

ACTION 2: Take a long step forward with the right foot and follow in the left foot a half-step to sit into a *santi* stance. Push and pull the staff base with the left hand, finishing with the hand under the right armpit, palm up. With the right hand, bring the staff up above the head then forward and down in a covering chop.[13] The right hand finishes with the palm down on top of the staff. The staff finishes level, the tip slightly below shoulder height. Press the head up and look past the tip. (image 4.9)

---

[13] Editor's note: Bend the right arm as you circle the staff at the side. The staff stays outside the right arm all the way around the circle, just tucks under the arm at the final strike.

Pointers

- Hook the staff tip down as the leading foot advances.
- Complete the chop as the right foot steps forward.

1d Hook Down to the Left, Reverse Grip Chop

zuǒ xiàguà fǎnpīgùn 　　　　　　　　左下挂反劈棍

Left retreat, hook down to the left;
Right advance, reverse grip chop.

ACTION 1: Retreat the left foot a half step and withdraw the right foot back to in front of the left foot. Control the staff with the right hand to bring the tip down and back at the left side, then to swing up. Turn the body leftward. Keep the left hand at the armpit, coordinating with the action of the right hand. Follow the movement of the staff tip with the eyes. (image 4.10)

ACTION 2: Take a long step forward and follow in the left foot a half-step to sit into a *santi* stance. Swing the staff up, forward, and then down with the right hand, finishing with the palm in a reverse grip – palm up and hand under the staff. The staff tip is at shoulder height. Follow the action of the staff with the left hand, sliding it back to the butt, pulling it back tight to the body at the left side. Focus power to the staff fore-section. Press the head up and look past the staff tip. (image 4.11)

Pointers

- The retreating and withdrawing steps must work together to enable the staff tip to hook around on the left side. Be sure to turn the body to the left.
- The staff must complete its chop as the right foot advances.
- The two actions must be completed as one with no hesitation between them.

210   STAFF CHOP

1e   Hook Down to the Right, Reverse Stance, Covering Chop

yòu xiàguà àobù gàipīgùn   右下挂拗步盖劈棍

Right advance, hook down to the right; Left step forward, covering chop.

ACTION 1: Advance the right foot a half-step and follow in the left foot to the right ankle. Control the staff with the right hand to circle the tip down and back at the right side. Coordinate with the left hand, lifting up and pushing forward to above the head. Turn the body right. Look at the staff tip. (image 4.12)

ACTION 2: Take a long step forward with the left foot and follow in a half-step with the right foot to sit into a *santi* stance. Continue to circle the staff with both hands, the right hand pulling the tip back, up, then forward and down, finishing with a strong covering chop. The left hand finishes pulled into the right armpit, palm up at the base end of the staff. The staff is level at shoulder height. Look past the staff tip. (image 4.13)

Pointers

- Hook down as the right foot advances. Be sure to turn the body to the right.
- Complete the covering chop as the left foot steps forward. The staff must arrive as the foot lands.

1f   Hook Down to the Left, Reverse Grip Chop

zuǒ xiàguà àobù fǎnpīgùn   左下挂拗步反劈棍

Left advance, hook down to the left; Right step forward, reverse grip chop.

ACTION 1: Advance the left foot a half-step and follow in the right foot to the left ankle. Control the staff tip with the right hand to circle it down at the left. Turn the body to the left. Keep the left hand at the right armpit to help coordinate the action of the staff. Follow the staff tip with the eyes. (image 4.14)

ACTION 2: Take a long step forward with the right foot and follow in the left foot a half-step. Continue to circle the staff with the right hand, to go back, up, and then forward and down with a reverse grip chop. The right hand is palm up, with the forearm under the staff. Keep a grip on the base of the staff with the left hand, and pull it back to the left side, finishing with the palm down tight to the body. The staff tip is at shoulder height. Press the head up and look past the staff tip. (image 4.15)

Pointers

- o The hook down and chop is one action; there cannot be any hesitation midway through. This pertains whether you're doing a covering chop or a reverse grip chop, and whether you're moving into an aligned stance or a reverse stance.
- o Hook forward and down as you step forward, fully coordinated.

• Continue to repeat the actions. When you are doing the reverse grip chop, you can change the footwork, sometimes retreating, sometimes advancing. When you are doing the covering chop you can change the stance, sometimes an aligned stance, sometimes a reverse stance. You should be able to do the techniques in a variety of ways.

1g Turn Around for the Hook Down and Chop

xiàguà pīgùn zhuànshēn 下挂劈棍转身

Using the *reverse stance covering chop* with the <u>left</u> foot forward as example. *Left hook-in, turn around, hook down to the right; Right step forward, covering chop.*

ACTION 1: Hook-in the left foot in front of the right foot and shift to the left leg. Lift the right foot and turn around 180 degrees to the right to face back. Bring the right hand around to circle the staff tip up, forward, and then to hook down at the right side. Lift the left hand to lift the staff base and push forward a bit. Follow the staff tip with the eyes. (image 4.16)

ACTION 2: Step the right foot forward and follow in the left foot a half-step. With the right hand, bring the staff tip up, forward, and then down to chop at

212   STAFF CHOP

chest height. Pull the staff base back under the right armpit with the left hand. Press the head up and look past the staff tip. (image 4.17)

If the <u>right</u> foot is forward in a *reverse grip chop*:

ACTION: Step the left foot forward, hooking in as it lands. Shift onto the left leg and turn around 180 degrees to the right. The rest of the turn around is the same as described above.

Pointers

- To complete the hook-in and turn, hook-in a considerable amount and turn quickly.
- When doing the turn around and hook down, coordinate the action of the hands.
- Complete the covering chop as the right foot lands. Launch power with a firm grip and a strong strike.

1h   Chop Closing Move   pīgùn shòushì   劈棍收势

On arriving back at the starting point, do a *turn around* to face the original direction. The *closing move* is: *Right retreat, raise the staff in both hands; Stand at attention with the staff.* If the <u>right</u> foot is forward in a *reverse grip chop* or a *covering chop*, then you need to first retreat the right foot and withdraw the left foot. The description is from a <u>left stance</u> *covering chop*.

ACTION 1: Retreat the right foot a half-step and withdraw the left foot beside the right foot. Turn the body forty-five degrees to the right. Straighten the legs and stand to attention. With the right hand on the shaft, pull it back to the right side of the body then raise it up above the head. With the left hand on the staff base, push it under the right armpit. The staff is now standing vertically. Press the head up and turn it

to look straight to the left. (image 4.18)

ACTION 2: Keep standing at attention. Lower the right hand to bring the staff butt to the ground so that the staff stands at the right side. Let go with the left hand and bring it to the left side. Turn the head to look straight ahead. (image 4.19)

Pointers

- Be sure to remain focused throughout the closing move. Do not let your attention dissipate.
- Stand up straight when standing to attention with the staff. Show good spirit, do not relax yet.
- When retreating or withdrawing the foot and shifting back, the right hand is bringing the staff tip through with a slicing action that hooks back. This is the hidden technique within the move.

POWER GENERATION FOR STAFF CHOP

Hook up: The hands must work together. Bend the right arm and pull back towards the chest. Extend the left arm and push forward. One pulling and one pushing, one bending and one extending – both arms do the hook up. Of course, the action of the arms comes from the shoulders, and that of the shoulders comes from the lower back. The torso should contract during the hook up, tucking the abdomen and closing the chest.

Chop: The chop must have a focal point and stop at chest height. Momentum must not carry it further down than that. It must chop down so quickly that the staff makes a whooshing sound. And it must stop so abruptly and accurately that the staff tip quivers. Turn the waist, reach the shoulder forward and use both arms – push with the right and pull with the left. At the instant of striking the hands' grip must tighten and stop the staff. The left hand stops tight to the body, between the waist and hips. The right arm should finish with a 150 degree bend in the elbow. The principle is that a firm grip is needed to strike. When chopping, lengthen the body slightly, press the head up, and tuck in the jaw. Send the power of the whole body forward into the chop. The whole body must be connected with no slackness in it. Coordinate the strike with an exhalation.

Hook down: The body should turn slightly in the direction of the hook down – whether to right or to left – so that the body leads the action of the hands. Turn the body to move the arms, and transfer from the hands to the staff. Keep the staff close to the body whenever moving it. Movement should be soft but without any slackness in the body.

- Be sure to slide the right hand along the shaft. Slide the hand down as you hook the staff down. The hook down is intended to knock aside the opponent's weapon with the fore-section of the staff – the right hand hooks down and the left hand pushes forward slightly. When the right hand is moving down it should slide forwards a bit to give more strength to the hooking action.

- Each hook down should draw a full circle to either side of the body. The initial action of circling down from the front is the actual 'hook down ', and this action should be gentle. The continuation – circling towards the rear – contains a drawing action, and a gathering of power for the chop. Circling upwards above the head is 'traveling ', and this should accelerate. The rest of the circle – down from above – is the chop. This is the final goal of the rest of the circle, and it should be fast and strong. The chop follows the principle of launching full power after the midpoint of the movement.

Turn around: The hands rotate during the turning lift. The left hand blocks up with the staff as the right hand pushes outwards. When wheeling the body around with the retreating step, turn the waist to gather power for the strong chop. Tuck in the abdomen, swing the arms, and press the head up.

BREATHING CYCLE FOR STAFF CHOP

In order to have whole body integrated power, in addition to moving the hands and feet together, making the body and weapon as one, sending power smoothly through to the focal point, and showing strong spirit, you need to coordinate your breathing with the movements. Only when the breath works exactly with the movements can you fully utilize your power.

- Inhale as you do the hook up or hook down.

- Exhale as you chop.

In general, breathe in during actions that are non forceful or gathering power, and breathe out during the forceful actions. Breathing out helps you to use *qi* to launch power, and you must settle the *qi* to the *dantian*.

PRACTICAL APPLICATIONS FOR STAFF CHOP

Hook up and chop: The hook up defends against a mid to high strike, and includes a slicing action. Use the fore-section of your staff to hook and scoop the mid-section of the opponent's long weapon – once it is knocked away you can enter with your chop. Use the hook to protect yourself so that you can get in with the chop. So the circle of the hook up should not be too large a movement, as that would slow you down and give the opponent an opportunity to get in. The action should be small, just knocking aside and entering, using your speed to your full advantage. Chop strongly to whatever you can reach – body or weapon. The key is to enter in as close as possible and to fully utilize the whole body power of Xingyi.

Hook down and chop: The hook down defends against a low stab down the midline. You hook down to knock away the opponent's weapon then quickly move in with a covering chop or reverse grip chop to his head. The hook down can draw back, or it can check away. When you do the hook down, contact the mid-section of the opponent's weapon with your fore-section – as soon as you make contact, stick to his weapon and draw it back. Then you can follow the line of action to chop.

- Your footwork must adjust to the situation. Whether you are hooking up or down you can enter or retreat. If the opponent comes in strongly you can retreat as you hook. But you must advance or step forward when you chop. Your feet, body, and staff must charge forward all at once. Chop to your opponent's head, body, arms or weapon.

- Chop can be used as a defensive action as well as the main attack. Used to defend, you can chop directly to the opponent's weapon. If you hit the tip of his weapon with full power he is likely to lose his grip. You can then follow up with a variety of techniques. Chop can either hit or break down, and can combine and alternate the two, taking care of attack and defense. It is a very practical technique that fully shows the flavour and character Xingyi staff.

THE POEM ABOUT STAFF CHOP

劈棍歌诀

劈棍气势要勇猛，
上挂前劈步要冲。
左右下挂侧身走，
劈械劈身紧连崩。

The staff chop must be fierce.

The footwork must charge in to do the hook up and chop forward.

Move in with the body turned to effectively hook down to left or right.

Chop to a weapon or a body, and follow up immediately with a poke.

2. STAFF DRILL

INTRODUCTION TO STAFF DRILL, *ZUAN GUN*

The definition of drilling fist in Xingyi is any punch that hits forward and upward. Staff drill is named from the drilling punch, so staff drill is a scoop that moves forward and up. The definition of a staff scoop in the wushu regulations is "with both hands holding the staff, either end of the staff is scooped forward and up from below. The action must be fast and the power must reach to the effective end." The scoop is a very practical technique. The staff drill combination uses both the tip and the butt to scoop. It is said that the staff has two heads, and the drill combination uses this characteristic fully.

Staff drill includes any technique that strikes forward and up with a slicing action, whether with the tip or butt, whether advancing or retreating, whether into an aligned stance or a reverse stance. All are within the range of staff drill.

The staff drill combinations include: *Left stance drill, right stance drill, aligned stance drill, reverse stance drill, advancing drill,* and *retreating drill.* The actions include *hook up and scoop, hook down and scoop,* and *hook up and scoop with the butt.*

METHOD ONE: HOOK DOWN AND SCOOP

2a Reverse Stance Drill   àobù zuāngùn   拗步钻棍

Start from *on guard. Right step forward, hook down to the right; Left step forward, sculling scoop.*

ACTION 1: Shift forward without moving the left foot. Take a step forward with the right foot. Slide the right hand forward along the shaft and hook the staff tip down past the right leg towards the rear. [First rotate the right palm away from the thumb, then hook with the arm rotated.] Hold the base with the left hand and raise it at the left front of the head. Turn to the right. Press the head forward and look at the staff tip. (image 4.20)

ACTION 2: Take a long step forward with the left foot and follow in the right foot a half-step to sit into a *santi* stance. Bring the right hand forward and up to do a sculling scoop with the staff tip. Rotate the right palm towards the thumb as the staff comes through so that it finishes with the palm up. Pull the base back with the left hand, pressing down at the left side, tight to the body. The staff tip is at head height. The right hand supports under the shaft with the elbow tucked in. Reach the right shoulder forward. Sit down into the stance. The left palm faces down. Press the head up and look past the staff tip. (image

4.21)

Pointers

- o   Complete the hooking down action as the right foot steps forward.
- o   Complete the sculling scoop forward and up as the left foot lands.
- o   The reverse stance drill is one continuous technique. Do not hesitate midway through the actions

• Continue on, repeating the actions.

METHOD TWO: HOOK UP SCULLING SCOOP

2b Right Aligned Stance Drill   yòu shùnbù zuāngùn 右顺步钻棍

Start from *on guard. Left advance, hook up; Right step forward, scoop.*

ACTION 1: Advance the left foot a half-step and follow in the right foot to the left ankle. Slide the right hand along the shaft and bring the staff tip up and then back. Raise the right arm above the head, then lower it behind the body. Turn to the right and reach the left shoulder forward. Push the staff base forward in front of the chest with the left hand. Look forward. (image 4.22)

ACTION 2: Take a long step forward with the right foot and follow in the left foot a half-step. Keep most weight on the left leg. Slide the left hand forward along the shaft and bring the base of the staff up and then hook back. Circle the right hand down at the right side to bring the staff tip forward and up, higher than the head. Rotate the right palm towards the thumb to turn the palm up as the staff scoops up. Tuck in the right elbow with the forearm under the staff. Pull the staff butt back to the left side, turning the left palm down. Turn the waist and reach the right shoulder forward. The staff is along the midline. Look past the staff tip. (image 4.23)

Pointers

- o   Complete the hook back as the left foot advances.

218 STAFF DRILL

- ○ Complete the sculling scoop as the right foot steps forward. The staff tip must finish the scoop as the right foot lands – upper and lower actions must work together.
- ○ Keep moving through the two actions; use the full movement to gain power.

2c Left Aligned Stance Scoop with the Butt

zuǒ shùnbù tiǎobà   左顺步挑把

Right advance, hook up; Left step forward, scoop with the butt.

ACTION 1: Advance the right foot a half-step and follow in the left foot to the right ankle. Pull the staff tip up and then back on the right side with the right hand, sliding it forward along the shaft to hook up. Continue on to lower the right hand to in front of the right shoulder. Slide the left hand along the shaft to about thirty to fifty centimetres from the butt and bring it to the left side. Look forward. (image 4.24)

ACTION 2: Take a long step forward with the left foot and follow in the right foot a half-step. Pull the staff down to the right waist with the right hand, putting it tight to the body. Scoop the staff butt up and forward to nose height with the left hand. Reach the left shoulder forward and bend the left arm under the staff, keeping the elbow tucked down. The left thumb/forefinger web is in front of the chest. Look past the staff butt. (image 4.25)

Pointers

- ○ Complete the hook up with the right hand as the right foot advances.
- ○ Complete the scoop up with the left hand as the left foot steps forward.
- ○ Three actions must be coordinated for the movement to work: scoop the left hand up, step the left foot forward, and pull the right hand back.
- ○ [Editor's note: make sure to slide the hands each time as you alternate left and right, so that the striking end sticks out.]

2d Right Aligned Stance Drill   yòu shùnbù zuāngùn   右顺步钻棍

Left advance, hook up with the butt; Right step forward, scoop.

ACTION 1: Advance the left foot a half-step and follow in the right foot to the left ankle. Hook the staff butt up and then back with the left hand, reaching the left shoulder forward. Keep the right hand at the right waist. Follow the movement of the staff butt with the eyes, then look forward. (image 4.26)

ACTION 2: This is the same as described above in 2b, action 2.

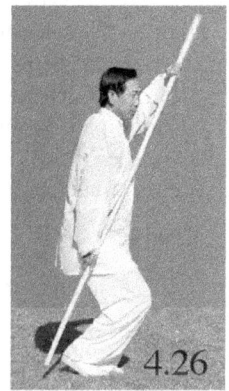

Pointers

- Complete the hook up with the butt as the left foot advances.
- Be sure to draw a full circle with the staff as it completes the hooking action.

• Repeat this combination as long as energy and space permit.

2e Drill Turn Around   zuāngùn zhuànshēn   钻棍转身

The drill combination uses the same turn around no matter which stance or footwork combination you are doing. You will always end up in a *reverse stance drill* after turning. You will hook-in the right foot and turn around leftward to turn, so the first step needs to adjust to accomplish this. If the <u>left</u> foot is in front then step the right foot forward, hooked in. If the <u>right</u> foot is in front, then hook-in on the spot.

Right hook-in step, hook down; Turn around, left step forward, sculling scoop.

ACTION 1: Hook the right foot in, and shift onto the right leg. Lift the left foot at the right ankle. Turn around 180 degrees to the left to face back in the opposite direction. Bring the right hand to the left, down, and then right so that the staff tip circles in a full hooking down action by the right thigh. The circle is full, but the tip should not hit the ground. Lift the staff base in front of the left shoulder to the left side of the head with the left hand. Look past the staff tip. (image 4.27)

ACTION 2: Take a long step forward with the left foot and follow in the right foot a half-step, keeping most weight on the right leg. Do a sculling scoop forward and up with the right hand controlling the staff tip, finishing

with the tip at head height. Pull the staff butt with the left hand back to the left side, turning the palm down and keeping it tight to the body. Rotate the right palm towards the thumb and tuck the forearm under the staff. Reach the right shoulder forward slightly. Press the head up. Follow the action of the staff with the eyes. (image 4.28)

Pointers

- Complete the hook up with the staff as the right foot does the hook-in step.
- Complete the scoop as the left foot steps forward. The points to consider and power are the same as the normal *reverse stance drill*.

2f   Drill Closing Move   zuāngùn shōushì   钻棍收势

The staff's action in the *closing move* is always the same, no matter which foot is forward. *Right retreat, raise the staff in both hands; Stand to attention with the staff.*

ACTION 1: If the right foot is forward it retreats behind the left foot. If the left foot is forward, the right foot retreats a half-step. Then the left foot withdraws to meet the right foot. Once the feet are together, stand to attention. Turn the body forty-five degrees to the right. Pull the staff to the right side with the right hand and raise it vertically above the head, almost fully extending the right arm. Push the left hand to under the right armpit to bring the staff base to the side. Look to the left. (image 4.29)

ACTION 2: Without moving the feet, lower the right hand to place the butt of the staff on the ground and stand it vertically at the right side of the body. Bring the left hand to hang at the left side. Press the head up and turn it to look straight forward. The closing is now complete. (image 4.30)

Pointers

- Points to consider are the same as the closing for *staff chop closing move*.

POWER GENERATION FOR STAFF DRILL

Opening: The first *right aligned stance drill*, coming from the ready stance, completes two upward hooks – one on the right side and one on the left. Both are completed while the left foot advances a half-step. When doing the hook up, the hands should slide along the shaft. This action should be quick but concealed. The mid-section of the shaft should always stay close to the body. The body action must use the principle of power loading during the drill – load back to go forward, load right to go left.

Reverse stance drill: The staff shaft must stay close to the right side of the body as it hooks back and down. The body must turn to the right as the right foot steps forward to accomplish this. The movement develops a smoothly flowing power by having one part move up as the other moves down, and one part move forward as the other moves backward. When the right hand hooks down the palm should rotate away from the thumb so that the palm faces back. The hand should also slide forward along the shaft. These actions increase the power of the hook down.

Sculling scoop: Transfer power from the waist to the shoulders – turn the waist and reach the shoulders into the movement. Lengthen the spine and sit into the buttocks to gain power from the body. Rotate the right palm towards the thumb and tuck the elbow in with the arm bent – in the usual drilling fist action. Add to this the pull back and press down of the left hand plus the driving forward from the rear leg, and the whole body has a power that charges forward. In this way the drill gains power from the whole body so that it hits strongly and cannot be defended against.

- The footwork for the staff drill must be quick, long, and fierce. The staff drill must have a focal point. The hands must slide to the appropriate places on the shaft. The hands must also rotate to apply power in the correct way. First practise slowly to get a feel for this, paying a lot of attention to the fine details.

Slicing up: The power must transfer from the waist to the shoulders, the shoulders to the hands, and the hands to the staff. The staff must stay tight to the body. The right hand should rotate palm towards thumb and the elbow should tuck in. The left hand should pull back and press down. The hands work together with their actions. At the instant of impact, sit down into the buttocks. Breathe out to connect the inner power with the outer actions, so that the body's power reaches to the fore-section of the staff.

- The hands must slide smoothly and quickly along the shaft. They slide as the staff is moving, as the steps are being taken, to get into the optimal position for the strike at the optimal time. Sliding the hands makes the technique work better and allows for better application of power.

- When the left hand does the scoop up with the butt, the elbow must stay snug to the ribs so that the staff stays close to the body.

PRACTICAL APPLICATIONS FOR STAFF DRILL

The drill is basically a scoop forward and up from below. The objective is to strike the opponent's weapon or body. If you are close enough, hit the body, if not, hit the weapon.

Left stance drill and *right stance drill*: These techniques both use a hooking back action before the strike, whether with the butt or the tip. First hook away a high strike from the opponent's weapon. If the right hand is forward then it hooks back on the right side. If the left hand is forward then it hooks back on the left side. When hooking back the hands must draw a full circle so that the staff makes contact with the opponent's weapon and then hooks it back. At this point you must step quickly forward and use the other end of the staff to do the slicing strike. The keys to the drill are daring to get in very close to the opponent and mastering the exact timing.

Reverse stance drill: This technique first hooks down then comes through with a sculling scoop up. The hook down defends against a low strike. Your staff tip just needs to touch the opponent's weapon to cause it to go off target. Then you stick to his weapon and follow the line of the shaft forward and up to strike his hand, arm, or body. The key lies in stepping in quickly and fearlessly with a strong technique.

> On the first touch, the defensive action of drill must create the circumstances that make it possible to get in with the other end of the staff. This applies to the positioning and the timing.
>
> If you have done a chop, then you can follow up with a scoop. Chop to the head then scoop to the groin so that your opponent has to defend high and low and may be thrown off. When he backs up you should follow up with a thrust to ensure victory. There are no fixed combinations, you need to adjust as opportunities present.

THE POEM ABOUT STAFF DRILL

钻棍歌诀
棍法挂挑谓之钻，
两臂拧旋腰催肩。
挂开敌械进身挑，
快步向前冲中间。

Drill with the staff is a hook and a scoop.
The arms twist and turn, and the body core sends the shoulder forward.
Hook away the enemy's weapon and enter to scoop,
Step in quickly to charge into his midline.

3. STAFF THRUST

INTRODUCTION TO STAFF THRUST, *BENG GUN*

The name 'thrust' comes from the five element fist techniques. Usually this staff technique is called 'poke'. In the wushu regulations, a poke is "to strike forward, back, or to the side in a straight line with the tip or the butt of the staff. Power is applied to the striking end." The main technique of the staff thrust is to forcefully poke straight forward with the tip or butt, and the thrust combination also includes an outer trap and a covering press down. In the martial world it is said that one would rather take a hit than a poke. A lot of power can be directed through the end of a staff due to its small surface area, so it can cause a lot of damage.

The thrust combinations include: *left stance thrust, right stance thrust, advance thrust,* and *retreat thrust*. Connecting moves include: *inner trap and press down, covering press down,* and *chop and pound*. There are also thrusts to front and back, left and right. The thrust combination is centered on the poke.

3a Right Stance Thrust   yòubù bēnggùn   右步崩棍

Start from *on guard. Left advance, inner trap to press; Right step forward, poke.*

ACTION 1: Advance the left foot a half-step and follow in the right foot to the left ankle. Circle the staff with the right hand so that the tip draws a full thirty centimetres circle in front of the body – down, right, and then up and left. Bend the right arm and draw it back a bit, tucking the elbow in towards the solar plexus, and pressing down on the staff. Keep the staff tight to the left side of the body with the left hand, also rotating. The staff tip finishes at chest height. Press the head up and look past the staff tip. (image 4.31)

ACTION 2: Take a long step forward with the right foot and follow in the left foot a half-step, keeping most weight back on the left leg. With the left hand, lift the staff base at the left ribs so that the shaft is horizontal, pointing straight forward. Poke the staff forcefully straight forward at chest height with both hands. Almost fully straighten the right arm, and keep the forearm tight to the shaft. Keep the left arm bent, the upper arm tight to the ribs, and the left hand in front of the chest. The striking surface is the tip of the staff. Press the head up and look past the staff tip. (image 4.32)

224 STAFF THRUST

Pointers

- Complete the inner trap as the left foot advances.
- Complete the poke as the right foot steps forward.

3b Left Stance Poke with the Butt   yòubù chuōbà   右步戳把

Right advance, cover and press with the butt; Left step forward, poke with the butt.

ACTION 1: Advance the right foot a half-step and follow in the left foot to the right ankle. Pull the staff butt back with the left hand, keep the right arm almost straight, sliding the shaft through the right hand. Then, gripping the staff, circle the right hand down then pull it back to the right armpit, palm up. Slide the shaft through the left hand, stopping at the middle, and circle the butt up, forward,  then down – to complete a covering press down. Reach the left shoulder forward. Turn the body ninety degrees to the right. The left palm is down, the thumb/forefinger web to the right, and the hand is pressing down in front of the left side of the chest. The right hand is behind the right ribs. The staff shaft is horizontal at chest height. Press the head up and look past the staff butt. (image 4.33)

ACTION 2: Take a long step forward with the left foot and follow in the right foot a half-step, keeping sixty percent of the weight on the right leg. Firmly grasp the staff with both hands and thrust forward with the staff butt at chest height. The left palm faces right and the right palm faces left. Almost fully extend the left arm and keep the right hand in front of the chest. The staff tip finishes on the right upper arm, under the shoulder. Press the head up and look past the staff butt. (image 4.34)

Pointers

o   Complete the covering press down as the right foot advances.
o   Complete the forward thrust as the left foot steps forward.

3c Right Stance Thrust   yòubù bēnggùn   右步崩棍

Left advance, hook with the butt, inner trap and press down; Right step forward, poke.

ACTION 1: Advance the left foot a half-step and follow in the right foot to the left ankle. Bring the staff butt down and hook back with the left hand, and as the hand arrives at the rear left, slide it back along the shaft. Bring the staff tip up, forward, then down with the right hand to do a pounding, covering press down. Turn the body to the left, tuck in the abdomen and contain the chest. Draw the right hand back slightly towards the chest. The right thumb/ forefinger web presses down on the staff, the right elbow tucks into the solar plexus. The left hand holds the staff base behind the left ribs. The staff shaft is horizontal at chest height. Follow the action of the left hand with the eyes as it hooks, then watch the right hand as it presses down. (image 4.35)

ACTION 2: This is the same as described above in movement 3a, action 2. (see image 4.32)

226 STAFF THRUST

Pointers

- Three actions are completed as one: advance the left foot, hook up the staff butt with the left hand, and pound / press down the staff tip forward with the right hand.
- The points to consider for *right stance poke* are the same as movement 3a.

3d Thrust Turn Around   bēnggùn huíshēn   崩棍回身

Starting from <u>*right*</u> *stance thrust: Left hook-in step, wheel around, hook down to the right; Right heel kick; Resting stance covering chop.*

ACTION 1: Hook-out the right foot on the spot and step the left foot forward, landing with it hooked in, in front of the right toes. Shift to the left leg and turn the body 180 degrees around to the right to face back behind. Scoop the staff tip up with the right hand, then, coming around with the body turn, hook forward and down to the right rear of the body. Lift the staff base up with the left hand, pushing forward slightly. Twist the waist a bit to the right. Look at the staff tip. (image 4.36)

ACTION 2: Stand firmly on the left leg and lift the right knee, then do a crossing heel kick forward and up to waist height. Look past the right foot. (image 4.37)

ACTION 3: Land the right foot forward, keeping it hooked out. Follow in the left foot a half-step, bend both legs, lift the left heel, and sit into a crossed leg stance (the dragon model stance). Bring the right hand forward and down to do a covering chop with the staff. Pull the left hand back to under the right armpit, so that the staff finishes horizontal at chest height. Press the head up and look past the staff tip. (image 4.38)

Pointers

- The turn around is one complete movement. Do not hesitate in the middle, but complete it in one go.
- Complete the scoop up with the staff tip as the right foot hooks out. Complete the hook down with the staff tip as the left foot hooks in and

CHAPTER FOUR: STAFF, *GUN* 227

the body turns around. Spread the lower back when doing the scoop up. Tuck in the abdomen when doing the hook down.
- o Kick as high as you can. Lift your leg to kick at the proper time and place – after the staff has hooked down to the right side.
- o You do not need to hit hard for the resting stance covering chop. Just do a coordinated movement and be sure that everything lands at once. Complete the chop as the right foot lands. Be sure to tuck in the abdomen and contain the chest.

3e Thrust Closing Move   bēnggùn shōushì   崩棍收势

Practise until you get back to your opening place, turn around, and then you may close. *Close the feet, raise the staff in both hands; Stand to attention with the staff.* From a <u>left</u> stance thrust:

ACTION 1: Retreat the right foot a half-step and shift back. Withdraw the left foot to beside the right foot, turn the body ninety degrees to the right, and stand up. Raise the staff in the right hand so that the tip points straight up. Slide the left hand along towards the base and push it out under the right ribs. Look to the left. (image 4.39)

ACTION 2: Lower the right hand so that the staff comes directly down to stand vertically at the right side, placing the butt on the ground. Release the left hand and let it hang at the left side. Look straight ahead. (image 4.40)

- From a <u>right</u> stance thrust, first retreat the right foot behind the left foot, then withdraw the left foot to beside the right. The rest of the actions are the same.

POWER GENERATION FOR STAFF THRUST

Right stance thrust: Prior to the poke, the inner trap combines two powers: pressing down and drawing back. The inner trap itself is a circular, coiling power that uses the movement of the body – tucking the abdomen and containing the chest – to press down. The right hand should slide forward along the shaft as you circle, and slide back towards the base as you draw back.

- *Poke with the tip*: The body and staff must move as one to poke forcefully forward. The step must go for distance and speed, as it is the step that takes the staff forward and gives distance to the strike. When poking, settle the shoulders down and close the elbows, so that the hands have a closing power between them. The actual strike is a 'one inch power' strike, and the footwork must have a charging power. Be very careful that the staff tip does not waver – it must poke straight forward. Gather all the power in your body and direct it to the tip of the staff.

Left stance poke with the butt: First slide the right hand forward along the shaft. The body must load in the opposite direction before striking, so that it leads the arms, which in turn move the staff, causing the staff to circle and hook down. The hands must work together – one pulls while the other pushes, one lifts while the other presses down – and this is accomplished by using the power from the body. The hands need to slide easily and comfortably along the shaft.

- When poking with the butt, there is only thirty to fifty centimetres of base sticking out, so you must use your footwork to the fullest. The footwork must charge forward for as much distance as possible. Adding a good step forward to the shaft of the staff give you about 1.5 meters. The key to a good thrust is in the charging footwork.

Turn around: The action of hooking with the butt with the left hand: The staff must first circle, drawn by the body, so the body must load in the opposite direction. As the hands do the trapping/ pressing down with the tip and covering/pressing down with the base, the waist must twist and the shoulders must reach. There is not just a pressing down power, but also a power drawing back. This gathers power for a strong thrust forward. Contain the chest and tuck in the abdomen, settling the body down slightly. Then, to thrust forward, lengthen the back and extend the arms. Always try to use the power of the body, not just the arms, to try to make the weapon one with the body.

PRACTICAL APPLICATIONS FOR STAFF THRUST

Poke: Poke is the main technique of the staff – the tip or the butt drives forward in a straight line. The small surface area applies a great deal of pressure. A well directed poke will always do considerable damage. The staff has two 'heads ', and the staff thrust uses both. To set up for the poke, a trapping action similar to that of the spear is used. The inner trap and the encoiling press down are the defensive actions that break the opponent's attack and control his weapon. Then you advance to get close, and poke directly forward to the chest or abdomen.

Inner trap, press down and poke: If the opponent stabs to your chest you use the right hand to do an inner trap and press down with the staff tip to take his weapon off target. Press down with the fore-section of your staff so that he has trouble pulling his weapon away or changing his attack. Then quickly move in and poke to his chest. The inner trap and press down must have a sticking, drawing power.

Encircle, press down and poke with the butt: If the opponent attacks your left side or turns and does a technique to the rear, you hook down or scoop up with tip. You need to slide your hands quickly on the shaft so that the right hand can hook or scoop with the tip. Then the left hand can pound and press down the butt, or scoop up to check away. Coordinate the defense with the footwork, either retreating or dodging. The poke, however, must be done with strong forward moving footwork, to direct the power strongly forward.

Staff thrust turn around: This is also called *leopard cat turns over whilst climbing a tree*. It is just a hook down, a kick, and a cover. If the opponent stabs towards you from behind, you step the left foot forward to get out of the way, hooking the foot in to get turned around. Use the staff tip to hook down, knocking his weapon away. If he is close, you can kick him, then immediately strike his head with the fore-section of the staff. Can you really use this technique? That depends on the situation – if everything is right then it would work, but this will rarely happen.

- The staff thrust is often linked with the chop. After you have chopped the staff is perfectly lined up for a thrust forward. This is a fierce and very practical attack.

THE POEM ABOUT STAFF THRUST

崩棍歌诀

崩棍技法是戳击，
戳时身械要合一。
拿压盖把侧身走，
对准心窝疾如急。

The technique of the thrust is to hit with a poke.

To poke, the body needs to unite with the weapon.

You must move in with the body sideways to trap, press down, or cover with the butt.

Aim accurately at the solar plexus and be quicker than quick.

4. STAFF SLASH

INTRODUCTION TO STAFF SLASH, *PAO GUN*

The staff slash is similar to the empty hand pounding punch – moving forward diagonally into a reverse stance as the staff blocks and slices up. There are a number of branch and regional variations, but they almost all hold the push, block up, slice and scull in common. The exact connecting movements and power use may differ. Each region performs according to their understanding as passed on from masters in their region, and all are correct for their style. Here I present two combinations that I think are the most practical, allow the smoothest power flow, and best show the flavour and characteristics of Xingyi.

STAFF SLASH

Slash combinations include *left slash, right slash,* and *slash turn around*. The first slash method includes *left advance entangling press down, step forward slicing block up and sculling slice with the butt, advance entangle and press down with the butt, step forward scoop to block up and sculling slice.* The second slash method includes *advance and change the grip, step forward and sculling slice.*

METHOD ONE: ALTERNATING ENDS

4a Right Stance Slash　　　　yòubù pàogùn　　　右步炮棍

Start from *on guard. Left advance entangling press down; Step forward, slicing block up and sculling slice with the butt.*

ACTION 1: Advance the left foot a half-step and follow in the right foot to the left ankle. Keep the legs together and squat slightly. Circle the staff tip with the right hand to the left, down, then right and up, then left to cover and press down. The tip draws a full counterclockwise circle. Slide the right hand forward along the shaft and press down with the thumb/forefinger web on top of the shaft. The staff is horizontal at waist height, and points diagonally to the forward right. Hold the base with the left hand and rotate it at the left waist. Press the head up and look past the staff tip. (image 4.41)

ACTION 2: Take a long step diagonally to the forward right with the right foot and follow in a half-step with the left foot, keeping most weight on the left leg. Slide the right hand forward along the shaft and slice up the staff tip. Keep the right arm bent, raised above the head at the right side, thumb/forefinger web back. Slide the left hand forward along the shaft to show more staff base. Push the left hand to the forward right so that the staff base does a sculling upward slice to the front and up. The butt stops at waist height so that the shaft completes a blocking up action in front of the body. Look past the staff butt. (image 4.42)

Pointers

o Complete the entangling press with the staff tip as the left foot

advances.
- o Complete the sculling slice with the staff butt as the right foot steps forward.
- o [Editor's note: the left hand pushes strongly, like punching.]
- o The two actions should be done without hesitation between them. Keep the body action soft, but with intended power, during the entangling press down. Launch power into the step forward sculling slice up. Take a long step forward and strike fiercely.

4b Left Stance Slash   zuǒbù pàogùn   左步炮棍

Start from *on guard. Right advance, entangle and press down with the butt; Left step forward, scoop to block up and sculling slice.*

ACTION 1: Advance the right foot a half-step and follow in the left foot to the right ankle. Squat down slightly, keeping the legs together. Controlling the staff with the right hand, bring it down to the right side of the ribs. With the left hand circle the staff base down, left, then up and right so that it entangles then presses down. The staff butt should draw a full clockwise circle and finish pointing to the forward left. Finish with the left elbow bent above shaft height, and the thumb/ forefinger web facing right. The staff shaft is level at waist height. Press the head up and look past the staff butt. (image 4.43)

ACTION 2: Take a long diagonal step to the forward left with the left foot and follow in the right foot a half-step, keeping most weight on the right leg. Slice up the staff base with the left hand, sliding the hand back to the butt and raising it up above and to the left of the head with the thumb/forefinger web down and the arm bent. Slide the right hand back on the shaft and do a sculling slice to the forward left with the staff tip.[14] The tip finishes at waist height. The

---

[14] Editor's note: be sure to move the shaft closely past the body, do not let it swing out.

STAFF SLASH

right arm is slightly bent, the palm facing forward, and the shoulder reaching forward. Look past the staff tip. (image 4.44)

Pointers

- Complete *entangle and press down* with the staff butt as the right foot advances.
- Complete both tip and butt actions as the left foot steps forward. The tip does a sculling slice up and the butt does a hooking back upper block.

• Continue on, repeating the actions to left and right as space permits.

METHOD TWO: CHANGING GRIP SLASH

4c Right Stance Slash   yòubù pàogùn   右步炮棍

Start from *on guard*. Continue with *Left advance, change the grip; Right step forward, scull and slice*.

ACTION 1: Advance the left foot a half-step and follow in the right foot to the left ankle. Loosen the grasp of the right hand and shoot the staff butt forward from the left hand, controlling it with the right hand. This makes the staff tip go forward and lift up above the head. When the tip arrives above the head, the right hand has slid along to the butt to grasp it. Slide the left hand up and back to the left along the shaft, controlling its action and finally grasping it as the tip arrives at the rear lower left. The right hand is now holding the butt in front of the left shoulder while the staff tip is about ten centimetres from the ground behind the body at the left side. Twist the body left. Follow the action of the staff tip with the eyes then look forward. (image 4.45)

ACTION 2: Take a long step diagonally to the forward right with the right foot and follow in the left foot a half-step, keeping most weight on the left leg. Grasp the staff butt in the right hand and bring it from the left side to lift and pull forward and up on the right side to above the head. Keep the arm slightly bent. Push the shaft forward with the left hand,

palm up, finishing with the staff tip at waist height. Reach the left shoulder forward. Press the head up and look past the staff tip. (image 4.46)

Pointers

- Change the hand grip as the left foot advances. The changeover is a smooth, gentle action and must be well coordinated. Pay attention to controlling the staff tip's line of action and the direction in which it points.
- Complete the sculling slice up as the right foot steps forward.
- [Editor's note: this is more a slice than a push, note that the left hand is palm up.]
- The two actions must be done as one, with no hesitation between them.

4d Left Stance Slash zuǒbù pàogùn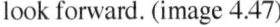

Right advance, slice and change the grip; Left step forward, sculling slice.

ACTION 1: Advance the right foot a half-step and follow in the left foot to the right ankle. Swing the staff tip to the forward left with the left hand, sliding the shaft through it. Push the staff base forward with the right hand so that the staff tip goes forward and up. When the staff tip arrives above the head, slide the left hand down the shaft to the base and slide the right hand up the shaft. Lower the right hand to the rear right to behind the body on the right side. Hold the staff base with the left hand in front of the right shoulder. The staff tip is about ten centimetres from the ground. Turn the body a bit to the right. Follow the action of the staff tip with the eyes, then look forward. (image 4.47)

ACTION 2: Take a long step diagonally to the forward left with the left foot and follow in a half-step with the right foot, keeping most weight on the left leg. Grip the staff base with the left hand and lift and pull it to above the head at the forward left. The arm is slightly bent to brace out. Push the staff shaft forcefully to the forward left with the right hand. The palm faces

forward at chest height. The combined actions make the staff tip do a sculling slice up forward to waist height. Reach the right shoulder forward. Press the head up and look past the staff tip. (image 4.48)

Pointers

- o Points to consider are the same as 4b, *left stance slash*.

- Continue on, alternating *right* and *left stance slash*.

4e Slash Turn Around for Method One   pàogùn huíshēn   炮棍回身

From the *left* stance slash. Left hook-in step, turn around, entangling press down; Right step forward, sculling slice.

ACTION 1: Hook-in the left foot in front of the right toes and shift to the left leg. Lift the right foot and turn around 270 degrees to the right. With the right hand, swing the staff tip around to the right as the body turns, and, after turning, draw a counterclockwise circle then press down. Lower the left hand to the left waist. The staff tip is at waist height. Look past the staff tip. (image 4.49)

ACTION 2: Continue on with *right stance slash*.

- From the *right* stance slash, hook-in the right foot in front of the left toes and do the encircling press down with the left hand. Then continue on with *left stance slash*.

Slash Turn Around for Method Two

From the *left* stance slash. Left hook-in step, turn around, change the grip; Right step forward, sculling slice.

ACTION 1: The footwork is the same as described above, just slide the hands to change the grip as usual for method two.

Pointers

- o The hook-in needs to be well placed and well turned so that the body can turn around quickly.
- o Press the head up and keep the body upright – don't look down, as this tends to make the body lean over.
- o Don't hesitate between the turn around and the following slash.
- o [Editor's note: Keep the shaft on the body as you turn and press down.

Step, bring the shaft to the body and turn, then circle and press.]

4f   Slash Closing Move   pàogùn shōushì   炮棍收势

If the <u>left</u> foot is forward, then withdraw the right foot further back. If the <u>right</u> foot is forward then retreat it behind the left foot. Then bring the left foot back to beside the right foot. The rest is the same as described in 1h, *staff chop closing move*: *raise the staff in both hands, stand at attention with the staff.*

POWER GENERATION FOR STAFF SLASH

FIRST METHOD

Use the power of the torso and waist to draw the counterclockwise circle of the encircling press down, so that the power transfers from the lower back to the arms, and the hands work in opposite directions. The fore-section of the staff should have coiling plus drawing actions. When encircling and coiling, reach the staff forward slightly. While the right hand draws a large circle in the front, the left hand draws a small circle in the rear. When pressing down and drawing, compress the body and draw back slightly. Tuck in the abdomen, contain the chest, and use the whole body as a unit.

The clockwise circle of the staff butt during the coiling press down should stay between shoulder and waist heights. Transfer power from the lower back to the shoulders, from the shoulders to the arms, and from the arms to the staff. Do not simply use the forearms. Keep the staff shaft snug to the body so that the body and staff move as one. The left hand draws a large circle in the front while the right hand draws a small circle behind.

SECOND METHOD

The hands must changeover quickly and smoothly. First slice up the staff base, then hook it back, and then change the hands. The right hand slices the staff tip up and then hooks it back. The hand change must be smooth and slide along the shaft easily, keeping it under control even during the switchover. Everything must be smooth – the body action, the power transfer, and the movement of the staff.

Left and right slash: Turn the waist and reach the leading shoulder forward, tucking in the leading elbow. The leading arm must strike with a focal point. The upper arm of the leading arm must stay close to the ribs with the elbow tucked in to push the staff with a quick, powerful, and focused sculling slice. The rear hand must brace out above the head. When launching power, lengthen the back and reach the shoulder forward to send power out to the fore-section of the staff. Exhale to assist the power launch and to put the power of the whole body into the strike.

> The power of the staff slash comes from the feet, centers in the lower back/waist, is expressed through the shoulders, and applies through the arms to reach the staff shaft. As the staff

tip comes through from the rear that is the *scull*. As it comes up from below that is the *slice up*. The leading hand has a lifting, pulling, bracing power. The rear hand has a pushing, sculling, slicing power. You have to practise over and over to get a feel for the power. Start out slowly to find the power, then gradually add speed and strength.

PRACTICAL APPLICATIONS FOR STAFF SLASH

Encircle and press down: The encircling press down uses the tip or the base of the staff to wrap around and press down the opponent's weapon. The action circles inward and sticks to the opponent's weapon to prevent him from withdrawing it.

Scoop up and hook back: This is one action with two phases. The scoop works forward and up, while the hook works to the rear. Scoop to knock the opponent's weapon forward and up. Then hook to control it, pulling it back.

Sculling slice up: Whichever end of the staff is below slices forward and up, and this is the main attack of the staff slash technique. The target is the leading hand, arm, leg or knee of the opponent. Or, if you can get in close, his groin.

> One important characteristic of the staff is that it has two 'heads' – you put either the tip or the butt to good use.

- It is interesting to analyse the application of a technique by looking at its structure and movement. But to actually use the weapon is another thing. You must be able to react to the actual situation and do what is necessary; nothing works 'by the book'. It is of utmost importance that you develop and train courage, the winning instinct, and your tactical sense.

THE POEM ABOUT STAFF SLASH

炮棍歌诀

左右擂撩是炮棍，
绞压挑架不停顿。
技法劲力腰肩找，
前冲后蹬脚下问。

The staff slash is a sculling slice up to either side.
Entangle and press down, slice up and block up without hesitation.
Look for the technique and power in the waist and shoulders.
Look to the feet to charge forward, pushing off strongly.

5. STAFF CROSSCUT

INTRODUCTION TO STAFF CROSSCUT, *HENG GUN*

Xingyi staff crosscut has its own unique characteristics and flavour, sharing characteristics with, but yet not quite the same as other staff techniques. Staff crosscut is basically a horizontal crossing strike to either side. This is classified as a sideways strike in staff terminology. The wushu regulations defines a sideways strike as "the tip or the butt of the staff strikes sideways, to either right or left, hitting with the striking end. " But the Xingyi crosscut is not performed exactly the same as a normal sideways strike. The striking surface of a sideways strike is the end of the staff, while that of the Xingyi crosscut is the entire fore-section. The crosscut also holds similarities with a horizontal swing. The definition of a horizontal swing is, "the tip is swung in a half circle to either side at a height above the chest and is then accelerated, and strikes with the fore-section. " But the horizontal swing is usually done with both hands holding the butt and swinging the staff for a full circle or more. The Xingyi crosscut holds the staff with the hands separated as usual on the shaft and completes only one circle to strike. It also holds similarities and differences to the flat action of a brandish. Brandish usually goes fully over the head, while the crosscut does not.

The crosscut combination includes *right stance crosscut, left stance crosscut, crosscut turn around,* and *closing move.*

5a Right Stance Crosscut   yòubù hénggùn   右步横棍

Start from *on guard. Left advance, checking brandish to the right; Right step forward right crosscut.*

ACTION 1: Advance the left foot a half-step and follow in the right foot to the left ankle. Move the staff with the right hand to check to the right with the fore-section, continuing on to circle to the rear, then circle above the head to arrive in front of the left shoulder. The right forearm finishes on top of the shaft with the right palm turned to face forward. Hold the base in the left hand and draw a small circle in front of the body, assisting the right hand by moving in the opposite direction. The left hand finishes under the right armpit with the palm turned up. Turn the body to the left and look at the staff tip. (image 4.50)

4.50

ACTION 2: Take a long step to the forward right with the right foot and follow in a half-step with the left foot, staying back on the left leg in a *santi* stance. Swing the staff to the right with the right hand, so that the tip passes horizontally in front of the body from the left to the right, stopping at a forty-five degree angle at the front right. Rotate the right palm to face right. Keep the left hand at the right armpit to keep the staff base snug to the right ribs. The staff tip is just above shoulder height. Press the head up, tuck the jaw in, and look past the staff tip.[15] (image 4.51)

Pointers

- Coordinate the swinging of the staff as the left foot advances. Complete the sideways strike as the right foot hands. Complete the two actions without a pause midway.

5b Left Stance Crosscut zuǒbù hénggùn 左步横棍

Right advance, check to the left; Left step forward crosscut.

ACTION 1: Advance the right foot a half-step and follow in the left foot to the right ankle. With the right hand, check with the staff to the left, then continue on, so that the staff tip circles forward, left, back, and over the head to the right side, in front of the right shoulder. Extend the right arm and rotate the palm towards the thumb so that the palm faces forward. Hold the staff base in the left hand and draw a small circle in front of the body in the opposite direction to coordinate with the action of the right hand. Bring the left hand to in front of the shoulders, rotating the palm away from the thumb to turn the palm down. Watch the staff tip as it starts to circle, then look forward once the tip is behind the head. (image 4.52)

---

[15] Editor's note: Get the left hand in to the body soon, to bring the staff tight to the body before the strike. The staff does not slap or hit the body.

ACTION 2: Take a long step to the forward left with the left foot and follow in the right foot a half-step, keeping the weight mostly back on the right leg. Swing the staff with both hands so that the tip comes across in front of the body from the right to the left in a horizontal strike. Hold the base in the left hand and pull it in to in front of the left shoulder, tucking the elbow down. Bend the right arm slightly and stop it at the forward left. Both palms face left. The staff tip is just higher than the shoulders. Turn the waist to the left and reach the right shoulder forward. Press the head up, tuck the jaw in, and look past the staff tip. (image 4.53)

Pointers

- Be sure to pull the left hand into place.
- Swing the staff as the right foot advances. Strike as the left foot lands.

5c Crosscut Turn Around   hénggùn huíshēn   横棍回身

Starting from a *left stance crosscut*. *Left hook-in turn around, checking brandish; Right step forward crosscut.*

ACTION 1: Hook-in the left foot towards the right toes and shift onto the left leg, lifting the right foot to the left ankle. Turn around to the right to face back. Bring the staff tip around with the right hand, following the turning of the body to check to the right. Then continue to circle the staff so that it goes right, back, around over the head, and out to the left to in front of the left shoulder. Rotate the right palm away from the thumb. Tuck the left hand in to the right armpit with the palm up. Look at the staff tip. (image 4.54)

ACTION 2: Complete the right crosscut, described in movement 5a.

- If turning from *right stance crosscut*, hook-in the right foot, turn around, and move into a *left stance crosscut*. The only difference in the actions is the direction of the turn.

Pointers

- Points to consider in the staff's actions during the turn around are the same as for the advancing crosscut. You just need to pay attention to getting a good hook-in step and turning around quickly.

5d Crosscut Closing Move   hénggùn shōushì   横棍收势

The closing move is always the same. Turn around when you arrive back where you started. If you are in a *left stance crosscut,* retreat the right foot a half-step and bring the left foot in. If you are in a *right stance crosscut,* retreat the right foot to behind the left foot, then bring the left foot to beside it. Then raise the staff and stand to attention as described in movement 1h, *staff chop closing move.*

POWER GENERATION FOR STAFF CROSSCUT

Checking brandish: First check to the side, then brandish over the head. Use the power of the body to check. Circle the hands in opposite directions to brandish. As the right hand does a large circle, the left hand does a small circle in the opposite direction. Turn the body to move the arms, which in turn move the staff. Remember the principle of counter movements to gather and release power – pre-load left to go right, pre-load right to go left.

Crosscut: The crossing strike must have a focal point. Use the strength of the waist turn to strike with the fore-section of the staff. Gradually accelerate during the brandish. The staff tip should move fast enough to whoosh, and stop sharply enough to vibrate.

> You must first gather power then launch. Gather gradually and launch immediately. Follow the principle of 'go past the midpoint, firm up the grip and launch power ' when doing the checking brandish. This means that you wait to accelerate until you get just past the midpoint of the circle. During the first half of the circle you need to gather power to prepare for the acceleration in the latter half. Gather power within the body – this is very important. If you do not do a preparatory gathering in the first half of the circle, then 'launch power at the midpoint ' is just idle talk. Also remember to firm up the grip before launching power – you can't strike anything with a loose hold on your weapon.
>
> All Xingyi staff techniques emphasize using the body and weapon moving as one, so the primary power comes from the lower back and torso. For the crosscut, you need to add a twist in the waist and a sit into the hip so that there is a pulling back and settling power in addition to the power striking directly to the side.

- You may adjust the placement of the right hand during the crosscut – slide forward and backward slightly along the shaft. The left hand may allow about fifteen centimetres of the base to show or may hold at the very end. Minor adjustments allow the staff to move more freely and smoothly, making the power application stronger.

PRACTICAL APPLICATIONS FOR STAFF CROSSCUT

Crosscut: Crosscut is a swinging strike across to the side, the main target being the opponent's head. The most effective target is the head, but anywhere on the torso is also effective. A strong crosscut can also break the opponent's weapon or knock it out of his hands. This sets you up for a following attack.

Right stance crosscut: If the opponent does a high stab towards your midline you check your staff tip across to the right with your right hand to knock his weapon offline. Then you quickly move in along the line and do a crossing strike to the right with the fore-section of your staff striking his head.

Left stance crosscut: If the opponent does a high stab towards your midline you check your staff tip across to the left with your right hand to knock his weapon offline. Then you use the leftward momentum to swing the staff around and do a crossing strike to his head, arm, body, or whatever you can get.

- When you check to the right or left you may step forward or back, whatever is necessary. When you strike you should step forward. Of course, though, you have to do whatever works for the situation.

- During practice you should swing the staff in a large circle to get a feel for the power, add to the momentum, and develop whole body power. When using the technique, though, the action should be small. The classics say that a large movement is never as effective as a small movement. The smaller the amplitude, the fiercer the technique, and the faster. Speed is the way to control and beat the opponent. As the classics say, "you can defend against everything but speed."

THE POEM ABOUT STAFF CROSSCUT

横棍歌诀

横棍劲力气势雄，
左右云拨任意行。
过中固把身发劲，
上步横棍似旋风。

The staff crosscut is fierce.

Brandish to right and left to go where you will.

Wait until the halfway point, then firm up your grip and shoot power from the body.

Step forward and swing the staff like a tornado

6. FIVE ELEMENTS LINKED STAFF FORM

INTRODUCTION TO THE FIVE ELEMENTS LINKED STAFF, *WUXING LIANHUAN GUN*

The Five Elements Linked Staff form is a widespread and popular form. It uses the pattern, movements, and characteristics of the five element fist form, but with the staff techniques. The form is short and sweet – once up and back – with postures that flow smoothly from one to the other. The techniques are simple and practical, the power is full, and the spirit is fierce. The main techniques are chop, drill, and crosscut, with the supplementary techniques of hook, scoop, block, check, and swing. The structure and performance style of this form shows very clearly the characteristics and flavour of Xingyi staff.

The rhythm of the form is as follows: The opening move is slow and steady. Moves two, three, and four hit strongly, linking together with smooth footwork. Be careful to make the footwork – both advance and retreat – clear. The fifth move emphasizes body technique, and should start gently and finish strongly. Use body technique to gently set it up, then finish with a power launch. Moves six, seven, eight and nine should connect together without hesitation. This combination should be fast and fierce, like 'chasing the wind and the moon without relief'. The moves all advance – charging forward as if nothing could stop them. The tenth move, the turn around, should be stable and firm. The landing should go to a low stance, and should not be rushed. The spirit and focus must remain full and connected throughout the closing movement.

NAMES OF THE MOVEMENTS

1. Opening Move (On guard)
2. Chop: Hook up and Chop
3. Chop: Hook down and Covering Chop
4. Chop: Hook down and Reverse Grip Chop
5. White Crane Flashes its Wings: Close the feet and Block
6. Crosscut: Right stance Crosscut
7. Crosscut: Left stance Crosscut
8. Drill: Reverse stance Drill
9. Chop: Hook up and Chop
10. Leopard Cat Turns Over Whilst Climbing a Tree: Turn Around with a Hook down, Heel Kick, and Resting stance Chop

(The following moves are a repetition, coming back in the returning direction.)

11. Chop
12. Chop
13. Chop
14. White Crane Flashes its Wings
15. Crosscut

CHAPTER FOUR: STAFF, *GUN*   243

16. Crosscut
17. Drill
18. Chop
19. Leopard Cat Turns Over Whilst Climbing a Tree

(The following moves are the closing combination)

20. Chop
21. Closing Move

Description of the Movements

1. Opening Move   qǐ shì   起势

Stand with the staff; Raise the staff in both hands; Left advance and chop.

ACTION 1: Stand with the feet together and the legs straight, facing in a forty-five degree angle to the line of the form. Stand the staff vertically with the butt on the ground at the right side of the body. Hold the staff midsection in the right hand with the thumb/forefinger web up as the arm hangs naturally straight. Let the left arm hang straight at the left side. Press the head up and look forward. (image 4.55)

ACTION 2: Raise the staff straight up with the right hand. Bring the left hand to the right armpit and grasp the staff about ten centimetres from the base. Turn the head left and look to the forward left. (image 4.56)

ACTION 3: Step the left foot to the forward left and turn a bit to the left, sitting into a *santi* stance. Chop forward and down by pulling the left hand back tight to the body between the left waist and hip, and extending the right arm forward. Keep the right arm slightly bent and tuck in the elbow, the right hand at chest height. The staff tip is at shoulder height. Press the head up and look past the staff. (image 4.57)

Pointers

- Turn the head left as you raise the staff.
- Complete the chop as the left foot lands.

2. Chop: Hook Up and Chop   pīgùn   劈棍

Right step forward, hook up; Left step forward and chop.

ACTION 1: Take a long step forward with the right foot and land firmly with the knee bent. Follow in the left foot to the right ankle. Controlling the staff with the right hand, bring the staff tip down to waist height, then bend the elbow and lift the hand back to above the right shoulder to hook up with the staff. Push the staff base forward with the left hand, the hand finishing at waist height. Tuck in the abdomen and contain the chest. Bring the right shoulder back. Look forward. (image 4.58)

ACTION 2: Take a long step forward with the left foot and follow in a half-step with the right foot, settling into a *santi* stance. Controlling the staff with the right hand, chop the staff tip forcefully down the midline to chest height. Pull the left hand back tight to the body between waist and hip crease height. Reach the right shoulder forward, keep the arm bent and the elbow tucked in, and press the thumb/ forefinger web down on the staff. Press the head up and look past the staff tip. (image 4.59)

Pointers

- Unite the hook up with the chop down, using the hook up to prepare for the chop down without any hesitation. Take long steps and follow in quickly.
- Complete the hook up with the staff as the right foot steps forward. Complete the chop down as the left foot steps forward. The staff must arrive at the same time as the feet so that upper and lower work together.

CHAPTER FOUR: STAFF, *GUN* 245

3. Chop: Hook Down and Covering Chop   pīgùn   劈棍

Left advance, hook down to the right; Right step forward, covering chop.

ACTION 1: Advance the left foot a half-step and follow in the right foot to the left ankle. Lift the staff base with the left hand, pushing it forward in front of the left shoulder. Pull the right hand back to hook down and back on the right side with the staff tip, then continue to swing it upwards. Turn the body to the right. Follow the staff tip with the eyes. (image 4.60)

ACTION 2: Take a long step forward with the right foot and follow in the left foot a half-step. Pull the left hand down to the right armpit with the palm up underneath the staff, so that the staff base is snug to the right ribs. With the right hand, bring the staff tip forward and down with a covering chop. The right arm in on top of the staff, palm down. The staff shaft is horizontal, the tip just below shoulder height. Press the head up and look forward. (image 4.61)

Pointers

- Complete the hook down as the left foot advances.
- Complete the covering chop as the right foot steps forward.

4. Chop: Hook Down and Reverse Chop   pīgùn   劈棍

Left retreat, hook down to the left; Right advance, reverse grip chop.

ACTION 1: Retreat the left foot a half-step and withdraw the right foot to just in front of the left foot. Circle the staff tip with the right hand down, back, and then up on the left side of the body. Turn the body to the left. Help the action with the left hand, keeping it at the right armpit. Follow the action of the staff tip with the eyes, turning the head to look back on the left side. (image 4.62)

STAFF CROSSCUT

ACTION 2: Advance the right foot a long step and follow in the left foot a half-step, keeping most weight back on the left leg. Circle the staff tip with the right hand up on the left side, then forward and down. The right hand finishes in a reverse grip, forearm under the staff with the palm up. The staff tip finishes at shoulder height. Hold the staff base in the left hand and pull it back to the left side, between hip and waist height. Focus power to

the fore-section of the shaft. press the head up and look past the staff tip. (image 4.63)

Pointers

- Complete the hook down to the left as the feet retreat and withdraw.
- Complete the covering chop as the right foot advances.
- Complete both actions as one, without a break in between. Lead the body with the staff during the hook down, then lead the staff with the body during the chop.

5. **White Crane Flashes its Wings: Stand and Block**

   báihé liàngchì　　　　　　　　　　白鹤亮翅

Left retreat, entangle; Feet together, block to the left.

ACTION 1: Shift forward to the right leg and retreat the left foot a half-step. Circle the staff tip with the right hand – up, left, and then down – drawing a circle of forty centimetres diameter. Keep the left hand in front of the abdomen and help with the encircling action. Look past the staff tip. (image 4.64)

ACTION 2: Shift back to the left leg and withdraw the right foot to beside the left foot, settling it on the ground with a thump. Both legs are bent. Rotate the right palm towards the thumb and block to the left side in front of the body with the staff tip. The right hand finishes about twenty centimetres in front of the left chest. Pull the staff base back with the left hand, placing it snugly on the left side. Turn the body left so that the right shoulder is directly forward. Look to the forward right. (image 4.65 and from behind)

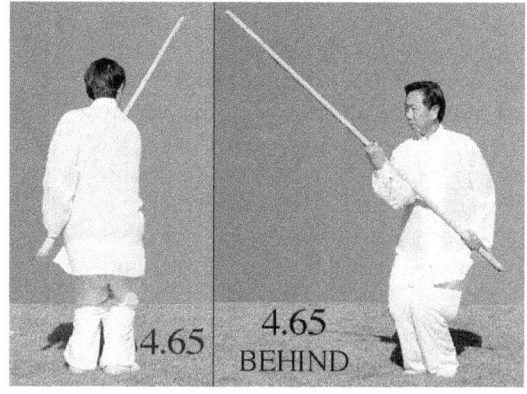

Pointers

- Complete the encircling action as the left foot retreats. Use the power of the body and waist, and keep the movement gentle.
- The right foot should stomp with a sound when it withdraws, but it should not lift and stamp. Complete the block with both hands as the foot lands. The power launch should be fierce and the block should have a focal point.

6. Crosscut: Right Stance Crosscut   hénggùn   横棍

Right checking brandish; Right step forward crossing cut.

ACTION 1: Shift onto the left leg without moving the feet. Swing the right hand to the right and turn the body right so that the staff tip moves forward then checks to the right. Do not stop at all, but continue to circle the staff back up over the head to brandish in a complete circle over to the left side. the right hand is in front of the left shoulder, palm rotated away from the thumb. Hold the staff base in the left hand and draw a smaller circle in the opposite direction in front of the body, bringing the base finally in to under the right armpit with the palm up under the shaft. Turn the body to the left. Look to the forward right. (image 4.66)

ACTION 2: Take a long step to the forward right with the right foot and follow in a half-step with the left foot, keeping most weight on the left leg. Swing the staff forcefully to the right with the right hand so that the tip strikes with a

crossing hit to the forward right, stopping at a forty-five degree angle to the right front. Rotate the right palm away from the thumb to turn the palm to the right. Keep the left hand under the right armpit to keep the staff base snug to the right ribs. The staff tip is at shoulder height. Press the head up, tuck the jaw in, and look past the staff tip. (image 4.67)

Pointers

- The staff draws a conical shape during the check, and then cuts across horizontally for the crossing strike. Gather power in the body during the check to pre-load for the strike in the opposite direction.
- Complete the crosscut as the right foot advances. Exhale to assist in getting power. Unite the staff and body as one, and send power to the staff tip.

7. **Crosscut: Left Stance Crosscut**   hénggùn   横棍

Right advance, left checking brandish; Left step forward crossing cut.

ACTION 1: Advance the right foot a half-step and follow in the left foot to the right ankle. Check the staff to the left with the right hand so that the staff tip moves across to the left in front of the body, and then circles back and around over the head. The right hand finishes palm up in front of the right shoulder with the arm extended. With the left hand, draw a smaller circle in the opposite direction with the staff base. Finish with the left hand in front of the right shoulder, the palm rotated away from the thumb with the palm down. Press the head up and look forward. (image 4.68)

ACTION 2: Take a long step to the forward left with the left foot and follow in the right foot a half-step, keeping most weight back on the right leg. Swing the staff with both hands so that the tip comes across the front to the left to strike sideways. Bend the right arm slightly and stop it at the forward left. The staff tip is at shoulder height. Hold the staff base in the left hand with the arm bent, pulling to in front of the left shoulder, elbow tucked down and back, palm facing left. Turn the body to the left and reach the right shoulder forward. Press the head up, tuck the jaw in, and look past the staff tip. (image 4.69)

Pointers

- Check the staff to the left as the right foot advances.
- Complete the swinging crosscut to the left as the left foot steps forward. Use both hands to strike, turn the waist and put the shoulders into the action. Hit with whole body power, uniting the staff and body as one.

8. **Drill: Reverse Stance Drill**   zuāngùn   钻棍

Right step forward, hook down; Left step forward, sculling scoop.

ACTION 1: Shift forward onto the left leg without moving the foot. Step the right foot forward. Slide the right hand a bit forward along the shaft and rotate the palm away from the thumb, taking the staff tip down outside the right leg to hook back to the rear right. Twist the body to the right. Lift the staff base up in front of the left shoulder with the left hand. Look at the staff tip. (image 4.70)

ACTION 2: Take a long step forward with the left foot and follow in the right foot a half-step, keeping most weight back on the right leg. Rotate the right palm towards the thumb so that the palm faces forward, and scull the staff tip forward then scoop up to nose height. The forearm is under the shaft, palm facing up. Lift the left hand then press it down beside the left side. Tuck the left elbow in close to the ribs. Straighten the back, settle the shoulders, and press the head up. Look forward. (image 4.71)

250   STAFF CROSSCUT

Pointers

- Hook the staff back as the right foot steps across to balance the action – forward and up with backward and down.
- Scoop the staff up as the left foot steps forward. Be sure to slide the right hand along the shaft and to rotate it palm towards thumb. You must first lift the left hand and then press down. These hand actions must coordinate to put power into the staff.

9.   Chop: Hook Up and Chop   pīgùn   劈棍

Right step forward, hook up; Left step forward, chop.

ACTION 1: Shift forward and step the right foot forward. Pull the right hand back to in front of the right shoulder so that the staff tip hooks up and back. Push the staff base forward with the left hand to waist height. Bring the right shoulder back. Look forward. (image 4.72)

ACTION 2: Take a long step forward with the left foot and follow in a half-step with the right foot. Extend the right arm forcefully straight forward to chop down with the staff, the tip at chest height. Pull the left hand back snug to the body between waist and hip height. Reach the right shoulder forward. Almost fully extend the right arm, but tuck the elbow in. Press the head up and look past the staff tip. (image 4.73)

Pointers

- All the points to consider are the same as movement 2.

10. Leopard Cat Turns Over Whilst Climbing a Tree: Turn Around, Hook Down, Heel Kick, Resting Stance Covering Chop   huíshēn 回身

Turn around hooking down; Right heel kick; Resting stance, covering chop.

ACTION 1: Hook-in the left foot to the outside of the right toes. Shift onto the left leg and turn the body around 180 degrees to the right to face back along the line of the form Pivot the right foot to face straight as well. Scoop up the staff tip with the right hand and bring it around as the body turns. Then hook down and back at the right side. Lift the staff butt with the left hand above the left shoulder. Twist the body around to the right. Follow the staff tip with the eyes then look forward. (image 4.74)

ACTION 2: Stand firmly on the left leg, lift the right knee, and kick forward and up with the foot turned out at chest height. Look past the kick. (image 4.75)

ACTION 3: Land the right foot forward, still turned out. Follow in the left foot and lift the heel to squat down into a resting stance – Xingyi's dragon stance. Continue to circle the staff with the right hand, bringing the tip up behind, then forward and down in a covering chop. Pull the left hand in to the right armpit, palm up, to settle the staff base at the right ribs. The staff is near horizontal with the tip at chest height. Press the head up and look forward. (image 4.76)

Pointers

- Hook-in the foot considerably so that the turn around is easily done.
- Time the kick so that the staff first hooks smoothly down outside the right leg.
- Complete the drop into resting stance and the staff chop together.
- Complete all three actions as one without hesitation between them.

252 STAFF CROSSCUT

- The following moves, 11 through 19, are a repetition of the first section, moves 2 through 10, going back in the returning direction.

11. **Chop**   See move 2.
12. **Covering Chop**   see move 3.
13. **Reverse Grip Chop** see move 4.
    (image 4.77)

14. **White Crane Flashes its Wings**

    See move 5. (image 4.78)

15. **Right Stance Crosscut**

    See move 6. (image 4.79)

16. **Left Stance Crosscut**   see move 7.

CHAPTER FOUR: STAFF, *GUN*   253

17. Drill

See move 8. (image 4.80)

18. Chop   see move 9.

19. Leopard Cat Turns Over Whilst Climbing a Tree see move 10.

20. Chop

This is the e same as move 2. This is now going in the original direction.

21. Closing Move   shōu shì   收势

Starting from *thrust. Right retreat, raise the staff in both hands; Stand to attention with the staff.*

ACTION 1: Retreat the right foot a half-step and withdraw the left foot to beside the right foot. Turn the body forty-five degrees and stand up straight. Pull the staff back to the right side, then raise the staff in the right hand straight up at the right side. Push the base of the staff with the left hand under the right armpit so that the staff is vertical. Press the head up and look to the left side. (image 4.81)

ACTION 2: Release the left hand and bring it to the left side. Lower the right hand, still holding the staff, to place the staff vertically on the ground at the right side. Turn the head to look straight forward. (image 4.82)

Pointers

- o   Straighten the back when holding the staff up, and show good spirit. Do not slack off when almost done. Keep focus and concentration to the very end of the form.

CHAPTER FIVE

TEACHING AND TRAINING SUGGESTIONS FOR WEAPONS

Teaching Suggestions For Weapons[16]

POST STANDING

Students must do post standing on both sides of each posture. This enables them to master the exact position, height, and direction of the weapon tip, the blade or shaft angle, the hand positions, the feeling of the hold on the weapon, the elbow position and the structure of every part of the body. This improves the kinesthetic awareness and sets the correct model into the body.

> The spear is a difficult weapon, so student absolutely must stand in *santishi* with it. Getting comfortable with the correct position with spear sets the foundation for all applications of power and all changes in techniques. The shoulders must be settled and released. The hands must work together with the lead hand bracing forward and the rear hand pulling back. The spear must always be aligned with the midline of the body so that the 'three points line up' – the tips of the foot, nose, and spear. The qi must be settled, the spirit must be at peace, and the mind must be focused.

FIXED STANCE PRACTICE

The students can practise any technique in a fixed stance. This means standing on the spot and repeating a move without stepping. This allows them to find the overall line of action, get used to the changes that the hand has to do on the grip, find the lines of power in the body, and get the details of the direction and height that the weapon points and which blade edge is where. Once they have basically mastered all of this, then they can combine it with the footwork.

SLOW PRACTICE

In a class, have the students learn and practise the movements slowly so that they can pay careful attention to all the details of each movement, getting the coordination between the hands and feet, finding the correct line of the weapon, finding the correct hand adjustments on the weapons, and seeking out the body

---

[16] Editor's note: I have gathered these teaching and training suggestions from throughout the original book and placed them together to save space and avoid repetition.

action to coordinate with the weapon. Be strict about them following the model for each movement; do not allow them to become casual. Even when they know the movements, make sure that they practise slowly for the first 10 to 20 minutes of a class, and then allow them to practise at normal speed. You may have them practise together on command so that you control the speed.

GROUP DRILLING

To watch the students, keep them together, and avoid accidents with weapons, the teacher can have them perform the movements together on command. Line them up with good spacing between them. Call the actions as broken up in the descriptions in the book to make sure that all students move at the same time. The interval between commands depends on the ability of the students to keep up. Leave time in between moves for beginners, then leave less time when the students can link the moves together better.

- Do not ever call too quickly. A characteristic of Xingyi is that you need time to gather power before each move. But do not call too slowly, either, as this will destroy the completeness of the movements.

  Example one. Call 'one', and the students perform action 1 of broadsword thrust: left advance right broadsword draw; call 'two' and the students perform action 2: right step forward broadsword thrust. Call 'two' quickly and strongly, so that the students respond with a fast, strong action.

  Example two. Call 'one' and the students perform action 1 of sword slash: advance block up and draw back. Call 'two' and the students perform action 2: step forward sword slice. For sword slash turn around, call 'one' and the students perform hook-in chop. Call 'two' and the students perform turn around step forward and slice.

WHOLE – PART – WHOLE TEACHING

When teaching the weapons, the teacher should first show the entire movement at the correct speed to give the students an impression of the proper model that they will follow. The best way to get an idea of the action at first is to carefully watch the teacher's demonstration. Watching a correct action creates a model in the head. So the teacher must show the movements correctly and do them with proper power, speed, and spirit to create the proper model.

Once the technique has been shown at normal power and speed, then 'part teaching' should be done. Break down the movement into its components for teaching purposes, and explain the practical and power applications. Show each movement slowly, pointing out the key points so that the students can understand the outline and get a feel in slow motion of the line of action and correct postures. With weapons, you must focus on placement and path of movement of the grip and tip of a weapon, the direction of the blade or shaft actions, and of the changes in grip. This must be in concert with the body work, arms, elbows, and shoulders. Have the students follow along as you do each component, explaining clearly. After three or four times they should be able to basically do the move. Then you may do the whole move with them, and they should practise the whole move.

Always first let the students get a rough idea of the movements and then gradually explain in more detail. Add more detail after the students have learned the basic moves – gradually adding in body action, power flow, and the smaller, detailed actions. Once the students have practised some more, then add further detail – breathing co-ordination and technique, and practical applications of all the moves. The student must then practise over and over for a long time to become comfortable, skilled, and consistent.

EXAMPLES OF TEACHING PROGRESSIONS

SWORD THRUST

The final stab position should be practised as a post standing exercise. Then have the students practise fixed stance hook and check, paying particular attention to the action of the wrist, the line of movement of the sword blade, and the placement of the blade after the hooking action. The correct movement and placement must become second nature. Then add the footwork. Pay attention to the whole body, but particularly the angle and placement of the arm and the height of the sword.

The same principle applies the second method of the sword thrust – first teach fixed stance circles with the sword, paying particular attention to the wrist and arm movement and how they control the size of the blade's circle. The students should practise circling in both directions, paying particular attention to adjusting the grip and the rotation of the hand until this becomes comfortable. Once the circling is comfortable, then add the draw back.

SWORD OR BROADSWORD CROSSCUT

Have the students practise fixed stance block and hook. Pay particular attention to adjusting the grip of the right hand and its placement in front of the body. Make the distinction between the block and the hook – the sword first blocks and then hooks, using the fore-section of the upper edge of the sword blade or spine of the broadsword blade.

SPEAR CHOP

The core of the spear chop combination is the actual chop. The students should practise the chop action separately in a fixed stance to get a feel for the action of the chop – how to use the hands together, the line of movement of the spear tip, the final position, and so on through all the details. The students should start out slowly then speed up, and start out without power then add power as the action becomes comfortable. The student should strive to make the movement correct and to find the feeling for each part of the body. The most important thing to learn first is the kinesthetic awareness.

Once the basic chop is correct, then the student should practise the full movements – check and chop, and scoop, chop and stab – again starting out with fixed stance techniques, then moving. The student must clarify the techniques – check, hook, and scoop. What are the similarities and what are the differences?

SPEAR THRUST

The main techniques of the spear thrust – outer trap, inner trap, and stab – are the most basic and important of all the techniques of the spear. If you can't do them properly then you are not a spear player. This is the key spear technique for any style, and it must be practised diligently. The spear classic says,

> "If you want to be a spear player then you must practise
> the circle long and hard. It must become more familiar
> than familiar, more refined than refined."

At first the student should practise the movement slowly, making large circles with the spear tip to learn the movement of the hands. The student should first practise in fixed stance. The spear must be stable and the positions must be correct, the line taken by the spear tip must be correct. The most important aspect in early learning is to make everything correct. During slow movement the student has time to find the correct body positioning, use of power and coordination, and to discover how to send power to the tip of the spear. Only after the techniques are correct should speed and power be added. The circle drawn by the spear tip should gradually decrease down to the size of a saucer – about 30 cm. Stepping may now be added as well – back-cross step, crossover step, and roundabout step.

- While this method of gradual additive learning – post standing, fixed stance training, slow practice, part practice, and moving on command – seems to advance slowly, the movements are learned more clearly and correctly. Once the basic movements are properly learned then the pieces can be put together with more success in the long run. The goal is whole body integration with the weapon, so the full movements should be put together fairly soon.

SMALL GROUP PRACTICE

You may put the students into groups and assign a certain time limit, a certain number of repetitions of a move, or a certain goal for them to achieve. When students practise together in groups they may help each other out, watching and correcting each other. This helps them advance together.

Have the students perform in front of each other frequently. In particular, have the students who have learned a bit better and mastered the moves a bit quicker perform in front of the others.

GIVE TIMELY AND POSITIVE CORRECTIONS

The teacher must constantly correct the positions and actions of the students. Corrections must be made as soon as possible, to catch the mistakes before they become habitual. Timely corrections will ensure better results.

- Whether the students are practising in small groups or on their own, correct mistakes in a timely way when you see them.

- When the students are practising, the teacher should use praise while correcting their errors. This encourages the students to try harder, rather than discouraging them. If there is nothing to praise in the actual technique, then praise their effort and give encouragement to those who are trying hard.

ADJUST TEACHING METHOD TO STUDENT AGE

Do not ask older students to do full power movements. Place more emphasis on developing the co-ordination of mind with movement, and of breathing with movement. Emphasize regulation of qi and development of the spirit.

With young students, do more demonstration and have them copy you more. Explain the movements and their requirements repeatedly and do more repetitions. You must also must try to keep the class interesting and to avoid overtiredness.

EXPLAIN APPLICATIONS

You should always explain the combative application when showing new moves, so that the students understand the techniques fully. This gives them more of a goal in their study and training, and makes it easier to learn and train as well.

> Example: the idea of sword drill is to drill into the smallest crack, following the line of the opponent's weapon. It is either a reverse grip low pierce to the knee or a twisted high pierce to the head. Four techniques are done within the sword drill practice – entwine, lift, draw, and pierce. Entwine, lift, and draw are the assisting techniques for the pierce, which is the

main technique. Entwine uses the sword tip to draw a vertical circle either in a clockwise or counterclockwise direction, sending the power to the front end of the blade. Lift is to use the lift the blade in an arc up to the right or left side, close to the body, finishing at shoulder height with the tip angled slightly down. When lifting to the left side, you must first externally rotate the arm to turn the palm up, and then lift at the left side. Draw uses the whole of the blade, either flat or vertical blade edges, to carry the opponent's weapon directly back or up and back. When doing right stance drill, you must first entwine, and then lift, but the lifting action must be part of the entwining action. Entwining and lifting are the defensive actions that prepare the way for the low pierce, which is the goal.

TRAINING SUGGESTIONS FOR WEAPONS

ATTITUDE TO TRAINING

When learning weapons you must first have a good foundation in the empty hand techniques. All of Xingyi's weapon techniques are based on footwork, body work, and power application of the empty hand techniques. If you perform a weapon without bringing out the footwork, body work and power of Xingyiquan, or without bringing out the flavour and characteristics of Xingyiquan, then you are not performing a Xingyi weapon. Also you should first know the standard techniques. Only do any alternate methods once you are comfortable with the standard method. You must be honest in the assessment of your skill level.

Once you have mastered the basic actions, then you need to practise over and over. That is the only way to develop real skill and power. You should not content yourself with learning the movements, but should work hard to develop power. During practice, gradually add intent, imagining what you are doing to an opponent. You should hit hard and fast with no mercy, as if pushing a mountain into the sea. If you use this type of intent and attitude in practice then you will progress quicker and further. The type of intent and attitude with which you practise determines the type of skill that you will develop.

Learning is just a stage, a process. The main thing is the training; you want to train until you can do the movements, until you understand the techniques, until you forge the deep skill, until you have developed a strong body and mind.

LEARNING FROM BOOKS

If you are using a book as study aid, you should look at the movements stance by stance, breaking them down clearly. First study the photographs or diagrams to get the general idea. Pay particular attention to the feet – is it the right or the left – is it advancing or retreating? Then look at the position and line of action of the hands and weapon – from where to where. Once you are clear on the diagrams then try out the movements yourself. Then read the accompanying text. Once you are pretty sure that you are doing the movements correctly then read the pointers and section on power application. Then you can practise to improve your mastery of the techniques, gradually getting a feel for the requirements and power. As you get more comfortable with the movements then you will gradually improve and have your own feelings and understanding of them,

POST STANDING

When learning weapons, always start out with post standing in the on guard position, and learn each and every part of it correctly. First you must understand the 'four methods and three structures'. The four methods are the hand technique, footwork, body technique, and weapon technique. The three structures are the hand shapes, stances, and body structure.

You must practise post standing with each technique to fix the model position into your body. For example, the final position of each technique of broadsword chop: withdraw lifting draw, advance pushing stab, and chop.

When doing post standing, be sure to have the proper structure, smoothly aligned strength, full power, and fully concentrated mind. You want to train your body to the model stance to guarantee that it will take an unerring stance when in the midst of quick action. Post standing is a means to an end; the end is to perform the movements.

SLOW TO FAST PROGRESSION

When learning weapons you must not try to go fast right away. The movements are simple and easy to learn, but they need to be practised over and over to find the right power to be able to use them properly. You must not be content with just being able to do the moves; you must train hard and persevere to get a feel for the moves and combinations in order to become really skilled.

First practise any new movement slowly and softly to seek out the correct coordination, power flow and technique. Once you have mastered the basic movements in slow motion, then you should speed up gradually, paying attention to the power flow and technique. This phase takes a long time but it is the phase that builds real skill and develops power. During this phase you should also try to better understand the applications and train the spirit.

Once you have achieved the required speed then you must practise repeatedly. The only way to master the techniques is through repeated practice – this is the path to deep skill. Once you are comfortable with the movement then increase the speed further, being careful that the movement and techniques do not become sloppy. Seek out the natural rhythm in fast movements – this is how they will become practical, which is the goal.

Even when you know the movements well, train a combination of fast and slow

– mainly fast, but also slow. Seek out the details of the techniques in slow movement, and seek out the power of the techniques in fast movement. Take this time to work on finding the power of each move. First gather then launch, the gathering period is drawn out, and the launching period is short – like the drawing of a bow is slow and the shooting of the arrow is quick.

AWARENESS OF THE WEAPON

When learning a movement, first try to do the large actions and then the small and more detailed ones. First learn the outer actions, and then the inner feelings. You must do the movements to feel and develop awareness – feel the position of your body, the line of movement and speed of the actions, the feeling of the hands on the hilt or shaft, and the feeling of using power through the weapon.

You must focus especially on placement and path of movement of the hilt, tip, and blade edge of a broadsword or sword, and the butt, shaft, and tip of the staff or spear, and the different holds used. The manner in which the hand holds the hilt is of vital importance, so you must learn to use each method appropriately. Your grip directly affects your ability to correctly transfer power to the blade. Each grip is a vital component of the technique, and the ability to perform and to apply power in each technique is directly related to the grip. The overall principle is that your grip must be versatile and your wrist must be supple. You must be able to slide freely along the shaft of the staff and spear, and to stop automatically in the correct place for each technique.

You must master the movements, be able to use whole body power, have agile and adjustable footwork, and practise often with a partner before you can say you can use a weapon.

EXAMPLES OF TRAINING PROGRESSIONS

SPEAR CROSSCUT

First of all, practise fixed stance circling and snapping. Stand in a comfortable stance and alternate circling and snapping in both directions. Draw a relatively large circle with the spear tip, keeping a smooth line. Work on coordinating the body and hands and on finding out how to transfer through from the body to the spear tip.

First work on the actions slowly. You can find the coordination better by working slowly. Find the cooperation between the hands. Find how to gather power and release. Find the smooth lines of the action. Start out with large circles and gradually shrink them. Start out gently and gradually put more and more power into the movement. Gradually speed up.

Once you are comfortable with the action then add the stepping. If you build up each skill gradually then you will be able to coordinate the entire action sooner than if you tried to do everything at once. A teacher's instruction is important, but your own diligent training is more important.

STAFF CHOP

First do fixed stance chop. Stand in *santi* stance with the left foot forward in a good ready stance and perform a simple chop. Keep the action gentle and slow to carefully feel the route of the chopping action. Pay attention to the hooking action of the right hand and the pushing and pulling action of the left hand. You should be looking for the power transfer from the body to the shoulders, and to the hands, and thus to the staff.

Once the movement is correct, gradually speed up and add more force. Be sure to have a focal point to the chop – do not lose control just because you are striking harder. The staff should make a whooshing sound as you swing it, and should vibrate when you stop it.

The next phase is to add the stepping. Go back to slow and gentle movement and add the retreat, forward, and follow in steps. Gradually speed up, paying attention to correct requirements and power application. Always learn actions slowing and gently, then add speed and power.

IMAGINATION

As you repeatedly practise and think about the actions, you should study the outer actions and seek the inner meanings. You need to find the application for each and every action before you can really understand them. Only with thorough understanding can you hope to show the true meaning of the actions and gain even deeper understanding and gain deeper performance levels.

During repetitive training you must be sure that you understand the combative use of each technique. Once you have the foundation of full understanding and hard training, you should imagine an opponent in front of you, and imagine what you are doing with the techniques.

As the masters said "Practise as if there is someone in front of you. " Imagine the attack and defense use of the techniques to develop the practical knowledge and instincts for combat with the weapon. If you train with this intent then you will progress quicker.

HEAVY WEAPONS

You may use a heavier weapon to improve your strength and deep skill. Chose a weight that you can control but cannot flash around. You must be able to do all the moves properly. The training effect is lost if it is so heavy that you cannot handle it.

Move slower with a heavier weapon, and do not change the movement requirements or techniques. Strengthen the arms, wrists, and body, and then gradually speed up. A heavy weapon also helps you to find the real meaning behind the left hand – placing it at the right wrist, and how to use it in coordination to gain power.

A TRAINING SESSION

Once you have basically mastered the movements then you should use 'three periods training' during a session of practice.

The first period is: Start out slowly and softly, diligently feeling the details of each movement, looking for all the requirements of the move and the application, feeling the path of each segment of the body, the placement and positioning of every part of the body, the body action and the power of the weapons. This is the time that you can fine-tune the actions. Do this for about 10 to 20 minutes.

The second period is: Increase your speed and put full power into the moves. Do not lose the correctness and techniques. Do not get sloppy or hasty. This is the period where you gain skills and develop power. Do this for about 30 minutes.

The third period is: Slow down the movements. Regulate the *qi* and gradually bring your heart rate and breathing back to normal. Do this for about 10 minutes.

PERSERVERENCE

You must not be content with learning and being able to do the moves. You must repeat them over and over to develop deep skill. The classics say, "skill comes from ripeness, essence comes from skill," and "to gain the true essence of techniques, deep skill comes from perseverance."

> Deep skill is not achieved in an instant; do not expect to reach your goal in one step. You must train and ponder for many years to fully develop deep skills. "Live to old age, learn to old age, train to old age."

There is no limit to mastery, hard training will bring real deep skill. You must have this attitude towards each and every movement. You must constantly polish and improve yourself, keep trying to make progress. The way to mastery is perseverance and training.

APPENDIX

GLOSSARY OF WEAPONS TERMS IN ENGLISH ORDER

SECTION ONE: PARTS OF WEAPONS

aft-section of blade or shaft, third nearest the grip or butt............	bà duàn	把段
base, butt, the thick end of a long weapon...............	bà	把
blade body, the whole blade...............	shēn	身
blade edge, the sharp edge...............	rèn, rènr	刃
blade spine, the non-sharp edge of a broadsword blade	bēi	背
fore-section of blade or shaft (the third nearest the tip)	qián duàn	前段
flat blade: blade edges side to side relative to the hand	píng rèn	平刃
guard of the grip of a short weapon...............	bǐng or pán	柄, 盘
hilt of a short weapon...............	bà	把
midsection of blade or shaft, middle third...............	zhōng duàn	中段
shaft, the wooden section of staff or spear...............	gǎn	杆
spear tassel...............	qiāng yīng	枪缨
spear head...............	qiāng tóu	枪头
standing blade: blade edges up and down relative to the hand...............	lì rèn	立刃
tip of sharp weapon...............	jiān, jiānr	尖
under edge: bottom edge (finger side) of blade.............	xià rèn	下刃
upper edge: top edge (the thumb side) of blade.............	shàng rèn	上刃

SECTION TWO: WEAPONS TERMINOLOGY

block across...............	gé	格
brandish horizontally, usually over the head...............	yún	云
broadsword, sabre: curved single edged blade............	dāo	刀
check, knock to the side...............	bō	拨

checking brandish, first check to the side with the tip, then swing over the head	bō yún	拨云
chop, strike vertically down	pī	劈
coil (a broadsword around) the head (from left shoulder to right shoulder)	chán tóu	缠头
covering chop, chop folding a staff in on the arm	gài pī	盖劈
crosscut	héng	横
cross-over stance, foot steps across in front	gài bù	盖步
cut	zhǎn	斩
draw back	dài	带
drill	zuān	钻
encircle with spear, full circles	quān qiāng	圈枪
entangle, stir with a blade or shaft tip	jiǎo	绞
flat blade of sword: edges horizontal relative to the strike	píng jiàn	平剑
grip, hold, grasp a weapon	bǎ	把
grip, full (on the grip of a short weapon): grip with all fingers and full palm contact	mǎn bǎ	满把
grip, hanging (on the grip of a short weapon): to let the tip drop	diāo bǎ (or diào?)	刁把, 吊把
grip, pincer (on the grip of a short weapon): hold mainly with the thumb, index, and middle fingers, and only lightly with the ring and little fingers	qián bǎ	钳把
grip, relaxed, can let shaft slide through	sōng wò	松握
grip, spiral (on the grip of a short weapon)	luó bǎ	螺把
hack, a short hard chop	kǎn	砍
hide a broadsword; draw a broadsword behind	cáng dāo	藏刀
hook down to trap with spine of weapon	xià guà	下挂
hook, trap with weapon, hook bladed weapons using the spine, or upper edge	guà	挂
hook up	shàng guà	上挂
level pierce	píng cì	平刺

APPENDIX 267

lift.	tī	提
outer trap, inner trap, stab: spear technique	lán ná zhā	拦拿扎
pierce, stab with a thin blade	cì	刺
poke in, point; an action like dotting in calligraphy	diǎn	点
poke; stab with a blunt weapon, with the tip or butt	chuō	戳
press down	yā	压
punt, a low block with a long weapon, almost stirring action	lū	撸
push with flat of the blade or shaft of a long weapon	tuī	推
reverse pierce, hand or weapon turned over	fǎn cì	反刺
reverse grip chop, hand or weapon turned over	fǎn pī	反劈
rub	cuò	错
scoop; bring a weapon up with the wrist cocked and/or elbow bent	tiǎo	挑
scoop with the butt	tiǎo bà	挑把
scull; a low drag on the side, from the rear	huō	攉
sculling scoop: start with a low drag from the rear, coming forward with a scoop up (elbow bent)	huō tiǎo	攉挑
sculling slice: start with a low drag from the rear, coming forward with a high slice	huō liāo	攉撩
slash	pào	炮
slice, slice up, arm relatively straight	liāo	撩
slice, usually down diagonally	xiāo	削
snap, also for crossing snap	bēng	崩
staff	gùn	棍
spear	qiāng	枪
stab, used for spear and broadsword	zhā	扎
standing blade of sword: edges vertical relative to the hand	lì jiàn	立剑
stir, entangle with a blade tip, hand draws a small circle to make the tip draw a large circle	jiǎo	绞
sword, straight blade double edged sword	jiàn	剑

sweep, a large, low circle	sǎo	扫
sword fingers palm; index and middle fingers straight, other fingers bent and pressed with thumb	jiàn zhǐ zhǎng	剑指掌
thrust, stab as one of the five elements; otherwise is to snap weapon up or across	bēng	崩
trap, inner (clockwise circle and press)	ná	拿
trap, outer (counterclockwise circle and press)	lán	拦
wrap (a broadsword around) the head (from right shoulder to left shoulder)	guǒ nǎo	裹脑

PRONUNCIATION OF PINYIN, THE CHINESE NATIONAL PHONETIC ALPHABET (WITH INTERNATIONAL PHONETIC ALPHABET EQUIVALENTS)

INITIALS (words can start with these consonants, or have a zero initial)

PINYIN	IPA	ROUGH PRONUNCIATION GUIDE
p	p^h	Like English pet with a considerable puff of air.
b	p	Similar to the *pinyin* "p" but without the puff of air (unvoiced, neither English pet nor bet).
t	t^h	Like English tag with a considerable puff of air.
d	t	Similar to the *pinyin* "t" but with no puff of air (unvoiced, not dog).
k	k^h	Like English kill with a considerable puff of air.
g	k	Similar to the *pinyin* "k" but with no puff of air (unvoiced, not English get).
c	ts^h	Like exaggerating English cats.
z	ts	Like the *pinyin* "c" but without the puff of air (unvoiced).
ch	$tṣ^h$	Somewhat similar to English chat with a puff of air, but with the tip of the tongue rolled back.
zh	tṣ	Like the *pinyin* "ch" but with no puff of air (unvoiced).
q	$tþ^h$	Somewhat similar to English chat with a puff of air, but with the front of the tongue raised and the tip on the lower teeth.
j	tþ	Like the *pinyin* "q" but without the puff of air (unvoiced).
m	m	Like English met.
n	n	Like English net.
f	f	Similar to English fat, but with the teeth just touching lightly behind the lower lip.
s	s	Similar to English set.

sh	ʂ	Somewhat similar to English <u>sh</u>ow, but with the same tongue placement as the *pinyin* "ch" and "zh."
x	þ	Somewhat similar to English <u>sh</u>ine but with the same tongue placement as the *pinyin* "q" and "j."
h	χ	Raise the back of the tongue and let the breath come through the obstructed passage without vibrating the vocal cords.
l	l	Like English <u>l</u>et.
r	ɹ	Like the *pinyin* "sh" but with voicing.

FINALS

n	n	Like English pi<u>n</u>.
ng	ŋ	Like English si<u>ng</u>.

VOWELS

a	A a ɛ	Usually close to English f<u>a</u>ther (not p<u>a</u>t). Like y<u>e</u>t when written "-ian" or "yan."
e	ɤ e ɛ ə	Usually similar to English p<u>e</u>t, can tend towards a mid vowel.
i	i ɪ	Usually similar to English b<u>ee</u>. Similar to w<u>e</u>t when written "ui." After c, z, s, ch, zh, sh, and r it is similar to s<u>i</u>r.
o	o u	Usually close to English r<u>o</u>ll. Similar to c<u>ow</u> when written "ao," and <u>ow</u>e when in "ou."
u	u y	Usually similar t English o b<u>oo</u>t. After the *pinyin* "x", "q", and "j" and in the vowel groups starting with these consonants, it is pronounced "ü".
ü	y	Similar to French <u>ü</u>. It is written after "n" or "l," because these are the only positions where both "u" and "ü" are possible
y	i	Partially like an English 'y', tending towards i.
w	u	Partially like an English 'w', tending towards u.

INITIAL CONSONANTS

place of articulation	manner of articulation						
	Unaspirated Stops	Aspirated Stops	Unaspirated Affricates	Aspirated Affricates	Nasals	Fricatives	Voiced Continuants
bilabials	b	p			m		
labio-dentals						f	
dental-alveolars	d	t	z	c	n	s	l
retroflexes			zh	ch		sh	r
palatals			j	q		x	
velars	g	k				h	

TONES IN PINYIN

NUMBER	PINYIN	NAME	RANGE
1	ˉ	high level	55
2	´	high rising	35
3	ˇ	dipping	214
4	`	high falling	51
none	° or blank	neutral	in context

With tone sandhi, tones may change according to the preceding or following tone. The tone marking is put over the main vowel when there are two vowels written together (usually involving the pronunciation of y or w).

ABOUT THE TRANSLATOR

Andrea Falk has practised external and internal Chinese martial arts since 1972, and has concentrated on internal styles since 1981. She met Di Guoyong in 2001 and has trained with him since then.

She moved from her hometown of Victoria to hone her skills in Vancouver, Beijing, and Shanghai –

with a Bachelor of Arts majoring in Chinese, a Bachelor of Physical Education and later a Master of Physical Education with an emphasis on biomechanics and coaching science from the University of British Columbia. She trained in wushu full time from 1980 to 1983 at the Beijing Physical Culture Institute, earning an advanced studies diploma in wushu under the tutelage of professor Xia Bohua and the instruction of Men Huifeng and others. There she gained the basics of Yang and Chen style Taijiquan, Baguazhang, Xingyiquan, Chaquan, and modern wushu (Changquan and weapons). She also spent extended summers in 1984 and 1986 at the Institute. She then started learning purely traditionally, visiting China on extended trips as often as possible. She has trained and/or is training Chen style Taijiquan and Baguazhang as an inside apprentice of Huan Dahai and elder martial brothers in Shanghai, and Xingyiquan and Baguazhang as a close student and friend of Di Guoyong in Beijing. When not in China or traveling to teach, she is usually in Québec city or at a cottage in the Laurentian hills, Canada.

Andrea has worked teaching and translating the Chinese martial arts since 1983. She founded **the wushu centre** in Montreal in 1984, in Victoria in 1992, and in Quebec city in 2007. She has taught Chen Taijiquan, Bagua, and Xingyi around the world, but mostly in Canada and England. For years Andrea translated books for her own students, and in 2000 established **tgl books** and the website www.thewushucentre.ca to bring the best Chinese martial arts books to a wider audience.

trois gros lapin traversent le chemin

www.ingramcontent.com/pod-product-compliance
Lightning Source LLC
Chambersburg PA
CBHW071815230426
43670CB00013B/2459